THE NE

The New Pasta Cuisine

Low-fat Noodle and Pasta Dishes from around the World

Aveline Kushi
and
Wendy Esko

Japan Publications, Inc.

Note to the reader: Those with health problems are advised to seek the guidance of a qualified medical or psychological professional in addition to qualified macrobiotic teacher before implementing any of the dietary or other approaches presented in this book. It is essential that any reader who has any reason to suspect serious illness seek appropriate medical, nutritional or psychological advice promptly. Neither this nor any other related book should be used as a substitute for qualified care or treatment.

Published by JAPAN PUBLICATIONS, INC., Tokyo and New York

Distributors:
UNITED STATES: *Kodansha America, Inc., through Farrar, Straus & Giroux, 19 Union Square West, New York, 10003.* CANADA: *Fitzhenry & Whiteside Ltd., 91 Granton Drive, Richmond Hill, Ontario, L4B 2N5.* BRITISH ISLES AND EUROPEAN CONTINENT: *Premier Book Marketing Ltd., 1 Gower Street, London WC1E 6HA.* AUSTRALIA AND NEW ZEALAND: *Bookwise International, 54 Crittenden Road, Findon, South Australia 5023.* THE FAR EAST AND JAPAN: *Japan Publications Trading Co., Ltd., 1–2–1, Sarugaku-cho, Chiyoda-ku, Tokyo 101.*

First edition: April 1992

ISBN 0–87040–798–8
LCCC No. 91–060392

Printed in U.S.A.

Preface

The New Pasta Cuisine appears at a defining moment in the history of the Western diet. Several years ago, in *The Quick and Natural Macrobiotic Cookbook*, we reviewed the negative health effects of the modern high-fat diet and suggested that a new "four food groups" (whole grains and grain products; beans and bean products such as tofu and tempeh; fresh local vegetables; and sea vegetables) based on the guidelines of macrobiotics would better serve the health needs of modern people. Our proposal was echoed in April 1991, when a group of several thousand doctors petitioned the U.S. Department of Agriculture to abandon the "traditional" four food groups and replace them with a new grouping of foods in which grains, beans, and vegetables are emphasized and meat and dairy are minor options.

The doctors stated in their report that "the risks associated with plant-based diets are quite small in comparison with the great benefit to be gained in terms of reduced risk of cancer, heart disease, diabetes, and obesity." The essence of the report, that trying to modify diet within the existing food groups is not enough to reduce the risk of chronic illness and that a more total realignment of diet is necessary, is in complete accord with macrobiotic thinking about food and health.

Around the world, a consensus is building that the current high-fat diet is inadequate for the changing health needs of modern people. Practical guidelines on healthful eating are urgently needed as old nutritional concepts fall by the wayside in light of rapidly increasing knowledge about diet and health. For the past three decades, in countless seminars and in a variety of books, we have explained how to prepare whole grains, beans, fresh organic vegetables, sea vegetables, and other healthful natural foods and how to translate preventive guidelines into delicious and appetizing meals. Experience has taught us that dietary goals are of little value unless people are able to apply them satisfactorily in the kitchen.

The New Pasta Cuisine is the latest in a series of health-oriented cookbooks. In it we offer step-by-step guidance on changing diet without sacrificing the pleasures and enjoyment of food. The noodle and pasta recipes in this book represent the best of East and West. They illustrate how easy it is to blend traditional Italian, Chinese, Japanese, eastern European, and other ethnic cuisines with macrobiotic nutritional guidelines. *The New Pasta Cuisine* is based around the use of complex carbohydrates and foods that are low in fat and high in fiber, and is designed to appeal to a wide variety of tastes without sacrificing nutritional quality. It can help beginning and advanced cooks make the transition to a healthful way of eating fun and enjoyable. As you will discover in this book, taste and enjoyment are perfectly compatible with health and nutrition.

Aveline has had a lifetime of experience in making and cooking noodles. She was born in Izumo, a region of Japan famous for its buckwheat. When she was a child, her mother would make fresh *soba* (buckwheat noodles) on a huge table with a long rolling pin. She would use cold mountain spring water for making dough. Instead of kneading the dough by hand, she would place a straw mat over it and walk on it— Aveline and her brothers and sisters would all join in this activity. Then they would cut the dough with a large knife. In summer, they served the noodles chilled, in winter, with a hot broth. Buckwheat noodles were especially favored on holidays, especially New Year's Eve.

We would like to thank everyone associated with the creation of this book. We thank Michio Kushi for developing the macrobiotic guidelines that we explain in the introductory sections, and for his untiring dedication to world health and world peace. We thank Edward Esko for overall supervision of the project and guidance in bringing the manuscript to completion. We thank Alex Jack for providing some of the background research used in the text, Lynda Shoup for helping with the typing, and Joy Winetski, who lives in Becket, Massachusetts, for her wonderful illustrations and photographs. We would also like to thank Mr. Iwao Yoshizaki and Mr. Yoshiro Fujiwara, president and New York representative of Japan Publications, Inc., for making *The New Pasta Cuisine* available to people throughout the world.

Aveline Kushi
Wendy Esko
Becket, Massachusetts
May, 1991

Contents

Chapter 1: The New Pasta Cuisine

Noodles and pasta have been enjoyed by people in East and West for centuries. From the *soba* and *udon* eaten in Japan, to the spaghetti, macaroni, fettuccine, and linguine eaten in Italy and throughout the West, people have found pasta to be one of the most convenient and delicious ways to enjoy the staff of life. Whole grain noodles and pasta are rich in complex carbohydrates, fiber, vitamins, and minerals, and today are enjoyed by health-conscious people everywhere as an important part of low-fat, low-cholesterol diets.

Noodle and pasta dishes can be prepared with a wide variety of healthful and delicious ingredients. It is not necessary to serve them with meat, chicken, cheese, tomatoes, or other nightshade vegetables, or with strong spices. They can be quickly boiled and eaten as is—either hot or cold—and are delicious when garnished with a pinch of fresh chopped scallion and a few drops of *tamari* soy sauce. They can be fried with a wide variety of fresh vegetables, or with *tofu, tempeh,* or seafood. Simple noodles in broth are a favorite in many households and are a quick, one-dish meal in themselves. In Japan, the preparation of broth is considered an art. The simplest broths are usually made with tamari soy sauce, water, and kombu, a highly nutritious sea vegetable with proven anticancer properties. *Shiitake* mushrooms, which also have antitumor effects, are often added to noodle broth. Noodles and pasta are also delicious when added to miso and other soups, when cooked in casseroles, or when used in making healthful and refreshing salads.

Today, healthful low-fat pasta cuisine is becoming popular around the world. Below we look at what is in and what is out in this new approach to cooking delicious noodle and pasta dishes.

IN	OUT
Low-fat pasta dishes	High-fat pasta dishes
Pasta cooked the long, slow way over a natural gas flame	Microwaved pasta dishes
Organic carrot sauce	Canned tomato sauce
Kombu-shiitake broth	Chicken or beef broth
Homemade noodle soup	Canned noodle soup
Whole grain pasta	White, refined, or egg pasta
Spaghetti with wheat balls	Spaghetti with meatballs
Tofu lasagne	Cheese or meat lasagne
Natural *shoyu* or tamari soy sauce	Chemicalized soy sauce
Pasta made at home from freshly ground whole flour (very in)	"Enriched" noodles or pasta (very out)
Fresh organic vegetables	Canned, frozen, or nonorganic vegetables

IN	OUT
Naturally seasoned pasta dishes	Overly spiced pasta dishes
Cholesterol-free pasta sauces	Rich creamy pasta sauces

The trend toward a new pasta cuisine is motivated largely by the desire for better health. Scientific evidence showing that a balanced, low-fat diet based on whole grains (including noodles and pasta), beans, and vegetables can help prevent, and in some cases reverse, chronic illness has led many people to reevaluate their way of eating and look for healthful alternatives to the modern high-fat diet. Much of the scientific evidence consists of epidemiological studies that compare the diets and disease patterns of different populations. In southern Italy, for example, where pasta is eaten daily, fresh vegetables are used frequently, and vegetable oil is used in cooking, the rates of cancer and heart disease are low. These illnesses are higher in northern Italy, where pasta is eaten less often and where meat and rich, buttery sauces are frequently consumed. Moreover, it has long been noted that people in China and Japan, where rice, noodles, and other grain products are used as staples, together with fresh local vegetables and fermented soybean products like miso, tamari soy sauce, and tofu, have lower rates of heart disease and cancer. When people from these areas move to the United States and adopt a typical high-fat diet rich in animal food, their rates of heart disease and cancer increase.

Low-fat Diets Are Better for Health

A recent study of diet and disease patterns in China, where noodles are eaten regularly, has added substantial weight to the evidence linking low-fat diets with reduced rates of illness. Touted as the "Grand Prix of epidemiology," the study, released in the spring of 1990, has turned modern dietary assumptions upside down. Among the study's chief findings:

• Fat consumption should ideally be reduced to 10 to 15 percent of calories to prevent degenerative disease, not 30 percent as usually recommended.
• Eating animal protein is linked with chronic disease. Compared to the Chinese who derive 7 percent of their protein from animal sources, Americans obtain 70 percent from animal food.
• A diet high in animal protein that promotes early menstruation may increase a woman's risk of breast cancer and cancer of the reproductive organs.
• Dairy food is not needed to prevent osteoporosis, the degenerative thinning of the bones that is common among older women.
• The consumption of meat is not needed to prevent iron-deficiency anemia. The average Chinese consumes twice the iron Americans do, primarily from plant sources, and shows no signs of anemia.

The study, sponsored by the U.S. National Cancer Institute and the Chinese Institute of Nutrition and Food Hygiene, was published by Cornell University Press. The director of the study, Dr. T. Colin Campbell, a Cornell biochemist, noted, "Usually, the first thing a country does in the course of economic development is to introduce a lot of livestock. Our data are showing that this is not a very smart move, and the Chinese are listening. They're realizing that animal-based agriculture is not the way to go."

The data also suggest that high-cholesterol levels may predispose one to cancer, heart disease, and diabetes. As Dr. Campbell stated in an interview: "So far, we've seen that plasma cholesterol is a good predictor of the kinds of diseases people are going to get. Those with higher cholesterol levels are prone to the diseases of affluence—cancer, heart disease, and diabetes." Cholesterol levels in China were found to range from 88 to 165 milligrams per 100 milliliters of blood. The researchers also found that the rates of colon cancer were lowest among people who had the lowest cholesterol levels. These results suggest that the high consumption of dairy products and other animal foods has a major influence on higher cholesterol levels and a higher incidence of these diseases. Dr. Campbell summarized the preliminary results of the study:

> We are basically a vegetarian species and should be eating a wide variety of plant foods and minimizing our intake of animal foods.

Modern eating patterns, based around foods that are high in saturated fat and cholesterol, put everyone in the high-risk category for chronic illness. This tendency often begins at a young age. For example, at an American Heart Association forum in January, 1990, Dr. Gerald Berenson, chief cardiologist at the Louisiana State University Medical Center, stated that children should be routinely checked for signs of heart disease at about age five. Dr. Berenson reported the results of a twenty-five-year study of more than 10,000 children showing that doctors can identify at six months those children who are likely to develop excessively high levels of blood cholesterol. He suggested that children at risk for heart disease should be taught as soon as they begin school to avoid fat in their diet, exercise, and keep their weight down.

Moreover, research is now showing that a naturally balanced low-fat diet based on whole grains and vegetables can play a key role in the prevention and reversal of chronic illness. Studies conducted in the 1970s by researchers at Harvard Medical School and elsewhere on people eating a macrobiotic diet have shown that their blood cholesterols average 125 mg/dl, placing them in the low-risk category for heart disease, cancer, and diabetes. In a study presented at the 1989 meeting of the American Heart Association and published in *The Lancet*, Dr. Dean Ornish and associates at the University of California and University of Texas tested forty-one patients with severe coronary blockage. Twenty-two patients were placed in an experimental group and nineteen were assigned to a control group. Patients in the experimental group ate a diet based on whole grains, beans, and vegetables with less than 10 percent fat, took daily half-hour walks, and practiced meditation, stretching, and breathing exercises twice a week. The members of the control group did not practice stress reduction and most of them ate a less balanced diet of about 30 percent fat.

After one year, eighteen of the experimental patients showed significant unblocking of the arteries. Members of the experimental group also experienced a 91 percent reduction in the frequency of chest pains. This study demonstrates that diet and lifestyle can be just as effective as cholesterol-lowering drugs in reversing blocked arteries.

Over the years, researchers have associated a diet high in animal fat with higher rates of certain cancers, especially cancer of the colon, breast, and prostate. At the same time, diets high in fiber, such as that in whole cereal grains (including whole grain noodles and pasta), vegetables, beans, and other plant foods have been associated with lower rates of these illnesses. In a study conducted at Brigham and Women's Hospital in Boston and released in December, 1990, persons who eat beef, pork, or lamb everyday were found to be twice as likely to get colon cancer as those who avoid red meat. The study was conducted on 88,751 women, and provides some of the strongest evidence yet that a diet high in red meat contributes to this form of cancer.

"Moderate red meat intake is certainly better than large amounts, but it's quite possible that no red meat intake is even better," stated the director of the study, Dr. Walter C. Willet. The study was based on a follow-up of the health and eating habits of nurses throughout the United States during the period from 1980 to 1986. The researchers discovered that women who ate pork, beef, or lamb as a main dish everyday were 2 1/2 times more likely to develop colon cancer than those who ate these foods less than once a month. Processed meats were significantly associated with a higher risk of colon cancer. As this and other research shows, it is probably a good idea to learn to enjoy spaghetti *without* meatballs.

Breast cancer currently effects one in ten women in the United States and high-fat diets are now suspected as a leading factor in this disease. The United States, Britain, the Netherlands, and other countries where high-fat diets are common have the highest incidences of breast cancer, while countries such as Japan, Singapore, and China, where fat consumption is much less, have much lower rates. When people from countries with low rates of breast cancer move to countries with higher rates, their breast cancer incidence rises to match the higher rate of their new country within one or two generations, reflecting changes in diet and lifestyle as they gradually adapt to their new environment and culture.

Commenting on the breast cancer and diet connection, Maureen Henderson, an epidemiologist at the Fred Hutchinson Cancer Research Center in Seattle told *Time* (January, 1991), "I'm sure of it. The results are too consistent to believe that the association is indirect." Japan has traditionally had a low rate of breast cancer. However, the traditional immunity to breast cancer enjoyed by the Japanese is now changing: the rate of breast cancer in Japan increased 58 percent between 1975 and 1985. Dr. Akira Eboshida, of the ministry of health and welfare in Japan attributes this rise to changes in the Japanese diet. He stated in *Time*, "The largest factor behind the sharp rise is the westernization of eating habits. We are eating more animal fat and less fiber." Other illnesses linked with increasing fat consumption are also increasing in Japan, including heart disease and cancer of the colon, ovaries, and prostate.

Pasta in the Macrobiotic Diet

In this book, we explain how to prepare a wide variety of low-fat noodle and pasta dishes within the context of a naturally balanced, macrobiotic diet. The ingredients in the recipes have been selected according to the principles of macrobiotics, which provide practical guidelines for achieving good health through balanced nutrition in harmony with the environment. We do not use extreme or unbalanced foods in these dishes. For example, we omit foods such as meat, cheese, chicken, eggs, butter, and other animal foods high in cholesterol and saturated fat. We do not use refined sugar or foods that contain it, nor do we recommend using tomatoes, peppers, potatoes, eggplant, and other nightshade vegetables.

Researchers have noted a link between the nightshades and illnesses such as arthritis. They have found that when people with arthritis omit them from their diets, their symptoms often improve. In macrobiotic thinking, nightshades are extremely *yin* or expansive. They have become popular in modern diets as a counterweight to the extreme *yang* or contractive effects of meat, cheese, chicken, and other animal foods. Often, pasta dishes that include meat or cheese call for the use of tomato sauce with spices (also extremely expansive). Since our recipes are meat- and dairy-free, we do not need the extremely expansive effects of nightshades or strong spices to make balance. Originally, Italian cuisine did not include tomatoes or potatoes. These vegetables were imported into Europe from Peru in the sixteenth century, and were at first considered poisonous. However, as consumption of meat and cheese increased, people ignored these considerations and started including these vegetables in their diets.

The recipes in this book call for the use of all-natural ingredients. They are based on whole grains, beans, fresh local vegetables, and other complex carbohydrate foods that are centrally balanced in terms of yin and yang energies. Whenever possible, try to obtain fresh organic vegetables, as well as noodles, pasta, and flour (for making noodles) processed from organically-grown grains. High-quality natural seasonings are also important for daily use. We recommend using naturally fermented tamari soy sauce (also known as *shoyu*) that is free of chemical additives, as well as cold-pressed vegetable oils. In the section that follows, we present comprehensive guidelines for selecting the highest-quality foods. These guidelines, known as the Standard Macrobiotic Diet, can help everyone eat in harmony with human needs, traditional dietary practices, and seasonal and climatic changes, as well as nutritional recommendations for the prevention of chronic illness.

Macrobiotic principles—including the principles of balance according to yin and yang—are explained at length in books such as *Macrobiotic Diet, The Book of Macrobiotics: The Universal Way of Health, Happiness and Peace, The Macrobiotic Way*, and others listed in the bibliography. These books are highly recommended for readers who would like to deepen their understanding of food and its relationship to health and well-being.

The foods in the Standard Macrobiotic Diet can be divided into primary and supplementary categories. Primary foods are those consumed on a daily basis and include: (1) whole cereal grains and their products (about 50 to 60 percent daily); (2) soups (5 to 10 percent, or approximately one or two small bowls daily); (3) fresh local vege-

Table 1 General Yin and Yang Classification of Food

The items in this table are generally listed from most yang (contractive) to most yin (expansive). Foods in the center column are generally recommended for consumption in temperate climates, while those in the strong yang and strong yin columns are generally not recommended for optimum health. The macrobiotic diet is based on certainly balanced foods. Like opposite poles of a magnet, yin and yang attract each other. The more extreme the diet becomes at one end, the more we need opposite extremes to make balance, for example, meat and sugar, cheese and wine, and consumption of animal food and consumption of tropical fruits, strong spices, and nightshade vegetables.

STRONG YANG FOODS

Refined salt	Chicken and poultry
Eggs	Lobster, crab, and other shellfish
Meat	Red-meat and blue-skinned fish
Hard chees	

MORE BALANCED FOODS

Unrefined white sea salt, miso, tamari soy sauce, and other naturally salty seasonings	Seeds and nuts (from temperate climates)
Tekka, gomashio, umeboshi, and other naturally processed salty condiments	Temperate-climate fruit
	Brown rice syrup, barley malt, and other natural grain-based sweeteners (when used moderately)
Low-fat, white-meat fish	Nonaromatic, nonstimulant beverages
Sea vegetables	Spring or well water
Whole cereal grains	Naturally processed vegetable oils
Beans and bean products	
Root, round, and leafy green vegetables (from temperate climates)	

STRONG YIN FOODS

White rice, white flour	Honey, sugar, and refined sweeteners
Frozen and canned foods	Alcohol
Tropical fruits and vegetables (including those originating in the tropics such as tomato and potato)	Foods containing chemicals, preservatives, dyes, and pesticides
	Artificial sweeteners
Milk, cream, yogurt, and ice cream	Drugs (marijuana, cocaine, and so on, with some exceptions)
Refined oils	
Spices (pepper, curry, nutmeg, and so on)	Medications (tranquilizers, antibiotics, and so on, with some exceptions)
Aromatic and stimulant beverages (coffee, black tea, mint tea, and so on)	

tables (about 25 to 30 percent daily); and (4) beans, bean products, and sea vegetables (about 10 percent daily). These categories comprise the macrobiotic "four food groups," and provide a healthful alternative to the modern "four food groups" based around meat and dairy food.

Supplementary foods are those which are eaten periodically, usually several times per week, or daily in very small amounts. Foods eaten periodically include low-fat, white-meat fish (on average, once or twice per week); seasonal fruits (about three or four times per week); and seeds and nuts (several times per week on average). Foods such as sea salt, miso, tamari soy sauce, and other natural seasonings; umeboshi plums and other condiments; pickled vegetables; sugar-free, grain-based sweeteners; snacks; and natural, caffeine-free beverages, some of which are eaten daily, are also included in the supplementary category.

The percentages of foods in the Standard Macrobiotic Diet are based on the overall volume of food consumed each day. They are calculated by volume and not by weight. It is not necessary to include them all every time you eat. However, we do recommend eating whole grains, or the staff of life, at each meal. Lunch, for example, can be as simple as a bowl of whole grain noodles in broth with *bancha* tea or cereal grain coffee, or can include homemade sushi, lightly steamed vegetables, pressed salad or pickles, whole grain bread, and other side dishes. The number and variety of side dishes you prepare to go with your grain dishes depends on your appetite, preferences, and how much time you have for cooking and eating.

The standard diet is generally appropriate for persons living in temperate, or four-season climates. These guidelines require modification if you live in a tropical or semitropical climate, or a polar or semipolar region. However, the percentages indicated below are generally valid in all but the most extreme polar climates. Whole grains, beans, fresh local vegetables, and sea vegetables are the ideal principal foods in the tropics as well as in northern zones. The main difference between temperate and tropical diets is in the varieties of these foods we select, and in the methods we use to cook them. These and other personal adjustments underscore the importance of adapting these principles flexibly to our personal needs. In this sense, macrobiotics is not a fixed "diet" that can be followed rigidly without considering individual circumstances.

Together with listing the foods in the Standard Macrobiotic Diet, we offer suggestions on selecting the highest-quality foods, as well as information on their nutritional values. We also explain how to use the primary categories of food when preparing noodle and pasta dishes. Although you probably will not use all of these foods when preparing noodle and pasta dishes, it is a good idea to familiarize yourself with the wide range of whole natural foods included in the practice of a balanced macrobiotic diet.

Standard Macrobiotic Diet

Whole Cereal Grains

Whole grains may comprise up to 50 to 60 percent of daily intake. They are the most centrally balanced foods in terms of expanding and contracting, or yin and yang energies, and can be included as principal foods at each meal. It is much easier to create balance in your meals if they are based around whole grains. Below are the varieties of whole grains and grain products for regular use:

Fig. 1 The Standard Macrobiotic Diet

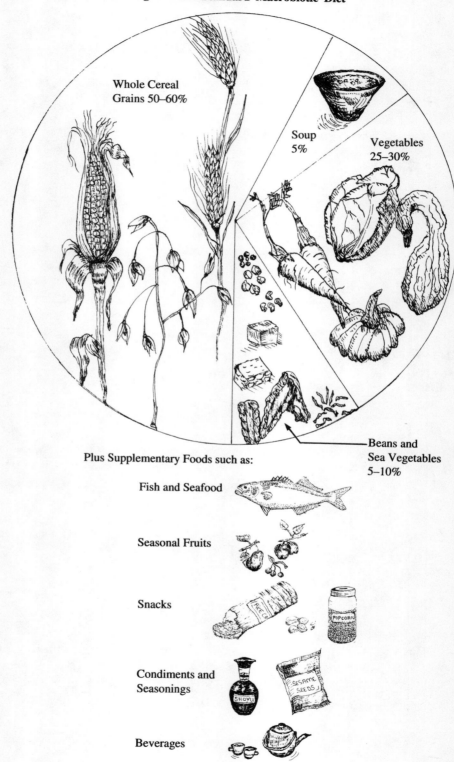

Whole Cereal
Grains 50–60%

Soup
5%

Vegetables
25–30%

Beans and
Sea Vegetables
5–10%

Plus Supplementary Foods such as:

Fish and Seafood

Seasonal Fruits

Snacks

Condiments and
Seasonings

Beverages

BROWN RICE
Brown rice—short, medium, and
  long grain
Genuine brown rice cream (the
  liquid squeezed from cooked
  brown rice)
Puffed brown rice
Brown rice flakes

SWEET BROWN RICE
Sweet brown rice grain (a more
  glutinous variety of brown rice)
Mochi (pounded sweet rice)
Sweet brown rice flour products

BARLEY
Barley grain
Pearl barley (a special variety of barley
  known in Japanese as *hato mugi*)
Pearled barley
Puffed barley
Barley flour products

WHOLE WHEAT
Whole wheat berries
Whole wheat bread
Whole wheat chapatis
Whole wheat noodles and pastas
Whole wheat flakes
Whole wheat flour
Whole wheat flour product such as
  crackers, matzos, muffins, and so on
Couscous
Bulgur
Fu (baked puffed wheat gluten)
Seitan (wheat gluten)

MILLET
Millet grain
Millet flour products
Puffed millet

OATS
Whole oats
Steel cut oats
Rolled oats
Oatmeal
Oat flakes
Oat flour products

CORN
Corn on the cob
Corn grits
Cornmeal
Arepas (traditional South
  Anerican cakes made from
  whole corn)
Corn flour products such as bread,
  muffins, and so on
Puffed corn
Popped corn

RYE
Rye grain
Rye bread
Rye flakes
Rye flour products

BUCKWHEAT
Buckwheat groats (*kasha*)
Buckwheat noodles (soba) and
  pastas
Buckwheat pancakes

Nutritional Quality: Cooked whole grains are easier to digest than flour products or cracked or rolled grains, and are preferred for regular use. In general, it is better to keep intake of flour products or cracked or rolled grains to less than 15 to 20 percent of your daily intake of grains.

The complex carbohydrates, or polysaccharides, in whole grains exist together with an ideal balance of minerals, proteins, fats, and vitamins. These complex sugars are gradually and smoothly assimilated through the digestive organs, providing a slow and steady source of energy to the body. In the mouth, an enzyme in saliva initiates predigestive activity and is the main reason why all foods, and especially whole grains, need to be chewed well. In contrast to the gradual burning of complex carbo-hydrates in grains, the predominately simple carbohydrates, or sugars, in fruits, milk, and other dairy food, sugar, honey, and other highly refined sweeteners, burn faster, contributing to rapid and uneven digestion, and erratic fluctuations in the body's me-tabolism. Refined sugar produces an immediate burst of energy—a sugar "high"—followed by the rapid depletion of energy in the inevitable "low" that comes after-ward.

Whole grains are also high in niacin and other B vitamins, vitamin E, and vitamin A. The B vitamin group, in particular, along with complex carbohydrates, contribute to mental clarity. Because whole grains contain an ideal balance of protein, carbo-hydrates, fat, and vitamins and minerals, they are, nutritionally speaking, very well suited as principal foods.

Use in Preparing Noodles and Pasta: Cereal grains are the primary ingredient in noodles and pasta. Western-style pastas are made primarily with durham wheat, a harder, more glutinous variety of wheat that allows the pasta to retain its shape. Oriental-style noodles, such as udon and *somen* are also made with whole wheat flour, while buckwheat flour is the primary ingredient of soba. Noodles can also be made from rice, corn, barley, and other whole grain flours.

While they are growing, whole grains are surrounded by a hard shell or husk, which is normally removed after harvest. The outer layer, the skin of the grain, contains pro-teins, enzymes, vitamins, and minerals. The inside portion is made up of complex carbohydrate. When grains are polished, or "refined," the outside skin is removed. The end product in the case of rice is white rice, or in the case of wheat, white flour, such as that used in white bread and commercial pastries. In brown rice or whole wheat, the outer skin is left intact and each grain retains its essential nutrients.

Many commercial noodles or pasta are made primarily from refined flour that is de-void of essential nutrients. These products are often "enriched," a process in which the nutrients removed through proceessing are artificially added to the flour. These prod-ucts are generally unsuitable for health and are best avoided. Other varieties are made from combinations of unrefined and refined flour and can be used on special occasions by those in good health. (Refined flour is added to give the noodles a finer texture.) High-quality noodles and pasta made without eggs or artificial ingredients can be en-joyed as a supplementary food three or four times a week by those in good overall health. However, we do not recommend using noodles or pasta in place of whole grains themselves. Whole grains are nutritionally and energetically superior to flour products and are ideally suited as principal foods in the human diet. In cultures where noodles and pasta are eaten regularly, such as China, Italy, and Japan, they were origi-nally eaten along with whole grains such as rice or barley.

Because they are boiled on top of the stove and have a soft texture, noodles and pasta are more easily digested than hard flour products such as bread, cookies, and crackers that are baked in enclosed ovens, and thus can be included more often in the diet.

Soups

Soups may comprise about 5 percent of each person's daily intake. For most people, that averages out to about one or two cups or small bowls of soup per day, depending on their needs and desires. Soups can include vegetables, grains, beans, sea vegetables, noodles or other grain products, bean products like tofu, tempeh, and others, or occasionally, fish or seafood. Soups are delicious when moderately seasoned with either miso, tamari soy sauce, sea salt, umeboshi plum or paste, or occasionally ginger. Spices and other highly expansive seasonings are best avoided in temperate climates.

Soups can be made thick and rich, or as simple clear broths. The texture of soups can vary with seasonal change and personal desire. Noodle, vegetable, grain, or bean stews can also be enjoyed, while a variety of garnishes, such as scallions, parsley, *nori* sea vegetable, and croutons may be used to enhance the appearance and flavor of soups.

Light miso soup, with vegetables and sea vegetables, is recommended for daily consumption, on average, one small bowl or cup per day. *Mugi* (barley) miso is normally the best for regular use, followed by soybean (*Hatcho*) miso. A second bowl or cup of soup may also be enjoyed, preferably mildly seasoned with tamari soy sauce or sea salt. Other varieties of soup include:

- Bean and vegetable soups
- Grain, noodle, and vegetable soups (i.e., brown rice, millet, barley, pearl barley, and so on)
- Puréed squash and other vegetable soups

Nutritional Quality: Natural miso contains living enzymes that aid digestion. This highly nutritious food strengthens the quality of the blood and provides a wonderful balance of complex carbohydrates, essential oils, protein, vitamins, and minerals. The best miso is naturally aged for several summers or longer, and is made from whole, round soybeans—without chemically treated ingredients or artificial aging procedures. It has a deep, rich flavor.

Similarly, natural soy sauce, known in macrobiotics as *tamari*, should also be the highest quality. Soy sauce is traditionally made from organically grown soybeans and wheat, good quality water, and unrefined sea salt that have fermented naturally for several years in well-aged cedar vats. Modern commercial soy sauces are a far different product. They are made with defatted soybean meal, chemically grown grains, refined salt, and usually contain monosodium glutamate, caramel, sugar, or other additives or preservatives. Moreover, commercial varieties are artificially aged in temperature-controlled stainless steel or epoxy coated vats to reduce their aging to several months. Their taste is harsh and flat in comparison to natural tamari soy sauce.

Natural miso and tamari soy sauce, used for centuries in traditional diets, are now gaining recognition as essential ingredients in a healthful way of eating. In 1981, the National Cancer Center of Japan completed a ten-year study on diet and cancer. They reported that people who ate miso soup daily were 33 percent less likely to develop stomach cancer than those who never ate it. The study also found that miso was effective in preventing heart and liver diseases.

Use in Preparing Noodles and Pasta: High-quality noodles and pasta are delicious when added to miso and other soups and stews. One of the most simple, nourishing, and delicious ways to serve noodles is in a clear broth made with water, *kombu* sea vegetable, shiitake mushrooms, and a small amount of tamari soy sauce.

Vegetables

Roughly one-fourth to one-third (25 to 30 percent) of each person's daily intake can include vegetables. Nature provides an incredible variety of fresh seasonal vegetables to choose from. For persons in temperate climates, centrally balanced vegetables from the same climate are recommended. Vegetables that originated in the tropics, such as tomatoes, potatoes, and eggplant, are too extreme for optimum health. Some of those recommended for regular use include:

Acorn squash
Bok choy
Broccoli
Burdock root (a long brown root that grows uncultivated throughout North America)
Buttercup squash
Butternut squash
Cabbage
Carrots
Carrot tops
Cauliflower
Celery
Celery root
Chinese cabbage
Chives
Collard greens
Cucumber
Daikon (long white radish)
Daikon greens
Dandelion greens
Dandelion root
Endive
Escarole
Green beans
Green peas
Hubbard squash
Hokkaido pumpkin (a variety of

winter squash originally grown in northern Japan)
Iceberg lettuce
Jerusalem artichoke
Jinenjo (Japanese mountain potato)
Kale
Kohlrabi
Leeks
Lotus root (the edible root of the lotus flower)
Mushrooms
Musterd greens
Onion
Parsley
Parsnips
Patty pan squash
Pumpkin
Radish
Red cabbage
Romaine lettuce
Scallions
Shiitake mushrooms (fresh or dried Japanese mushrooms)
Snap beans
Summer squash
Turnip
Turnip greens
Watercress
Wax beans

Vegetables can be served in soups, or with grains, beans, or sea vegetables. They can also be used in making rice rolls (homemade sushi), served with noodles or pasta, cooked with fish, or served alone. The methods for cooking vegetables include boiling, steaming, pressing, sautéing (both waterless and with oil), and pickling. A variety of natural seasonings, including miso, tamari soy sauce, sea salt, and brown rice or umeboshi vinegar are recommended to add taste and nutrients to vegetable dishes.

Nutritional Quality: As much as possible, try to use vegetables that are organic and natural in quality. Canned, frozen, and vegetables of tropical origin are best avoided (in temperate zones). Scientific tests show that organic produce contains up to three times more minerals and trace elements than inorganic produce. In one study, supermarket vegetables were found to have as little as 25 percent as much mineral content as organic vegetables. If you are unable to start a backyard organic garden, look for high-quality vegetables at the natural food store, coop, or farmer's market. In many outlets, organic produce is clearly marked and certified by an organic grower's association or state agency which periodically tests soil conditions and monitors cultivation standards.

Fresh vegetables are high in complex carbohydrates, fiber, vitamins, such as A and C, and minerals, including calcium. As part of a balanced whole food diet, they help provide all of the essential nutrients necessary for optimal health and vitality.

The importance of eating fresh vegetables is gaining recognition among many scientific and medical associations, especially their role in preventing chronic illness. In its report *Diet, Nutrition and Cancer*, the National Academy of Sciences recommended daily consumption of yellow and orange vegetables such as carrots and winter squashes high in beta-carotene (a precursor to vitamin A) and cruciferous vegetables such as cabbage, broccoli, cauliflower, and Brussels sprouts as part of a prudent diet to help prevent cancer. The American Heart Association, the American Diabetes Association, and many other organizations have issued guidelines on vegetable consumption that are similar in direction to the macrobiotic diet.

Use in Preparing Noodles and Pasta: Noodles and pasta are delicious when cooked along with a wide variety of fresh local vegetables. They can be added to noodles in broth, noodle soups or stews, or can be used in making delicious fried noodle dishes. Whole wheat spaghetti or pasta is often made with a delicious sauce made from miso, carrots, and other vegetables. This sauce is very tasty, deep orange in color, and much more healthy than the tomato sauce commonly served. Chopped raw scallions are frequently used as a garnish in noodle and pasta dishes, while shiitake mushrooms are often used in noodle broths. Deep-fried vegetables (*tempura*) are delicious when served on top of noodles and broth. Noodles and pasta can also be combined with fresh garden vegetables to make a variety of refreshing noodle salads.

Beans

About 5 to 10 percent of daily meals may include beans or bean products. Beans that are smaller in size (such as *azuki*, chick-peas, and lentils) and contain less fat are preferred for regular use. Persons in good overall health may select from any of the following:

BEANS
Azuki beans
Black-eyed peas
Black turtle beans
Black soybeans
Chick-peas (garbanzo beans)
Great northern beans
Kidney beans
Lentils (green and red)
Lima beans
Mung beans
Navy beans
Pinto beans
Soybeans
Split peas

Whole dried peas
Bean sprouts

BEAN PRODUCTS
Dried tofu (soybean curd that has been naturally dried)
Fresh tofu
Okara (pulp or residue left from making tofu)
Natto (fermented soybeans)
Yuba (dried soy milk)
Tempeh (fermented soybeans or combination of soybeans and grains)

Beans and bean products are more easily digested when cooked with a small volume of seasonings such as sea salt, miso, or kombu. They may also be prepared with vegetables, chestnuts, dried apples, or raisins, or occasionally sweetened with grain sweeteners like barley malt and rice honey. Beans and bean products may be served in soups and side dishes, or cooked with grains or sea vegetables.

Nutritional Quality: Beans and bean products are proportionally higher in protein and fat than whole grains and lower in complex carbohydrates. With grains, they make a complete protein and provide all of the amino acids needed by the body.

A variety of other nutrients are found in beans. They are very high in calcium, phosphorus, iron, thiamine, niacin, and vitamin E. Although they contain only modest amounts of vitamin A, beans contain phosphatides that increase the absorption of beta-carotene, the precursor to vitamin A found in carrots and other yellow and orange vegetables. Like whole grains, beans are rich in substances called *protease inhibitors* which are thought to inhibit the development of cancer. Fermented soybean foods, especially tempeh and miso, all contain vitamin B_{12}, an important nutrient otherwise found primarily in animal foods, and eating these foods regularly ensures an adequate supply.

For centuries, beans have formed a central part in the cuisine of all traditional cultures, and their nutritional superiority to animal foods is beginning to be recognized by modern scientists. Beans and bean products contain about twice as much protein as a comparable amount of meat or dairy food, their fat is unsaturated in quality, and they are entirely free of cholesterol. Beans and bean products are also very high in calcium. Tofu, for example, contains more calcium by weight than dairy milk.

Use in Preparing Noodles and Pasta: Beans are delicious when cooked along with noodles and pasta in soups, stews, and casseroles. Soybean products, such as tofu and tempeh can be prepared with noodles and pasta in a variety of ways. Tofu and tempeh are delicious when served with noodles in broth or fried along with noodles, and make wonderful stuffings for pasta shells. Deep-fried tofu and tempeh are especially delicious when served with noodles and broth. Beans, as well as tofu and tempeh, can be used in making a variety of noodle salads, and soybean foods, including natto, can be used in making noodle sushi.

Sea Vegetables

Sea vegetables may be used daily in cooking. Side dishes can be made with *arame* or *hijiki* and included several times per week. *Wakame* and kombu can be used daily in miso and other soups, in vegetable and bean dishes, or as condiments. Toasted nori is also recommended for daily or regular use, while agar-agar can be used from time to time in making a natural jelled desserts known as *kanten* (agar-agar also has natural laxative properties). Below is a list of the sea vegetables for use in macrobiotic cooking:

Arame	Irish moss
Agar-agar	Kombu
Dulse	Nori
Hijiki	Wakame

Nutritional Quality: Sea vegetables are among the most nutritious foods and have long been valued for their health-giving properties. Dried sea vegetables are high in complex carbohydrates, fiber, protein, vitamins, and minerals and low in fat. Polysaccharides account for about 50 to 60 percent of their weight, protein up to 7 percent, and minerals and vitamins up to 30 percent. The remaining 10 to 20 percent is water and only about 1 to 2 percent fat.

Sea vegetables contain proportionally more minerals than any other type of food. Nori, for instance, has from two to four times more vitamin A than carrots and ten times more than spinach. Hijiki, wakame, and arame have from eleven to fourteen times more calcium than milk. Kombu, wakame, arame, hijiki, and nori have from three to eight times more iron than beef.

In the Far East, sea vegetables are the main source of iodine in the diet, so that refined, chemically iodized salt is not necessary. Sea vegetables are also proportionately higher in vitamin A, thiamine, riboflavin, vitamin B_6, vitamin B_{12}, and niacin than most land vegetables and fruits. Nori is also rich in vitamin C and protein.

Recent scientific studies have upheld many of the traditional benefits associating sea vegetables with a variety of health benefits. In 1984, medical researchers at Harvard University reported that a diet containing 5 percent kombu significantly delayed the inducement of breast cancer in experimental animals. Extrapolating these results to human subjects, the investigators concluded, "Seaweed may be an important factor in explaining the low rates of certain cancers in Japan." Japanese women, whose diet normally includes about 3 to 5 percent sea vegetables, have from three to nine times less breast cancer incidence than American women, for whom sea vegetables are not a part of their usual diet.

Use in Preparing Noodles and Pasta: Sea vegetables such as kombu and wakame are primary ingredients in noodle broths and soups. Nori is commonly used as a garnish for noodle dishes (especially noodles in broth) and is also used in making noodle sushi. Nori flakes and other sea vegetable condiments are also delicious on noodle and pasta dishes.

Fish and Seafood

Fish and seafood can be eaten on occasion to supplement the foods listed above. Amounts eaten can vary, depending upon each person's needs and desires, but generally, it can be eaten several times per week as a part of a balanced meal. White-meat varieties that are lowest in saturated fat and most easily digested are recommended for regular use.

REGULAR USE	*OCCASIONAL USE*
Carp	Cherrystone clams
Cod	Littleneck clams
Small dried fish (*iriko*)	Crab
Flounder	Oyster
Haddock	Lobster
Halibut	Shrimp
Herring	
Scrod	*INFREQUENT USE*
Dried fish	Bluefish
Smelt	Salmon
Snapper	Sardines
Sole	Swordfish
Trout	Tuna
Other white-meat fish	Other blue-skinned and red-meat fish

Garnishes are especially important in balancing fish and seafood. Recommended garnishes include: chopped scallions or parsley, grated raw daikon, ginger, radish, and horseradish or Japanese horseradish (*wasabi*), raw salad, and shredded daikon.

Nutritional Quality: Fish and seafood are high in protein, contain unsaturated rather than saturated fat, and have plenty of B vitamins. In northern regions where the growing season is short and whole grains and vegetables are less plentiful, these foods are an important supplementary source of these nutrients.

An increasing number of nutritionists and scientists are recommending that meat and dairy foods be substantially reduced and replaced in the diet with fish and seafood that are low in fat and cholesterol. Researchers have recently identified a fatty acid found in fish, in some marine oils, and in sea vegetables and other plant foods that is protective against thrombosis, the formation or presence of a blood clot inside a blood vessel or the heart itself. The substance in the fish, EPA or eicosapentanoic acid (also known as omega-3), was shown to lower serum cholesterol up to 17 percent in healthy persons and 20 percent or more in heart patients. EPA has also been shown to lower triglycerides (fats that circulate in the blood) and to reduce inflammatory arthritis.

EPA has been found in sea vegetables, as well as in soybeans and soybean foods such as tofu.

Until recently, fish was one of the most uncontaminated and least processed foods. However, in modern times, its quality has been greatly affected by pollution and seafood has been subjected to many potentially harmful industrial processing techniques. Finding a reliable source of truly fresh and uncontaminated fish is very important for people who wish to include this supplementary food in their diet. As a general rule, seawater species are less polluted than freshwater varieties. Among deep-water species, moreover, white-meat fish are less fatty and oily than red-meat and blue-skinned varieties. Store bought fish and seafood should be obtained as fresh as much as possible rather than frozen, smoked, canned, prestuffed, prebreaded, concentrated, or otherwise commercially processed. However, fish or seafood that has been dried, pickled, or naturally processed without artificial preservatives may occasionally be used.

Use in Preparing Noodles and Pasta: Fish and seafood can be used in making sauces for noodle and pasta dishes, as well as in soups, stews, and casseroles. They can also be used in making stuffing for pasta shells, and can be deep fried (tempura) and served over noodles in broth. Traditional Japanese dishes such as *nabeyaki* udon often include fish and seafood among the ingredients cooked with noodles.

Fruit

The energy in fruits is expansive in comparison to most grains, beans, and temperate vegetables. In most cases, fruit can be enjoyed three or four times per week. Locally grown or temperate climate fruits are preferable, while tropical fruits—which are extremely expansive—are not recommended for regular use in temperate zones. The fruits listed below are suitable for consumption in temperate climates:

Apples	Peaches
Apricots	Plums
Blackberries	Raisins
Cantaloup	Raspberries
Grapes	Strawberries
Honeydew melon	Tangerines
Lemons	Watermelon
Mulberries	Wild berries
Persimmon	

Nutritional Quality: In the macrobiotic diet, fruits are regarded as supplemental foods and eaten mainly for variety and enjoyment. Compared to whole grains, beans, and vegetables from land and sea, they contain much smaller amounts of complex carbohydrates, fiber, protein, unsaturated fat, and essential vitamins and minerals. They are largely made up of water. Fructose, the primary carbohydrate in fruit, is a simple sugar and enters the bloodstream more rapidly than the complex carbohydrates found in grains and vegetables. Moreover, the energy fruits give is very light and expansive and needs to be balanced by the strong centering energy of the other foods recommended in macrobiotics to maintain health and vitality.

Obtaining good quality fruit is essential because of the poor quality of most commercially available varieties. Whenever possible, try to obtain organically grown fruit. Organic or more naturally grown fruit will generally be slightly smaller in size, duller in appearance, and contain more blemishes and evidence of nibbling by small insects than commercially grown fruit. However, it will generally have a more symmetrical shape, fresher aroma, and sweeter taste than the other kind.

Pickles

Pickles can be eaten frequently as a supplement to main dishes. They stimulate appetite and help digestion. Some varieties—such as pickled daikon, or *takuan*—can be bought prepackaged in natural food stores. Other quick pickles can be prepared at home. Certain varieties take just a few hours to prepare, while others require more time.

A wide variety of pickles are fine for regular use, including salt, salt brine, bran, miso, tamari soy sauce, umeboshi vinegar, and others. Sauerkraut may also be used in small volume on a regular basis.

Nutritional Quality: The best pickles are made from natural ingredients, such as fresh organic vegetables, high-quality natural sea salt, and naturally fermented miso, tamari soy sauce, umeboshi, and vinegars. Pickles processed with strong spices, sugar, artificial vinegar, or chemicals are best avoided for maximum health. Spicy pickles, for example, are often eaten to balance the consumption of meat and other animal foods. However, in temperate climates, the intake of strong spices or artificial vinegar creates imbalance with the surrounding environment and can weaken health.

Seeds and Nuts

Seeds and nuts can be eaten from time to time as snacks and garnishes. They can be roasted with or without sea salt, sweetened with barley or rice malt, or seasoned with tamari soy sauce. Seeds and nuts can be ground into butter, shaved and served as a topping, garnish, or ingredient in desserts and other dishes. Below are varieties that can be used:

NUTS (More regular use)	*NUTS (Infrequent use)*
Almonds	Brazil nuts
Chestnuts	Cashews
Fiberts	Macadamia nuts
Peanuts	Others
Pecans	
Pinenuts	
Small Spanish nuts	*SEEDS*
Walnuts	Black and white sesame seeds
	Pumpkin seeds

Squash seeds
Sunflower seeds
Poppy seeds

Umeboshi plum seeds
Alfalfa seeds
Others

Nutritional Quality: Seeds and nuts contain many essential nutrients. Compared to meat and dairy products, they are a much better source of protein, and their fat and oil are either neutral or unsaturated in quality. However, compared to whole grains, their composition is not as balanced. Seeds and nuts are much higher in fat, higher in protein, and much lower in complex carbohydrates. Chestnuts, which are more like grains, are an exception. They contain up to fifty times less fat than other common nuts, less protein, and from two to four times as much complex carbohydrates.

Seeds and nuts are also very high in fiber, iron, calcium, vitamins A, B, and E, and other minerals and vitamins. Sesame seeds and pumpkin seeds are especially rich in iron, containing about five times more than meat and more than any other plant foods except sea vegetables. Sesame seeds are also a major source of calcium, containing about ten times that of a comparable amount of dairy milk. In medical studies, cancer researchers have recently identified an ingredient in seeds called a *protease inhibitor* that helps protect against tumor development. Whenever possible, try to find seeds and nuts that are organically grown and unprocessed.

Snacks

A variety of natural snacks may be enjoyed from time to time, including those made from whole grains, like cookies, bread, puffed cereals, mochi (pounded sweet brown rice), rice cakes, rice balls, and homemade sushi. Nuts and seeds may also be used as snacks, for example by roasting them with sea salt, tamari soy sauce, or sweetening them with grain-based sweeteners.

Nutritional Quality: For optimal health, it is best to select the highest-quality natural snacks, while avoiding items made with refined sweeteners, honey, carob, tropical fruits, or poor quality oils. Snacks made from foods within the Standard Macrobiotic Diet are preferred and can often be made simply at home. Those that are easiest to digest, such as rice balls, homemade sushi, mochi, noodles, and steamed whole grain bread are preferred for regular use. Hard, baked flour products, such as crackers, cookies, and muffins can interfere with digestion when eaten in excess.

Condiments

A variety of condiments may be used, some daily and others occasionally. Small amounts can be sprinkled on foods to adjust taste and nutritional value, and to stimulate appetite. They can be used on grains (including on noodle and pasta dishes), soups, vegetables, beans, and sometimes desserts. The most frequently used varieties include:

Gomashio (roasted sesame seeds and
   sea salt)

Sea vegetable powders (with or
   without roasted sesame seeds)

Tekka (a special condiment made with soybean miso, sesame oil, burdock, lotus root, carrots, and ginger)
Umeboshi plum (pickled plum)

CONDIMENTS THAT CAN BE USED OCCASIONALLY
Roasted sesame seeds

Roasted and chopped *shiso* (pickled beefsteak plant) leaves

Shio kombu (kombu cooked with tamari soy sauce and water)
Green nori flakes
Cooked nori condiment
Cooked miso with scallions or onions
Umeboshi or brown rice vinegar

Nutritional Quality: In macrobiotic cooking, condiments and garnishes provide nutritional and energetic balance to the meal. Among regular condiments, gomashio, or sesame salt, is especially nutritious. It is rich in calcium, iron, and other nutrients and is an excellent way to obtain polyunsaturated vegetable oil in whole form. Also, because they are roasted, the sesame seeds in gomashio are easier to digest. The roasted salt with which they are combined provides a harmonious balance to the oil in the seeds.

The proportion of sesame seeds to sea salt can vary from about ten to one to eighteen to one, depending on individual condition and need. The best quality sesame seeds for use in gomashio are natural black sesame seeds. It is important to be careful when choosing seeds, however, because some black seeds are dyed. To distinguish dyed seeds from natural black seeds, put them in warm water. If the seeds have been dyed, the artificial coloring in them will gradually dissolve and the water will turn black. A small amount of gomashio can be used daily; it is especially delicious on brown rice and other whole grains.

Tekka, a traditional condiment made of burdock, carrots, lotus root, Hatcho miso, and ginger that have been cooked down into a concentrated black powder, is also recommended for regular use. Since it provides very strong, concentrated energy, tekka is best used in small amounts sprinkled on grains, noodles, and other dishes. Since it takes about sixteen hours to prepare, tekka can be bought ready-made at the natural food store.

Umeboshi plums, which are available ready to eat at most natural food stores, are also recommended for regular use. They grow in the warmer, southern and middle regions of Japan and are related to the apricot. Traditionally fermented with sea salt and pickled with shiso leaves, umeboshi plums combine a sour and salty taste. They are a very balanced food, giving a strong centering energy, and have a wide range of uses. Once again, the quality of modern commercially prepared umeboshi is different from the quality of the past. Their aging is artificially speeded up, and synthetic colorings are often added to give them a deep red color that naturally comes from aging.

Even though umeboshi plums in natural food stores are generally good quality, their taste and energy differ widely. Those that have aged the longest are less tart and salty and give stronger energy, and are especially recommended for regular use.

Seasonings

A variety of seasonings can be used when preparing noodle, pasta, and other dishes. The point of seasoning in macrobiotic cooking is to bring forth the natural flavor of the ingredients in your dishes rather than trying to cover them up. For optimum health, it is better to avoid strongly expansive seasonings such as curry, hot pepper, basil, oregano, and other spices, and use those which are naturally processed from vegetable products or natural sea salt. These traditional seasonings have more centrally balanced energy when used in small amounts. Garlic is a common ingredient in many pasta dishes. A small amount can be used several times a week by those in good overall health. A list of recommended seasonings is presented below:

Unrefined sea salt
Soy sauce
Tamari soy sauce (fermented soybean and grain sauce)
Miso (fermented soybean and grain paste, i.e., rice barley, soybean, and other misos)
Brown rice and umeboshi vinegar
Barley malt and rice syrup
Grated daikon, radish, and ginger

Umeboshi plum and paste
Lemon, tangerine, and orange juice
Green and yellow mustard paste
Sesame, corn, safflower, mustard seed, and olive oil
Mirin (fermented sweet brown rice sweetener)
Amazaké (fermented sweet brown rice beverage)
Other traditional natural seasonings

Nutritional Quality: Salt is essential to life. The discovery of fire and salt enabled our ancestors to adapt to practically any environment on the earth and signalled the beginning of civilization. In choosing the quality of salt, the amount consumed, and the way salt is used in cooking are paramount questions in the life of an individual, family, community, and culture. In proper volume, high-quality unrefined natural sea salt, containing trace minerals and elements, contributes to smooth metabolism, steady energy and vitality, and a clear, focused mind. Unrefined sea salt made in the largely traditional manner contains compounds of several minerals such as magnesium as well as trace amounts of about sixty other elements naturally found in the sea. The proportion of trace minerals varies according the way in which the salt is processed, usually from a high of about 3 percent to a low of 0.5 percent.

Regular table salt is a highly industrialized product containing about 99.5 percent sodium chloride. While it is made from either sea salt or rock salt, most of the natural trace elements have been removed in processing and magnesium carbonate, sodium carbonate, and potassium iodide have been substituted in their place. Furthermore, dextrose, a highly refined industrial sugar, is customarily added to table salt to stabilize the iodine.

The overuse of poor quality refined table salt is one of the major factors in the rise of chronic illness in modern society. Compared to the macrobiotic way of eating, the usual modern diet contains about three to four times the amount of sodium. In addition to the large amount of refined salt used in frozen, canned, and convenience foods and salt added to foods at the table, sodium is consumed in large volume in animal foods, including eggs, meat, poultry, and dairy products. Excessive sodium from these sources as well as refined salt is a major factor in some forms of cardiovascular disease and other degenerative conditions.

Garnishes

A variety of garnishes can be used to create balance in your noodle, pasta, and other dishes and facilitate digestion. The use of garnishes depends upon the needs and desires of each person. Chopped raw scallions are frequently used as a garnish for noodles in broth. They add a wonderful balance to these dishes and help harmonize the energies in the broth and noodles. A thorough discussion of the art of garnishing is presented in Chapter 2. The following garnishes can be used when preparing noodle, pasta, and other dishes:

Grated daikon (for fish, mochi, noodles, and other dishes)

Grated radish (used like grated daikon)

Grated horseradish (used mostly for fish and seafood)

Chopped scallions (for noodles, fish, and seafood, and so on)

Parsley

Lemon, tangerine, and orange slices (mainly for fish and seafood)

Others

Desserts

A variety of natural desserts may be eaten from time to time, usually at the end of the main meal. Desserts can be made from azuki beans (sweetened with grain syrup, chestnuts, squash, or raisins); cooked or dried fruit; agar-agar (natural sea vegetable gelatin); grains (i.e., rice pudding, couscous cake, Indian pudding, and so on); and flour products (i.e., cookies, cakes, pies, muffins, and so on, prepared with fruit or grain sweeteners).

Nutritional Quality: The sweet flavor in macrobiotic cooking comes primarily from the complex carbohydrates in whole grains, beans, and fresh vegetables. Carbohydrates are generally known as sugars, but in speaking of sugar it is important to specify the variety. Single sugars, or monosaccharides, are found in fruit and honey and include glucose and fructose. Double sugars or disaccharides are found in cane sugar and milk and include sucrose and lactose. Complex sugars or polysaccharides are found in grains, beans, and vegetables. In the normal digestive process, complex sugars are decomposed gradually and at a nearly even rate by various enzymes in the mouth, stomach, pancreas, and intestines. Complex sugars enter the bloodstream slowly after being broken down into smaller saccharide units. During the process, the pH of the blood maintains a normally healthy slightly alkaline quality.

By contrast, simple (single and double) sugars are metabolized quickly, causing the blood to become overacidic. To compensate, our chemical metabolism uses stored minerals, including calcium, for buffer reactions that are necessary to maintain blood alkalinity. This process produces excessive carbon dioxide and water which are normally eliminated through breathing and urination. Moreover, the intake of refined sugar causes the pancreas to secrete insulin which allows excess sugar in the blood to be removed and enter the cells of the body. This produces a burst of energy as the glucose (the end product of all sugar metabolism) is oxidized and carbon dioxide and water are given off as waste products.

Much of the sugar that enters the bloodstream is originally stored in the liver in the form of glycogen until needed, when it is again changed into glucose. When the amount of glycogen exceeds the liver's storage capacity of about 50 grams, it is released into the bloodstream in the form of fatty acid. This fatty acid is stored first in the more inactive places of the body, such as the buttocks, thighs, and midsection. Then, if cane sugar, fruit sugar, dairy sugar, and other simple sugars are eaten excessively, fatty acid continuously becomes attracted to organs such as the heart, liver, and kidneys, which gradually become filled with fatty mucus.

As these accumulations penetrate the inner tissues, the normal functioning of the organs begins to weaken. In some cases, blockage—as in atherosclerosis—can occur. The buildup of fat can also lead to the formation of cysts, tumors, and eventually cancer. Still another form of degeneration may occur when the body's internal supply of minerals is mobilized to offset the effects of simple sugar consumption. For example, calcium from the teeth and bones may be depleted to balance the excessive intake of candy, soft drinks, and sugary desserts.

In order to prevent these degenerative effects, it is important to minimize or limit eating refined carbohydrates, especially simple sugar, as well as naturally occuring lactose and fructose in dairy foods and fruits, and to derive the sweetness of complex carvohydrates primarily in the form of grains, beans, bean products, and fresh vegetables.

Beverages

A variety of beverages may be consumed daily or occasionally. Amounts can vary according to each person's needs and weather conditions. Soft drinks, frozen orange juice, coffee, commercial tea, and other drinks with more extreme expanding energy are best avoided. The beverages listed below can be used to comfortably satisfy the desire for liquid.

Bancha twig and stem tea
Roasted brown rice or barley tea
Cereal grain coffee
Spring or well water
Amazaké
Dandelion tea
Soy milk (prepared with kombu)
Kombu tea
Lotus root tea
Mu tea

Other traditional nonstimulant and nonaromatic natural herbal beverages
Saké (fermented rice wine, without chemicals or sugar)
Beer (more natural quality)
Apple, grape, and apricot juice
Apple cider
Carrot, celery, and other vegetable juices

Nutritional Quality: A source of good quality water is essential for daily cooking and drinking. Natural spring or well water that is moving and alive (charged with natural energy from the earth) is best. City tap water often contains chlorine, as well as pesticide residues, detergents, nitrates, and heavy metals such as lead. These are several mechanical methods used to filter tap water of impurities, but it is still preferable to natural spring water that comes up from the earth before it is bottled or clear well water from an underground vein. However, it is important to have spring or well water tested before using it to see if it is safe.

Bancha is the most frequently consumed beverage in most macrobiotic households. It is picked in midsummer from the large and mature leaves, stems, and twigs of the tea bush. These are called respectively bancha leaf tea, bancha stem tea, and bancha twig tea. Traditionally picked by hand in the high mountains, the bancha leaves, stems, and twigs are roasted and cooled up to four separate times in large iron caldrons. This procedure, as well as the late harvest when the caffeine has naturally receded from the tea bush, makes for a tea containing virtually no caffeine or tannin, especially in the stem and twig parts. Also, unlike other teas which are acidic, bancha is slightly alkaline and thus has a soothing, beneficial effect on digestion, blood quality, and the mind. Bancha twig tea is also known as *kukicha*, from the Japanese word for "twig tea."

Eating Healthfully

The way in which we eat can be just as important as the choice of foods. Regular meals are better and the amount of food eaten depends on each person's needs. Snacking is best kept moderate, so that it does not replace meals, while tea and other beverages can be enjoyed throughout the day as desired.

Chewing is also very important; try to chew each mouthful of food until it becomes liquid. Thorough chewing allows for the efficient digestion and absorption of foods. Moreover, chewing mixes food with saliva, a natural substance that helps protect the body from illness. You can eat whenever you feel hungry, but try to avoid eating before bedtime, preferably for three hours, except in unusual circumstances. Finally learn to appreciate your foods and the health-giving properties they contain. Let your gratitude overflow to include nature, the universe, other people, and all forms of life on this wonderful planet.

Chapter 2: Getting Started

In this chapter we present background information that will come in handy before you actually start cooking. We discuss preliminary steps such as how to wash your foods properly and how to soak, roast, and purée them. We also explain how to cut vegetables and other foods for your noodle and pasta dishes. Let us begin with a review of the important utensils you will need when getting started.

Basic Equipment

We do not recommend using aluminum, teflon, or plastic-coated cookware. Cookware of this type is easily scratched or chipped, thus releasing toxic metals and plastic into foods. Plastic-coated cookware is chemically treated and is also not recommended for optimum health. Glass pots and skillets used on top of the stove can make it more difficult to cook foods properly. These utensils cook food at a much higher temperature than cookware made of stainless steel. After you remove these pots from the burner, the food continues to cook in them, often for several minutes, and this can result in overcooking. These utensils are produced by bonding plastic particles with glass.

We recommend avoiding electric skillets and cooking pots, as electric current disturbs the natural energy of food. Foods heated by electricity are not recommended for optimum health and are not as delicious as those cooked over more natural energy such as gas or wood.

Stainless Steel Pressure Cooker—Although a pressure cooker is not necessary when preparing most noodle and pasta dishes, it is an essential item in a macrobiotic whole food kitchen. A pressure cooker is used to prepare the brown rice and other whole grain dishes served along with noodles or pasta and can be useful when cooking beans used in pasta dishes. Pressure cookers are available at most natural food stores and come in both stainless and enameled steel. A small five liter cooker is probably the most suitable for the average family.

Flame Deflector—Flame deflectors are metal discs with wood handles. They are made of metal with hundreds of tiny holes and are inserted under pots on the stove. They cause the flame to be evenly distributed under the pot, thus lessening the chances of burning. We usually place a deflector under the pressure cooker when preparing brown rice, other grains, or beans, or under pots in which food is being kept warm. Flame deflectors are inexpensive and can be found in most natural food or hardware stores.

Stainless Steel Cookware—High-quality stainless steel cookware is essential when preparing noodles, pasta, and other dishes. You can begin with a large- or medium-sized pot for preparing soups and stews, and for boiling noodles and pasta, vegetables, and beans; two or three smaller saucepans; and one or two skillets for frying and sautéing. These should be sufficient to begin cooking delicious meals.

Cast Iron Cookware—A cast iron skillet can be used to sauté vegetables or prepare noodle *sukiyaki*. To season a new skillet, first roast a small amount of sea salt in it for several minutes, then brush the skillet with sesame oil and sauté onion in it. Discard the onion. Bake the oil-coated skillet in a 300° to 350° F oven for several hours. The skillet will turn dark or black when properly seasoned. Remove the skillet and allow it to cool. Then wash and place it on a low flame until it is completely dry. This will prevent the skillet from rusting. Do not use metal scrubbers when washing the skillet as they may cause some of the seasoning to come off. Also, it is not a good idea to plunge a hot cast iron skillet into cold water. This may cause the metal to become pitted or develop little holes in it. Always allow the skillet to completely cool off before washing it. Treated carefully, a cast iron skillet will last for many years.

Deep-frying Pot—A cast iron Dutch oven is very useful to deep fry tofu, tempeh, seitan, fu, vegetables, or other items for noodle and pasta dishes. It is especially nice to use when making tempura topping for noodles in broth. Season the Dutch oven in the same manner as a skillet.

Oil Skimmer—This utensil is available in fine or large wire mesh with either wood or steel handles or in stainless steel. This is inexpensive and very useful for removing deep-fried or tempuraed foods from oil, or for removing steamed or boiled vegetables from a pot.

Stainless Steel Baking Ware—Although not used directly in noodle and pasta cookery, baking ware comes in handy when you wish to oven roast nuts, seeds, croutons, or sea vegetables for garnishing noodle and pasta dishes.

Glass and Earthenware Baking Dishes—There are a variety of casserole dishes that can be very helpful when cooking lasagna, stuffed shells, tofu manacotti, and other noodle and pasta dishes.

Nabe—These earthenware casserole bowls can be used to make various vegetable and noodle dishes. They are made in Japan and come in a variety of sizes. They are hand-designed and painted, and properly glazed to ensure good health. They can be used to prepare nabeyaki udon or noodle dishes.

Wood Utensils—Wood utensils help keep your metal cookware from scratching. Wood spoons, forks, spatulas, ladles, rice paddles, cooking chopsticks, spaghetti or pasta forks, and rolling pins are helpful for sautéing, stirring, removing food from pots, serving, and other uses. They are fairly inexpensive and can be purchased in most natural food or kitchenware stores.

Fig. 2 Pasta Rolling Pin

Fig. 3 Pasta Machine

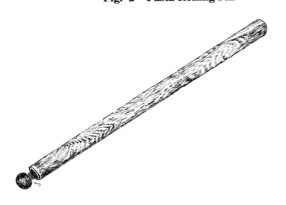

Pasta Rolling Pin—You will need a pasta rolling pin if you plan to make your own pasta and do not have a pasta machine. These specially-designed rolling pins make it easier to produce very thin sheets of dough which are cut into noodles or pasta. They are usually from 24 to 35 inches in length and are made of beechwood. Without a special rolling pin, pasta making is much more time-consuming, as you have to roll out smaller amounts of dough in order to get the desired thickness for good pasta. These pins allow you to roll out large sheets of dough, and because of their design, you can exert more pressure than you are able to with an ordinary rolling pin.

Pastry Rolling Pin—These wood rolling pins are designed for rolling pastry dough and are very handy for making pastry crust for dishes such as seitan-noodle pie. Most rolling pins are made of hardwood and come in a variety of styles. They can be found in kitchen specialty or department stores.

Pasta Machine—Stainless steel machines that roll out and cut pasta dough are now available. They can be used to make udon (both wide and thin), soba, spaghetti, fettucinne, lasagna, and other varieties of noodles and pasta. You can purchase attachable rollers for cutting dough into different sizes and thicknesses. The machine can be clamped to a table and has a handle that is turned by hand in order to roll or cut dough. There is a gauge built into the side of the machine that can be adjusted to change the thickness of your noodles and pasta. The machine is easy to operate and comes with complete instructions. Pasta machines are available at kitchenware stores, Italian markets, or through mail order kitchenware companies. Moderately priced and expensive models are available.

Blender—Although not used regularly in macrobiotic cooking, an electric blender can be used on special occasions to purée tofu to a very creamy consistency when making lasagna or other stuffed pasta dishes.

Natural Bristle Brush—Natural bristle brushes from Japan are recommended for scrubbing root or ground vegetables. They can also be used to clean the groves of your *suribachi* (earthenware grinding bowl), or clean foods from the bamboo mats used in making noodle sushi. They are inexpensive and can be purchased at most natural food stores.

Vegetable Knife—A sharp Japanese vegetable knife is an essential item in a macrobiotic kitchen. It permits you to cut vegetables smoothly and elegantly, and to cut homemade noodles and pasta. Several types are available including those made of stainless steel, carbon steel, and high-grade carbon steel. To care for your knife, wash and dry it after each use, and store it in a wood knife rack or wrap it in a kitchen towel and store it in a safe place. You may lightly oil your knife, if it is made of carbon steel, to prevent rusting. Carbon steel knives can be scrubbed with natural scouring powder to remove rust, rinsed, wiped completely dry, and stored as above. Knives come in different sizes and shapes for various uses.

Paring Knife—A stainless steel paring knife is useful in preparing fancy vegetable garnishes, or for mincing or peeling foods.

Serrated Pasta Knife—This knife is useful if you want to prepare fresh homemade pasta, or for making fancy vegetable garnishes for noodle and pasta dishes.

Sharpening Stone—Several types of stones are available for sharpening your knives. Whet stones are moistened with water before use, while oil stones are rubbed with oil. (Sharpening rods are not recommended for Japanese knives.) Sharpening stones can be obtained in most natural food and hardware stores.

Pasta Wheel (Fluted Pastry Wheel)—This tool is useful when making homemade lasagna, twists, or other pasta with fluted or curled edges. It has a wood handle that is attached to a fluted, stainless steel wheel. It is an inexpensive and practical tool for the serious pasta maker.

Fig. 4   Fluted Pastry Wheel

Ravioli Cutters—These tools are used to make homemade ravioli. They are not essential if you already have a fluted pastry wheel. They come in both round and square shapes for making either round or square ravioli.

Fig. 5   Ravioli Cutters

Pasta Drying Rack—Wood racks for drying homemade pasta are available at kitchen specialty stores. You can also hang fresh pasta over clothesline or bamboo chopsticks to dry. Pasta takes about three days to dry.

Wood Cutting Boards—It is useful to have several cutting boards: one for vegetables or noodles and another for fish and seafood. It is best not to cut fish or seafood on your vegetable-cutting board. The juices from fish and seafood are absorbed into the porous surface of the wood and are difficult to remove. To properly season a cutting board, rub the surface with either corn or light sesame oil. Allow the board to sit and absorb the oil for at least several hours. Then wipe the board dry with paper towels to absorb any surface oil. Cutting boards may be oiled once a month or so to keep them from absorbing the juices of the foods cut on them. To clean, simply wipe with a wet sponge after using, instead of plunging into water. Do not use soap on wood boards and utensils as it is easily absorbed into the wood and detracts from the taste of food. Oiling cutting boards also helps prevent bending or buckling. High-quality hardwood boards last many years if properly cared for.

Colander or Strainer—Colanders and strainers are available in stainless steel, wire mesh, or ceramic varieties and are essential for washing, rinsing, and draining noodles, pasta, and other foods. It is helpful to have one colander and two strainers: one larger mesh and one finer mesh for washing small grains or seeds. They are fairly inexpensive and can be purchased in natural food stores with a kitchen section or in department stores.

Bamboo Strainers—Bamboo strainers are available in natural food and Oriental markets and are especially nice for rinsing and draining Oriental noodles. Small strainers can be used as serving dishes for cold noodles.

Flat Grater—Flat metal or porcelain graters from Japan are used for finely grating ginger, daikon, and other root vegetables. They are used frequently in macrobiotic kitchens to prepare vegetable garnishes for noodle, pasta, and other dishes. They are inexpensive and can be found in most natural food stores.

Box Graters—Stainless steel Western-style box graters are used to grate vegetables for noodle and pasta salads.

Fig. 6   Box Grater

Tamari Soy Sauce Dispenser—Glass dispensers are very useful for pouring tamari soy sauce by the dropful on soups and noodles or for seasoning dishes while cooking. They can be found at most natural food stores and come in various sizes and shapes. Larger ones can be purchased sealed and prefilled with tamari soy sauce. Most macrobiotic cooks could not do without them.

Suribachi and *Surikogi*—A suribachi is a grooved, earthenware grinding bowl used to purée and grind

Fig. 7 *Suribachi* **and** *Surikogi*

foods by hand. It is useful in preparing condiments, dips, and sauces, in puréeing foods, or making soft foods for babies. These bowls come in small, medium, and large sizes, and are found in most natural food stores. The small- or medium-sized bowls are suitable for most households. A surikogi is the wood pestle that comes with the suribachi.

Serving Bowls—Serving bowls come in many sizes, shapes, colors, and designs and enhance the presentation of your noodle and pasta dishes. They are available in wood, earthenware, bamboo, glass, porcelain, and other natural materials.

Mixing Bowls—Wood, glass, or stainless steel mixing bowls are useful when kneading pastry dough, mixing foods, or sometimes when serving finished dishes.

Flour Sifter—Hand held flour sifters are useful to sift out the bran in flour when making homemade pasta. They are available in most department or kitchen supply stores.

Containers—Glass, ceramic, or wood containers can be purchased over time to store noodles, pasta, beans, sea vegetables, seeds, nuts, condiments, seasonings, flours, and other dried foods. They are fairly inexpensive and are well worth the investment. Proper storage of food prevents spoilage and make it easier to find the items needed in cooking. We do not recommend storing food in plastic containers, as the taste of the plastic may be absorbed by food and detract from its delicious natural flavor.

Fig. 8 **Bamboo Sushi Mat (*Sudare*)**

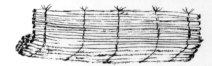

Bamboo Sushi Mat (*Sudare*)—These sushi mats are made of thin strips of bamboo that have been tied together. They can be used to cover leftovers or keep food warm. Bamboo mats help prevent food from drying out. Air circulates freely through the thin strips of bamboo, thus reducing spoilage of cooked leftovers. We also use them in making noodle sushi. They are inexpensive and it is well worth purchasing several. They can be found in most natural food stores.

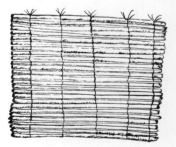

Steamer Basket—Steamer baskets are useful for reheating foods and steaming vegetables for noodle dishes. They come in two varieties: collapsible stainless steel steamers that fit inside cooking pots, and bamboo steamers that are placed on top of a pot. They can be found in most natural food or Oriental markets. Bamboo steamers need to be seasoned before use by steaming vegetable odds and ends in them several times to remove the taste of the wood.

Stainless Steel Hand Food Mill—Food mills, although not essential, are useful for puréeing soups or beans, making sauces, puréeing tofu fillings for pasta and noodle dishes, and puréeing seitan to make wheat balls. Mills can be found in most natural food or kitchen supply stores. They come in both steel coated tin and plastic varieties.

Wood Bowls—Wood bowls are useful for kneading pasta dough or serving noodle or pasta dishes when sauces or dressings are added in the individual servings. Wood is porous and allows cooked food to breathe but can absorb sauces or dressings, resulting in drier noodle or pasta dishes. At least one medium-sized bowl can be purchased right away. Wood bowls come in various sizes and shapes and are made of different types of wood. Choose ones that are appealing and suitable for your needs. Wood bowls need to be periodically seasoned with oil in the same manner as a cutting board to ensure long life and attractiveness.

Flour Mill—If you are considering making fresh pasta on a regular basis, you may want to purchase a flour mill for grinding fresh flour. Freshly ground flour produces superior quality pasta. There are many varieties available.

Organic Soap—High-quality, organic dishwashing soap is helpful for removing oil from skillets after frying, but is often not necessary for most other utensils. A simple washing in hot water is often sufficient.

Electric Appliances—As mentioned previously, we recommend using electric appliances as little as possible. For optimum health, convert from electric to gas cooking as soon as it is convenient. Electric blenders, waffle irons, popcorn poppers, food processors, and other appliances are best reserved for use on special occasions only. Microwave ovens are not recommended for cooking or reheating foods.

Washing Vegetables and Dried Foods

Washing foods properly greatly enhances their flavor. Cutting vegetables before you wash them is not recommended. Once you slice a vegetable, there is more exposed surface from which nutrients and flavor can escape. It is also more difficult to remove soil from cut vegetables than it is from whole ones.

Washing Grains, Beans, and Seeds—Prior to washing these foods, place a handful at a time on a plate and sort out the damaged pieces, stones, or other debris. After sorting, place them in a bowl and cover with cold water. Using one hand, stir in one direction. Wash these foods quickly, as this helps them retain nutrients. Pour off the water and repeat once or twice more until the water is clean. Finally, place the grains, beans, or seeds in a colander or wire-mesh strainer with the appropriate sized mesh and quickly rinse under cold water to remove any remaining dust. Allow to drain for a minute or so. These items are now ready to be cooked.

Washing Sea Vegetables—Most sea vegetables can be washed as above, although there are some exceptions. Kombu, for instance, needs only to be gently wiped on both sides with a clean damp sponge before being soaked and sliced. Flat sheets of nori do not require washing; simply toast and use them as is. (Fresh nori that is not in sheet form must be washed as above in advance of soaking and cooking.) All other sea vegetables can be washed in the following manner: Place the sea vegetable on a plate or table and sort out any hard clumps, stones, shells, or other debris. Then place in a bowl and cover with cold water. Quickly rinse by moving the sea vegetables around with your hand. Pour off the rinsing water and cover again with cold water. Rinse again, quickly, with your hand, and pour off the water. Place the sea vegetable in a colander or strainer and quickly rinse under cold water from the faucet. The sea vegetable is now ready to be soaked, sliced, and cooked.

Washing Root or Ground Vegetables—The skin of these vegetables is usually firm and soil can be difficult to remove completely by simply rinsing. Root or smooth round vegetables can be scrubbed with a natural bristle brush to properly remove soil. Place the vegetables in the sink and run cold water over them. Gently but firmly scrub with the vegetable brush, making sure not to damage the nutrient-rich skin. Below are guidelines for washing vegetables used commonly in macrobiotic cooking.

• Burdock has a rather delicate brown or dark brown skin that is often mistaken for soil. If the skin becomes white while scrubbing, you have scrubbed too hard.
• When washing green cabbage, most types of lettuce, and Chinese cabbage, remove some or all of the leaves from the core and wash them separately under cold water. Vegetables that have waxed skins require peeling to remove the skin and can be simply rinsed under cold water.
• Leeks need to be split, with a knife, lengthwise down the center and each layer needs to be carefully washed to remove soil. Scallions and chives do not need to be split with a knife; simply rinse the upper portion with cold water. The root portion of leeks, scallions, and chives can be held under cold running water and scrubbed firmly with a vegetable brush to remove soil between the roots.
• Celery sometimes has soil caked between the ribs that run up the stalk. To remove it, take a vegetable brush and lightly scrub.
• Cucumbers, if unwaxed, can be washed in the same manner as roots. If waxed, remove the skin and rinse under cold water before using.
• For root vegetables with the greens still attached (radishes, celery root, turnip and greens, daikon and greens, carrot and tops, and so on), remove the green portion with a knife and wash as you would other leafy greens. The root can be washed as above.
• Onions are first peeled and then rinsed quickly under cold water until clean.
• If vegetables that require peeling are heavily caked with soil, it is a good idea to soak them first in cold water for several minutes. Then scrub the vegetable (with the

skin left on) before peeling and rinsing under cold water so that the heavy soil does not discolor the inside.

• Fresh shiitake and other mushrooms can simply be rinsed thoroughly by hand under cold water, instead of using a vegetable brush.

Washing Leafy Greens—First sort through the green leaves and remove any yellowed or damaged leaves or grasses that may be mixed in with the leaves, and discard them. Next, place the greens in a large bowl or pot and completely cover with cold water. Let them soak for several seconds. Wash by swishing the leaves around in the water. Remove the leaves and pour off the water. If the leaves are heavily covered with sand, you may have to repeat this step two or three times. Take one leaf at a time and wash it thoroughly under cold running water to remove any remaining soil or dust. With tightly curled leaves, such as kale or chard, make sure to gently unfurl the leaves while rinsing to remove any hidden matter. Wash each leaf individually under cold water until completely clean. Watercress may have small shells in it, so it is important to wash each leaf thoroughly.

• Leafy greens such as collards, cabbage, or Chinese cabbage have smoother leaves and usually do not require as much effort to wash as green vegetables with jagged edges. When washing lettuce, cabbage, and Chinese cabbage remove the outer leaves on which soil is more likely to be attached, and rinse them separately from the inner portion. The inner core can be rinsed whole.

• Turnip, rutabaga, radish, carrot, and daikon tops sometimes have sandy soil attached to them. Rinsing an entire bunch in a pot once or twice is not sufficient to remove soil. Do this first and then make sure to rinse each leaf individually under cold water. Broccoli can also be difficult to clean, as it has hundreds of tiny flowerettes tightly packed together. It may require soaking for several minutes before washing and rinsing. Once the greens are thoroughly washed, place them in a colander and allow them to drain before slicing or cooking.

• String beans and peas are very easy to clean and can simply be rinsed individually or in a colander under cold water.

• Wild leafy greens such as dandelion and chives are best if picked in fields that are not close to roads or highways. They can be washed in the same manner as cultivated greens.

Washing Dried Foods—Foods such as dried daikon, lotus seeds, and dried lotus root require a quick rinsing under cold water before being soaked. Simply place in a colander, quickly rinse and pour off the water. Dried chestnuts require sorting before being washed and rinsed as above. Foods as shiitake mushrooms or dried tofu do not require washing; simply soak prior to using. Nuts roast more evenly if they are quickly rinsed and drained before roasting.

Other Helpful Hints

Some of the whole foods used in this book require soaking, puréeing, diluting, grinding, and roasting prior to cooking or during the cooking process. Below are instructions for various foods that require these preliminary steps.

Soaking—Beans, sea vegetables, dried chestnuts, lotus seeds, dried lotus root, dried tofu, dried daikon, shiitake mushrooms, and other dried foods need to be soaked prior to cooking in order to help them cook properly or to make them soft enough to cut smoothly. The amount of time for soaking varies from food to food, but the basic procedure is generally the same.

First wash or rinse the dried food item as instructed previously. Place in a bowl and add enough cold water to cover. Let the food soak for the length of time indicated in the recipe or in the chart below before slicing or cooking. Items such as dried tofu and shiitake mushrooms are best soaked in warm water rather than cold water.

Using Soaking Water—In most cases soaking water can be saved and recycled as part of your water measurement in the recipe. However, there are a few exceptions to this. Sea vegetable soaking water, if very salty, can be discarded. Azuki bean and black soybean soaking water can be used in cooking, while the soaking water from beans that are higher in fat is usually discarded. If the soaking water from dried daikon is very dark brown, it may make the dish taste quite bitter. In this case discard the soaking water. If the soaking water is light in color, it is more sweet and can be used in the recipe. Soaking water from dried tofu is discarded as it has an unpleasant taste. Soaking waters from items such as fu, shiitake mushrooms, lotus seeds, dried lotus root, and dried chestnuts can be used in cooking.

When dried foods are called for in a recipe, you can refer to the table below for the approximate amount of time needed for soaking.

Table 2

Food	Appropriate Soaking Time
Sea vegetables	3–5 minutes
Dried daikon	5–10 minutes
Dried tofu	5–10 minutes
Fu	7–10 minutes
Dried lotus root	30–60 minutes
Dried lotus seeds	30–60 minutes
Shiitake mushrooms	10–15 minutes
Dried chestnuts	10–15 minutes (after roasting)
Beans	6–8 hours
Grains	6–8 hours
Dried fruits	15–20 minutes

Diluting—A few dried food items require diluting before use. Kuzu, used often in making sauce for noodles, is one of these. To dilute kuzu, place in a cup or small bowl and add an equal amount or slightly more cold water. Stir to dilute and remove lumps. The kuzu is now ready to use as a thickener in making sauces or gravies.

Puréed Miso—In this book you will come across recipes that require puréed miso. To purée miso, place the amount of miso called for in the recipe in a suribachi. Add slightly more water than miso. Purée the miso with an even, circular motion, using the wood pestle (surikogi). Continue until the miso has a smooth, pastelike consistency. It is now ready to use.

Grinding—The suribachi can also be used to prepare pesto and other sauces, as well as condiments and dressings. To do this, place the whole, chopped, or roasted food in the suribachi and grind with the pestle in an even, circular motion. Sea vegetables are usually ground to a fine powder, while seeds and nuts are more lightly ground until half-crushed. (If you grind roasted seeds and nuts for a long time they will turn into a thick seed or nut butter that can be used as a dressing for noodle salad.) Large roasted nuts or pumpkin seeds usually need to be slightly chopped before grinding to make this process easier. Vegetables for making pesto, or for adding to fresh pasta dough, are chopped or minced prior to grinding.

Marinating—Some of the recipes call for marinating vegetables, tofu, fish, seafood, or other items in a mixture of tamari soy sauce and water, or in ginger, umeboshi vinegar, or miso. To marinate, follow the instructions in the recipe for preparing the marinade, then place the required food item in a bowl. Pour the marinade over the food item, and allow it to sit and absorb the marinade for the length of time indicated in the recipe. The marinated food is now ready to eat or be cooked.

Grating—Two types of graters are used in the recipes—a flat grater for fine grating and a box grater for coarse grating. To finely grate ginger, daikon, or other root vegetables for use in salads, sauces, condiments, dressings, or garnishes, take a flat grater and set it on a cutting board, table, or other flat surface. Hold it securely by the handle with one hand, while holding the item to be grated firmly in the other hand. Move the vegetables in a back-and-forth or circular motion over the teeth of the grater until the proper amount is grated. Place the gratings in a bowl until ready to use. The box-style grater has four or more sides which you can use depending the coarseness desired. It stands upright and can be placed in a bowl, on a plate, or on a cutting board. Hold the handle firmly and grate in a downward motion until you have grated the desired amount.

Using a Suribachi and Hand Food Mill—A suribachi is useful for grinding or puréeing food items for use in making pesto, sauces, garnishes, dressings, or condiments. Place the ingredients in the suribachi. Hold the wooden pestle securely with one hand while holding the suribachi with the other. Grind in an even, circular motion, preferably in one direction, using the grooved sides of the bowl to grind to the desired consistency.

A hand food mill can also be used to purée items such as tofu, soft-cooked vegetables, fruits, or grains, and can be used in preparing sauces and dressings. Simply set the food mill on top of a bowl so that it fits securely and place the food item in the mill. Hold the handle with one hand and turn the hand grinder with the other until the food is smooth and is squeezed through the little holes in the bottom of the mill, thus allowing the ground food to fall into the bowl underneath the mill. The food is now ready to use in preparing the dish.

Roasting—Items such as seeds, nuts, grains, beans, or sea vegetables can be oven roasted or pan roasted on top of the stove. Oven roasting is used most often when preparing sea vegetable condiments. Simply place the unwashed sea vegetable (kombu, wakame, dulse, kelp) on a dry baking or cookie sheet. Place in a 350° F oven for about 15 to 20 minutes or until crisp but not burnt or black. Remove and grind in a suribachi until it becomes a fine powder. Seeds, dried chestnuts, grains, beans, and nuts often roast more evenly when placed in a dry skillet on top of the stove. First wash or rinse the item to be roasted and then allow it to drain. Next, place the damp item in a skillet over a high flame. Take a bamboo rice paddle, and using a back-and-forth wrist motion, quickly but gently move the food back and forth to evenly roast. When the water has evaporated, reduce the flame to medium and continue roasting until golden. Often seeds and grains will begin to pop when they are done and release nutty fragrance. Beans are roasted only until the skin of the bean splits slightly and then only for a few seconds more.

You may occasionally shake the skillet gently back and forth to bring seeds, grains, nuts, or beans from the bottom to the top, thus roasting more evenly. When done remove immediately from the hot skillet to prevent further cooking and possible burning.

Elegant Garnishing

Garnishing noodle and pasta dishes properly is an important aspect of cooking. Garnishes add harmony to your dishes—both in terms of visual appeal and in terms of nutrient and energy balance. The use of simple garnishes as well as fancy, attractive cutting techniques transforms noodle and pasta cookery into an art. Garnishes add color and beauty, stimulate the appetite, and harmonize the tastes, colors, and energies of the ingredients. Most garnishes require little energy and time to prepare, and usually no special utensils other than a sharp vegetable or paring knife. Simple garnishes are often enough for daily meals served at home, while for special occasions, fancier garnishes are sometimes nice. Some of the garnishes used in noodle and pasta cooking include:

> Sprigs of parsley or watercress
> Sliced scallions, chives, or parsley
> Roasted seeds
> Roasted and chopped nuts
> Green nori flakes
> Powdered sea vegetable condiments

Croutons (deep-fried or dry-roasted)
Sliced red radish rounds
Grated daikon
Grated gingerroot
Toasted nori squares or strips
Grated horseradish or wasabi
Lemon, lime, or tangerine slices, wedges, or twists
Pine needles
Clean leaves
Flowers
Cooked, thinly sliced shiitake mushrooms
Marinated tofu cubes
Tofu cheese cubes
Fancy vegetable and fruit garnishes
Whole lettuce leaves
Bonito (shaved dried fish) flakes

Please note that these garnishes are fine for use by persons in generally good health. Those with specific health concerns may omit any of these ingredients until their condition improves. Now let us see how to make some of the more unfamiliar garnishes listed above.

Toasted Nori Strips or Squares—Toasted nori is often used as a garnish for noodle and pasta dishes. To toast or roast the nori, hold the sheet over the flame on a gas burner so that the shiny, smooth side faces up. Hold the nori about 10 to 12 inches above the flame and rotate it over the flame until the color changes from dark green or black-purple to a light green. This will take only a few seconds.

Once the nori is toasted, fold the sheet in half and tear or cut along the fold with a pair of scissors. Then fold in half again and tear or cut. You now have four equal-sized squares. Stack the squares on top of each other and cut them into strips 1 to 2 inches wide. Next, cut the strips into 1-inch squares or thin, matchstick-style strips. The nori is now ready to use as a garnish.

Croutons—Croutons are nice for occasional use on pasta or noodle soups and salads. As described below, they can be dry roasted, oven roasted, or deep fried.

• *Dry Roasting*—Dice fresh or slightly dried whole wheat, sourdough, or rice bread. Place a dry skillet on a medium flame and heat up. Place the diced bread in the skillet and dry roast until golden brown, stirring constantly to evenly toast and prevent burning. When dry, sprinkle with a few drops of tamari soy sauce, if desired, and roast another minute or so. If you do not wish to season the cubes with tamari soy sauce, omit it. The croutons are now ready to use.

Persons who do not have to watch their oil intake may occasionally roast the diced cubes in a small amount of light or dark sesame or corn oil instead of dry roasting them.

• *Oven Roasting*—Dice bread as above and place on a baking sheet. Place in a 350°

F oven and dry roast, stirring occasionally to evenly roast, until completely dried out and golden brown. Season with a small amount of tamari soy sauce as above, mix, and dry roast several more minutes until completely dry.

• *Deep Frying*—Dice the bread as above and dip into hot, light or dark sesame oil. Deep fry until golden brown. Drain on paper towels to remove excess oil. The croutons are now ready to use.

Roasted Sesame Seeds (Tan or Black)—Wash a small amount (1/8 to 1/4 cup) of sesame seeds as instructed earlier in this chapter. Place in a fine-mesh strainer and allow them to drain for several minutes. Heat a stainless steel skillet and place the damp seeds in it. Set the flame to high. Dry roast, stirring or moving the seeds back and forth with a rice paddle until most of the water has evaporated from the outside of the seeds. Then reduce the flame to medium and continue to roast until the seeds begin to pop. To test the seeds for doneness, take a clean, dry tablespoon and fill it with seeds. Now pour the seeds from the spoon back into the skillet. If any seeds stick to the spoon, this means that the seeds still contain moisture and are not yet done. Continue to roast, occasionally checking with the spoon, until no seeds adhere to the spoon. The seeds are now done. Remove quickly to prevent further roasting and possible scorching. The seeds are now ready to use as a garnish or in making various sauces, condiments, or dressings.

Roasted Sunflower or Pumpkin Seeds—Wash, drain, and dry roast these seeds as you would sesame seeds. Pumpkin seeds are done when they begin to pop and turn slightly brown. Sunflower seeds do not pop but are done when they turn golden in color. You may use the seeds as is for garnishes, or in preparing dressings for noodle salads. You may also season them with a few drops of tamari soy sauce at the very end of cooking for a slightly salty flavor. When you do this, roast the seeds for several more seconds until the tamari soy sauce dries on them.

Roasted Nuts—Occasionally, roasted nuts are used in making pasta sauces. Place shelled nuts in a hot skillet and dry roast or place on a baking sheet and oven roast. Stir occasionally to evenly roast and prevent burning. You may season with several drops of tamari soy sauce at the end of cooking or remove and use unseasoned (either whole or chopped) as a garnish or in dressings.

Try not to roast nuts until they become scorched or burnt, as this causes them to have a bitter flavor.

Chopped Nuts or Seeds—Roast the nuts or seeds as above, then place them in a circular mound on a cutting board. Hold the knife with the tip on the board. Using a circular rocking motion, move the blade from the tip to the hilt or opposite end, gradually cutting or working in a half-circle, until all the nuts or seeds are chopped. If large pieces are desired, such as when walnuts or pecans are used, simply break them into the desired size with your fingers.

Minced Vegetables—Mincing is simply a method of chopping vegetables very finely. Minced scallions, parsley, chives, or onions can be used often in sauces, dressings or to garnish noodles and broth or pasta soups. Minced vegetables are often much more flavorful than larger slices. Simply place the vegetable on a cutting board and chop into very small pieces.

Grated Vegetables—Sometimes vegetables can be finely grated and used as a garnish or in preparing dressings. Please refer to the previous section in this chapter for instructions on using graters. Grated daikon or ginger is often used to help digest oily foods such as tempura served on top of noodles and broth or when fish or seafood is served in or with these dishes.

Marinated Tofu—Cubes of marinated tofu are often very nice in summer noodle and pasta salads. Drain a cake of tofu and slice into bite-sized cubes. Place in a bowl and sprinkle with several drops of tamari soy sauce or umeboshi vinegar, gently mix, and let sit for 30 minutes or so.

As a variation, you may prepare a marinade by combining a small amount of water, tamari soy sauce or umeboshi vinegar, and a dab of grated ginger. Mix the marinade and pour it over the tofu. Gently mix and allow to marinate for 30 minutes or so.

Pickled Tofu—A slightly fermented flavor is sometimes nice in noodle and pasta salads and this can be achieved by adding pickled tofu. Pickled tofu is made by coating whole or halved cakes of tofu with barley miso, umeboshi vinegar and water, or tamari soy sauce and water, and allowing it to sit for 3 to 4 days.

To pickle tofu in miso, take a cake of very fresh firm-style tofu and drain it for several minutes. Wrap a layer of clean cotton cheesecloth around the tofu cake. Pack barley miso all around the covered tofu cake until it is completely covered with miso. Place in a bowl or ceramic crock. Cover the crock or bowl with a piece of cheesecloth and let it sit for 2 to 4 days. For mild-tasting tofu, let it sit for 2 days. For a stronger flavor, let it sit for 3 to 4 days.

When finished, remove the miso-coated cheesecloth from the tofu cake. Rinse the tofu under cold water. Slice into cubes for use as a garnish.

The miso can be removed from the cheesecloth and saved to be used again, or to season soups, although it will have a milder flavor, as the tofu absorbs much of the salt it contains.

These are just a few of the many natural foods that can be used to garnish and enhance the flavor and beauty of your noodle or pasta dishes.

Basic Cutting

To enhance the flavor and the appearance of foods prepared in a macrobiotic kitchen we use a variety of vegetable cutting techniques. In this section we introduce the techniques used most frequently.

Using a Japanese Vegetable Knife—The proper use of your knife is essential in smooth and effortless cutting. Grip the knife handle firmly with either hand. If you are right-handed, curl your index, middle, ring, and little fingers firmly around the right side of the handle. Rest your thumb firmly against the left side of the handle. Grip firmly with all of your fingers, but not too tightly. Holding your knife too tightly can make your arm tire quickly, especially if you have a lot of cutting to do. It can also interfere with your ability to make smooth, clean cuts. Actually, the thumb and index finger can be used to apply the most pressure. The other fingers can be used to balance the handle, thus making knife control easier.

When holding the vegetables that are being cut, curl your fingers in slightly at the first joint. This prevents or reduces the chance of cutting yourself while slicing. Tilt the blade slightly away from your fingers, with the upper portion of the blade resting gently against the middle or end joint of your middle finger. Place the blade on the vegetable and slide it firmly but gently forward through the vegetable, with a slight downward pressure.

Cut with the entire length of the blade. It is best not to saw or push down too hard to the extent that the knife tears through the vegetable. This produces jagged slices that are not so attractive or harmonious in terms of their energy balance.

Sometimes, when slicing long vegetables or leafy greens, we use a cutting technique known as the "drawing motion." In this method, we use only the tip of the knife. Place the tip on the vegetable and draw the blade back toward you until the entire length of the vegetable is cut.

With continual practice, your knife technique and speed of cutting will improve, so do not be overwhelmed if vegetable cutting seems difficult at first.

The most commonly used methods for cutting vegetables are presented in the diagram below.

Fig. 9   Vegetable Cutting Styles

Cutting in Thin Rounds

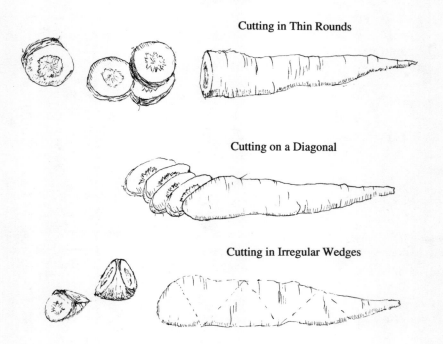

Cutting on a Diagonal

Cutting in Irregular Wedges

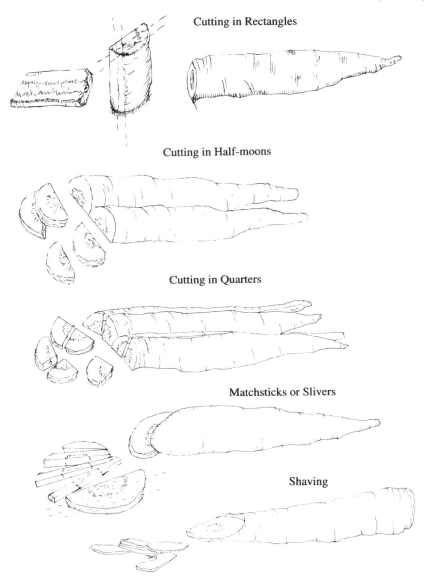

Cutting in Rectangles

Cutting in Half-moons

Cutting in Quarters

Matchsticks or Slivers

Shaving

Fancy Cutting

Sometimes more fancy cutting techniques are appropriate for garnishing noodle and pasta dishes for special occasions or holiday cooking. Vegetables can be cut into shapes that resemble roses and other flowers, fans, baskets, brushes, chains, springs, loops, curls, twigs, pine needles, combs, birds, trees, mushrooms, butterflies, fishnets, and so on, in order to enhance the beauty of your dishes. Most of these colorful garnishes are quick and simple to prepare. Instructions for preparing fancy garnishes are presented in our book, *Aveline Kushi's Wonderful World of Salads*. Feel free to use these fancy garnishes on your noodle and pasta dishes.

Chapter 3: Unraveling the History of Noodles and Pasta

The history of food is a fascinating study. Interestingly, many food items cannot be traced to one specific part of the world. Quite often we find that certain foods appeared simultaneously in various parts of the world and were influenced by contact with other cultures. This seems to be the case with noodles and pasta. Trying to unravel the long and convoluted history of noodles and pasta can be as fascinating as watching a person trying to unravel his first bowl of spaghetti!

It is safe to assume that wherever grains, especially wheat, barley, rice, and millet grew, our ancestors at first gathered them in their wild state and eventually began to cultivate them. It has been suggested that they roasted the grains in the husk, thrashed them to remove the husk, and then boiled them in their whole form. The next step was discovering that whole grains could be crushed by grinding them, very roughly at first, with stones, and then cooking them into a thick paste, porridge, or gruel. From this point, ancient people discovered that they could use their flour to make flat bread or cakes, then unleavened or sourdough breads. Eventually, the flour was ground finely enough and sifted so that people could make pasta or noodles from it. At first, pasta was freshly made and cooked immediately. Eventually, it was discovered that fresh pasta could be allowed to dry out completely, stored in paper or wood chests, and cooked at some future time.

It is easiest to follow the origin and development of pasta by researching the Italian, Chinese, and Japanese cuisines, as these are the countries that have incorporated noodles and pasta on a large scale into their daily diets, whereas other countries have not embraced noodle and pasta cookery on such a grand scale. In other countries, pasta was used more as a supplement to other traditional foods.

Pasta in the West

Just about everyone has heard the story of how the young Marco Polo journeyed to China and brought spaghetti back to Italy. With a little research, however, we find that pasta existed in Italy long before Marco Polo left for China.

Marco Polo set off for China in 1271 and did not return to Italy until 1295. According to the well-known story, when Polo's ship reached Sumatra, on the return voyage to Italy, a crew was dispatched to shore in search of fresh water. It was here that the crew members encountered the native people making long strands of pasta out of breadfruit flour. The crew returned to the ship with these strands and the knowledge of how to make them. As the story goes, the crewman who presented these strands to Polo was named Spaghetti. As we can see, this is one way in which pasta may have reached Italy, especially the long strands known as *spaghetti*.

However, a variety of documents and paintings suggest that pasta existed in Italy hundreds of years before Marco Polo. These include paintings depicting pasta making tools such as long pasta rolling pins, pasta or pastry wheels with fluted edges, cutting boards, and other items. Some ancient documents even suggest that pasta (lasagna type) existed at the time of Cicero (106–43 B.C.). The earliest recorded Italian documents that mention pasta making are dated around A.D. 1279. These documents speak of lasagna, tortellini (a half-moon-shaped ravioli), and tagtiatelle-trenette. The word *lasagna* is derived from the Greek *laganon*, which may indicate that this form of pasta existed at the time of Cicero. The word *spaghetti* comes from the Italian word *spago*, or "string," and was not used in these earlier references to pasta.

The oldest mentions of pasta in Italy refer to it as *macco, maccherone,* or *maccherroni,* which means a dough made of only flour and water and from which the word *macaroni* comes. This type of macaroni was more flat and wide in comparison to the more round spaghetti.

Apparently pasta was well known in the Arab countries by the eleventh century. Wheat grew abundantly in the Middle East and people there may have discovered pasta on their own. By the tenth or eleventh centuries, traders from the Middle East had traveled to China and India and brought knowledge of noodles and pasta back with them. Knowledge of pasta making reached Greece and Italy via Saracen traders on their trade routes across the deserts. In fact it is suggested that the Arabs were the first to discover and dry pasta on lines hung outside in the sun. One of the earliest words for pasta was *tri* which comes from the Arabic word *itriyah,* meaning "string" or "little threads." Apparently, pasta and spaghetti were dried and used as a quick meal while traveling. They were dried and stored in chests or wrapped in paper and would keep well for a long time. When these travelers reached Italy, they may have introduced pasta to merchants in Venice.

Wheat was grown in Samaria, as were rice and barley, for thousands of years. The Persians had a type of spaghetti called *rishta,* meaning "thread." People in this area knew that when dried, pasta became very light, did not need much care in handling, and cooked quickly. It was a perfect food for travelers headed East or West across the desert.

In cultures such as China, India, Samaria, and Italy, pasta was first used by farmers and villagers, and only later adapted by the nobility. Pasta was a very resourceful way of making food go further, as well as a way to preserve food for long periods of time. Initially, pasta was not used widely or often in Italian cooking. It was a special treat, quite often being a way in which to use leftovers. Most of the time, people in Italy used whole grains such as rice or barley in the form of *risotto* which means "great rice." Risottos contained rice or barley, beans, and vegetables.

In northern Europe, including northern Italy, people developed more yang, hearty or warming methods for cooking pasta, including dishes such as lasagna, stuffed pasta, and noodle casseroles. In the coastal and southern areas of Italy, where the climate was warm and sunny, people preferred their pasta dishes slightly under-cooked or "al dente," which is still true today. Vegetables and sometimes fish and shellfish were used to make light and simple sauces. Quite often these sauces were simply made with olive oil, garlic, and other herbs that naturally grew in the area. In Roman times there are references made to serving pasta with olive oil, salt, and fermented fish

Table 3 Climatic Variations in the Use of Pasta

Colder Climates	Warmer Climates
Heartier, warming pasta dishes	Lighter pasta dishes
Greater use of animal food	Less use of animal food
Higher in fat and protein	Higher in carbohydrates
Heavier, thicker sauces	Lighter sauces
Fewer spices	More spices

sauces, which had a somewhat cheese-like flavor because of the fermented fish. Meat sauces were used much less frequently.

Pasta Sauces and Seasonings

Contrary to popular belief, Italian cooks did not always use tomatoes in making sauces. Although the tomato, or "golden apple" as it was called, arrived in Italy from South America in the sixteenth century, it was not accepted as a food until later. Prior to that time most people believed the tomato was poison and did not wish to eat it. Until the end of the seventeenth century, pasta was served most often with olive oil, a few herbs, vegetables, and sometimes fish or seafood. Vegetable fillings were used to stuff pasta. These pastas were traditionally stuffed with such vegetables as pumpkin and carrots. Stuffed pasta is believed to have originated around the fourteenth century as a way of using leftovers, thus making food go further. Meat stuffings were used infrequently and more in the cold northern or mountainous areas, while vegetable and seafood stuffings were common in the southern and coastal regions.

Today if you try to buy *gnocchi* (a special thick pasta), you can only find it made with potatoes. Potatoes arrived in Italy from Peru in the sixteenth century but were not used widely in Italian (or European) cooking until later. Originally, gnocchi was made only from wheat flour and water. Sometimes puréed or minced pumpkin, carrot, or other vegetables were kneaded into the dough, as were bran and chestnut flour. Gnocchi was served with a pesto sauce, not with tomato sauce as it is today. In Sardinia you can still find gnocchi made the old way with flour and water.

Basil and oregano were not used in pasta sauces until spices from India and China began to arrive in Italy. Basil came from India and did not grow naturally in Italy. Originally, local plants suited to a warm Mediterranean climate such as onions, thyme, parsley, chives, mint, garlic, rosemary, and marjoram were combined with olive oil to prepare sauces. Lemon and vinegar were also introduced as a result of the spice trade and were originally used to disguise the taste of meat or fish that had spoiled.

Pasta Making

Pasta at first was served freshly made in all areas of Italy, but in the coastal and southern areas, where there was more sunshine, less humidity, a constant breeze from the sea, and little if any fog or mist, it was discovered that when fresh pasta was hung outside in the sun or in a well-ventilated room, it would completely dry out in about three days. The pasta could then be wrapped in paper and stored for long periods with no special care. Of course, most of the time, fresh pasta was preferred over dried pasta, as it is much more flavorful and light.

Originally, pasta was prepared by hand. A simple dough was prepared from whole wheat flour and water. After kneading, the dough was rolled out with large rolling pins and cut by hand into a broad and thick form of pasta. Eventually, simple machines were developed to knead and cut the dough. One simple cutting device was the *chitarro*, or "guitar." It consisted of a simple wood frame with metal strings stretched across it. Dough was laid across the strings and a rolling pin was used to roll it over the strings until it was cut into long strands. The next simple device to be developed was a hinged knife box with blades inlaid into the top. Long strands of dough or spaghetti were laid across the bottom of the box. The top of the box would be closed, bringing the blades down on the strands and cutting them into equal-sized lengths. This was the standard way of preparing pasta for many years until simple, hand-cranked devices, known as *extruders*, were invented. The dough was placed in the device and slowly extruded through metal plates and dies with holes in them. The end result was threads of spaghetti, linguini, and the like.

At first pasta making was done on a small scale at home, usually as a special treat. Eventually, however, pasta making became such an art that it started to become controlled and regulated. In the fifteenth century a pasta makers guild was formed in Genoa, Italy, and the art of making pasta became very secretive and guarded. In order to sell pasta, one had to be a member of the guild. When mechanical rolling machines were developed by a French inventor, the process of making pasta was sped up considerably. Small-scale pasta makers often referred to these modern machines as machines of starvation, because they replaced men with machines and put people out of work. By the eighteenth century, the English had developed the machinery to mass-produce pasta and to dry it in rooms that were temperature controlled. The first fully mechanized factory was established for producing pasta for worldwide export in 1939.

Together with mechanization of the pasta industry came the technology to produce white flour. At first this was done on a small scale, and rather crudely, as pasta makers were unable to fully remove the endosperm of the grain without crushing it. The endosperm causes flour to have an off-white or yellowish color. In the 1840s a machine that produced white flour was invented in Hungary. It had iron rollers that squeezed the grains in such a way that the endosperm popped out without crushing the rest of the grain. The germ and bran were then sifted from the flour.

Many nutritional deficiencies came about as a result of mass-produced refined white flour. People began eating less whole grains and more white pasta and white bread. In the seventeenth century a man named G.B. Basile wrote in his work, *Pen-*

Table 4 Nutrients Lost in Refining Wheat Flour

When whole wheat flour is milled into white flour, much of the germ (embryo), bran, and surface endosperm are removed. As a result, the flour loses most of its energy and vitality as well as its natural oils and nutrients. Though a few of the vitamins and minerals are artificially returned in enriching, the resulting quality is not the same. This table shows the typical loss of nutrients in producing white flour.

Nutrient Loss (percent)		Nutrient Loss (percent)	
Thiamine (B1)	77.1	Sodium	78.3
Riboflavin(B2)	80.0	Chromium	40.0
Niacin	80.8	Manganese	85.8
Vitamin B6	71.8	Iron	75.6
Panthothenic acid	50.0	Cobalt	88.5
Vitamin E	86.3	Copper	67.9
Calcium	60.0	Zinc	77.7
Phosphorus	70.9	Selenium	15.9
Magnesium	84.7	Molybdenum	48.0
Potassium	77.0		

Sources: Henry A. Schroeder, "Losses of Vitamins and Trace Minerals Resulting from Processing and Preservation of Foods," *American Journal of Clinical Nutrition*, 1971; *Macrobiotic Diet*, by Michio and Aveline Kushi with Alex Jack, Japan Publications, Inc., 1985.

tamerone, that three things could ruin families: "fried pastries, white bread, and pasta." From this point, flour was further refined by bleaching it pure white. Eventually, nutrients were put back into the flour through a process known as "enrichment." However, many Italian pasta makers, even today, believe enriching pasta is of little use, since most of the added nutrients may be leached into the cooking water during the cooking process. But the American and German companies that import pasta insist that the public wants eggs and various nutrients added to their pasta, and so the Italian companies who make pasta for export comply with this request. Originally, however, pasta did not contain eggs. Egg pasta developed in the colder northern parts of Italy. Bologna has long taken credit for discovering egg pasta, but with further research we find that egg pasta was known in Florence many years before. Even today, egg pasta is not used much in the southern or coastal regions of Italy, while the most authentic pasta eaten there today is also not enriched. In Sicily and Sardinia especially, pasta is still made the old way with only flour and water.

After pasta appeared in Italy, it eventually spread throughout Europe. When Catherine de Medici married the heir to the French throne in 1533, she brought several Italian chefs and a variety of pasta recipes with her. Marie de Medici also brought pasta with her when she went to France at the end of the sixteenth century to marry Henry IV. During that century, Princess Bona Sforza from Milan introduced pasta to Cracow when she married the heir to the Polish throne. However, pasta may have already existed in northern and eastern Europe before being introduced from Italy. Traders going to and coming from India and China often passed through Russia and may have brought pasta with them on their travels. The Polish dish known as *pierogi* is very similar to ravioli and to Chinese dumplings or egg rolls. In the northern parts of Europe, pasta was often used to make dumplings, as well as in puddings and desserts.

Thicker, more coarse pasta (such as the German *nudeln*) developed more in the northen regions of Europe, while light, thin pastas were used more in Italy and the south. Also, in the northern countries, pasta was not used as a main course but as a supplement to whole grain and other dishes.

In North America, pasta was not common until people from Italy, Poland, and China began to arrive in the eighteenth century. Even then, noodles and pasta were available mostly in large cities such as New York, San Francisco, Chicago, and others where ethnic communities thrived. Noodles and pasta did not really catch on as popular foods in the American diet until the early part of this century.

Noodles in the East

As it is in the West, it is difficult to pinpoint the exact origin of noodles in the East. However, unlike the West, the documented history of noodles in the East, especially in China, is very ancient. This leads us to believe that noodles may have originated in China and spread from there to other parts of Asia.

Grains such as wheat, millet, and barley were formally cultivated some 8,000 years ago in China. Rice is believed to have been cultivated initially in countries bordering the southern part of China, such as Thailand, Laos, Burma, Cambodia, and Vietnam, as well as in Indonesia and Japan. It may have been introduced in China after these other grains were cultivated.

It is generally assumed that noodles were invented by farmers and common people in China. Old documents state that the Chinese were making noodles as far back 7,000 years ago. According to one theory, noodle making developed because of a scarcity of food and fuel. Noodles are an efficient way to store grains, and because they cook quickly, they require less fuel to cook than whole grain or animal food dishes. Although whole millet cooks quickly and is easily digested, whole wheat berries require extensive cooking and are more difficult to digest. Noodles made from whole flour are much easier to cook and digest. Whole barley and rice also require longer cooking time, but unlike wheat, are easily digested in their whole form. The need to conserve fuel may have been a factor in the development of quick cooking, including methods such as stir frying, noodles in broth, and deep-fried noodle dishes such as ramen. By the time of the Sung Dynasty (A.D. 960–1280) noodles were widely accepted by all but the nobility. It seems that the nobility did not totally accept them until sometime in the sixteenth century.

Interestingly, one of the oldest noodle recipes in China describes a type of noodle made from cooked whole brown rice and not from whole wheat flour. The rice was cooked with a large amount of water to a creamy consistency, mashed, and spread out to dry in the sun. The dry paste was then ground to a fine powder, mixed with water, and formed into a dough. The dough was then separated by pulling off small pieces of it. The pieces were rolled between the hands to form a thick, round, short noodle, a little larger than a grain of rice. These fresh brown rice noodles were then boiled in soup. Another old recipe describes small hand-rolled rice noodles being deep fried and eaten with soy milk. Perhaps these were the first rice crispies!

The Chinese *lo mein*, or long noodles, were probably the earliest form of spaghetti. The Chinse as well as other Far Eastern peoples, also have their own, probably original, version of ravioli, in the form of stuffed dumplings that are steamed, boiled, or deep fried. Along with eating fresh noodles, the Chinese have for hundreds of years dried noodles by hanging them over bamboo poles, a practice that can still be observed today.

The Chinese mastered the art of noodle making, not only with whole wheat flour, but also with rice, barley, oat, millet, corn, wheat, buckwheat, soybean, mung bean, and chick-pea flour. Even today, many Chinese households serve long rice noodles on birthdays. These long noodles are a symbol of longevity and are thought to ensure long life. It is considered bad luck to break these noodles before cooking them.

Noodles were well known in India by A.D. 1200. They may have developed independently, or been introduced from China or other Asian countries. The Indian word for noodles is *seivka*, or "threads," and the transparent type of noodle made from mung bean flour and cooked in desserts is called *sevian*, or "China grass."

The art of noodle making was brought to Japan by Buddhist monks who returned from China. Although noodles may have existed earlier, the first written reference to them in Japan dates from the Heian period (A.D. 794–1185). The monks who returned from China with the knowledge of noodles soon began to make homemade (*te-uchi*) noodles in the temples. Eventually, the knowledge of noodles reached the common people, as they were often served noodles when visiting temples on religious holidays and other occasions. The earliest written reference to soba (buckwheat noodles) dates from around 1185. In another early reference, the Japanese historian, Shigeru Niijima describes eating noodles at a temple in the sixteenth century.

Noodles quickly spread beyond the Buddhist temples and became a popular food in Japanese cuisine. Japanese noodle makers have become expert at producing noodles from whole wheat (udon and somen), buckwheat (soba), and ingredients such as mung beans, rice, herbs, wild mountain potatoes, and kuzu starch.

Selecting High-quality Noodles and Pasta

A wide variety of noodles and pastas are available today in natural food stores and other food markets. Choosing the highest-quality products is important not only for the flavor of your dishes, but most importantly, for optimum health. As much as possible, select noodles and pasta made from organic flours, sea salt, and spring or well water as staples for regular use.

Types of Noodles and Pasta

Udon—These light colored Japanese noodles are made from whole wheat flour, sea salt, and water. They are available in varying amounts of whole wheat flour, unbleached white flour, sea salt, and water. Udon come in various widths, from *kishi-*

men, which are flat and wide and similar to fettucine, to common udon which are thick, round, and narrow and similar to linguine. Udon are wonderful when used in noodles and broth, soups, nabe, sukiyaki, sushi, or casseroles.

Brown Rice Udon—Udon noodles are also made from sifted whole wheat and brown rice flour, sea salt, and water. Brown rice udon can be used in the same manner as other varieties.

Somen—These very thin, delicate, Japanese noodles are shorter than udon. Somen are made with varying amounts of sifted whole wheat flour, high-gluten unbleached white flour, sea salt, and water. Traditionally served in broth, or served cool in the summer, somen can also be used in salads and sushi.

Hiyamugi—These are a thinner, longer variety of somen. They are a little more hardy than regular somen and are made with varying amounts of whole wheat, sifted whole wheat, or unbleached white flour. Hiyamugi are often served chilled or with a cool broth during the summer.

Soba—Japanese buckwheat noodles are called *soba*. They are made from 100 percent buckwheat flour, sea salt, and water or varying amounts of buckwheat flour combined with sifted whole wheat or unbleached white flours. Other ingredients are added to them as well. Some of the many varieties of soba include:

• *Ito Soba*—A thin, short, 40 percent buckwheat flour soba, similar in texture to somen
• *Jinenjo Soba*—A type of soba made from combining buckwheat flour and wild mountain potato (jinenjo) flour
• *Cha Soba*—Soba made from combining buckwheat flour and powdered Japanese green tea

Table 5 Yin and Yang (Expansive and Contractive) Classification of Common Noodles

More Yin (lighter, thinner, more delicate)

Clear Noodles
rice or kuzu—bean thread
Somen
more whole flour—more white flour
Udon
more whole flour—more white flour
Soba
more buckwheat flour—less buckwheat flour

More Yang (darker, thicker, more coarse)

In general, noodles that are yang or contractive are more resistant to heat and take longer to cook than more yin varieties. Adding vegetables or herbs to flour gives noodles a more yin quality, while adding salt (a very contractive substance) makes them more yang.

• *Yomogi Soba*—Soba made from combining buckwheat flour with powdered mugwort (an edible wild plant)

Soba can be served in hot or cold broth, nabe, sushi, casseroles, and in a variety of other ways.

Baifun—These clear Chinese rice noodles are made from white rice flour, 10 percent wild potato starch, water, and salt. They are sometimes called "rice sticks" or *maifun*, and are often served in broth, sukiyaki, nabe, salads, or plain with simple garnishes and natural soy sauce. Baifun can be deep fried and used to make *chow mein*.

Saifun—These clear Chinese noodles are made from mung bean flour, water, and salt. They are sometimes referred to as "bean threads," "cellophane noodles," or *fun-see*, and are used to make *chop suey*. Saifun can also be eaten in broth or used in salads and other dishes.

Ramen—These deep-fried, dried noodles are originally from China. Vegetable-quality ramen fried in vegetable oil rather than in animal fat are now available from Japan. Natural, prepackaged ramens can be found in natural food stores and come in soba, udon, or brown rice noodles. Natural ramen come with packets of instant miso or tamari flavored broth. The powdered broth packets often contain spices such as ginger or pepper.

Kuzu Noodles—These clear Japanese noodles are made from kuzu starch flour. Their use is similar to baifun or saifun.

Shirataki—These Japanese noodles are made from the starchy flour of a wild plant known as *konnyaku*. They are sometimes used in sukiyaki or nabe-style dishes.

Brown Rice Spaghetti—This pasta, made in Canada, is new to the market. It is made from 100 percent brown rice flour steamed and extruded by temperature and pressure-controlled machines that keep the brown rice dough from falling apart. Brown rice spaghetti contains no wheat or gluten.

Whole Wheat Spaghetti and Pasta—A variety of whole wheat Italian pastas made from high-gluten hard durum wheat flour and water are available in natural food stores. They come in a variety of shapes and sizes such as shells, spirals, wheels, bows, tubes, alphabets, and thin strands of spaghetti. Powdered herbs and vegetables are sometimes added for color and flavor.

American Jerusalem Artichoke Pasta—This Italian-style pasta is made from the flour of the tuber, Jerusalem artichoke, and durum semolina (high-gluten wheat) flour. It is less hearty than 100 percent whole wheat pasta and has a flavor, texture, and color similar to that of high-quality durum semolina pasta from Italy. It comes in a variety of shapes.

Corn Pasta—This American-made wheat-free pasta contains 100 percent corn flour. It is available in curls, elbows, and other shapes.

Spelt Pasta—This new variety of pasta is made from an ancient grain called *spelt.* Spelt looks and tastes like wheat but does not contain gluten. It is made of 100 percent spelt flour and can be used by those with wheat allergies. It is now available in shells and spaghetti shapes.

Semolina Pasta—Some companies import dried pastas from Italy made in the old-fashioned way with 100 percent semolina flour and no additives. Read the labels to make sure no eggs, vitamins, or chemicals are added.

Basic Noodle Cookery

Noodles from the Far East and pasta from Italy or America are cooked in a slightly different manner. Japanese and Chinese noodles generally contain salt, and so it is not necessary to add salt to the cooking water. Italian pasta is made without salt, therefore, salt is added to the cooking water to ensure proper cooking and to enhance the flavor of the pasta. In general, several small pinches of sea salt are adequate when preparing these noodles.

Regardless of whether you are cooking Italian, American, Japanese, Chinese, or other styles of noodles or pasta, the rule of thumb is to use plenty of water to cook them in. Adding plenty of water helps prevent noodles from sticking to each other and ensures thorough cooking. Use about 4 to 5 quarts of water per pound of noodles or pasta; 2 1/2 to 3 quarts for 1/2 pound; and 2 to 2 1/2 quarts of water for 1/4 pound.

When serving noodles or pasta as a main dish, you will need about 4 ounces (1/4 pound) per person. If noodles or pasta are being served as an appetizer or entrée, you will need about 2 ounces (1/8 pound) per person. Serving noodles and pasta with plenty of vegetables of course makes them go further than serving them simply as is.

You may follow the directions on the label of packaged noodles and pasta when preparing them, or use the guidelines presented below.

Cooking Oriental-style Noodles

Place 4 to 5 quarts of water in a large pot, cover, and bring to a boil. Remove the cover and add one pound of noodles. Stir back and forth gently to prevent sticking. Do not replace the cover. Bring the water to a boil again. When the water starts to boil rapidly and swell with foam, add 1/2 cup of cold water to the boiling noodles to halt the cooking action. Reduce the flame just slightly, bring to a boil again, and repeat the above process once more. Bring to a boil a third time. Several times during the cooking process, check the noodles for doneness by removing one noodle and breaking it in half. Before or by the time the noodles come to a boil the third time the noodles should be the same color all the way through. If they are white in the center and darker around the outside, the noodles need to cook longer. When properly prepared, noodles are usually a little on the firm or al dente side rather than soft or mushy.

When the noodles are done, remove the pot quickly from the burner and pour the noodles into a colander or strainer. Rinse under cold water until completely cool. Allow the noodles to drain.

Table 6 Cooking Times for Noodles and Pasta

Noodles and pasta contain different combinations of ingredients and come in different sizes and shapes. These factors influence the amount of time needed for cooking. Smaller, thinner, and lighter varieties take less time to cook than thicker, heavier, or larger varieties. Below are guidelines for cooking common varieties of noodles and pasta:

Variety	*Appropriate Cooking Time (in minutes)*
Common udon	15–20
Kishimen udon	20
Somen	5–7
Hiyamugi	6–7
Soba	7
Ito soba	5–7
Baifun	5–7
Saifun	Soak 5–15 minutes (cooking is unnecessary)
Brown rice spaghetti	10–12
Corn ribbons	7–9
Ramen	5–7
Spelt pasta	10
Whole wheat spaghetti	10–12
Whole wheat elbows	8–10
Whole wheat lasagne	8–10
Spaghetti	10-12
Fettucine	8-10
Elbows	8–10
Jerusalem artichoke	8–10
Lasagne	7–9
Semolina spaghetti	10–12
Semolina lasagne	7–10
Semolina rigatoni	10
Semolina rotoni (wheels)	7–8
Semolina shells:	
large	12–15
small	10

Cooking Italian-style Pasta and Spaghetti

Place 4 to 5 quarts of water in a large pot and add several small pinches of sea salt. Cover and bring the water to a boil. Place the pasta or spaghetti in the boiling pot of water. For small pasta such as elbows and shells, simply stir to prevent sticking. For longer spaghetti or linguine take a wooden spoon or pasta fork and slowly fan out the pasta, until it softens and is completely covered with water. Bring the water to a boil again. Do not cover the pot. Continue boiling until the pasta is done. To test for doneness, remove a piece of pasta from the pot and break it in half. The pasta should be slightly firm and the same color all the way through. If the pasta is white in the center and dark around the periphery, continue cooking until it is one uniform color. If you plan on cooking the pasta again in a baked casserole (such as lasagne or stuffed shells) it is best to under cook the pasta slightly, as it will cook further while baking.

If Italian or American pasta is to be served immediately with a sauce, simply drain, and place the hot pasta in serving dishes. Then add the sauce. If the pasta is to be used later in a soup or salad, you may place in a colander or strainer, and rinse under cold water, drain, and set aside until you are ready to use.

Chapter 4: Noodles in Broth

In Japan, China, and other Far Eastern countries, the most popular way to serve noodles is in a slightly salty broth topped with elegant vegetable garnishes. Noodles in broth are a delicious and nourishing one-dish meal. The noodle in broth dishes in this chapter are similar to chicken-noodle soup, minus the chicken. They are quick and easy to prepare, and are favorites among health-conscious noodle lovers everywhere.

In Japan, it is considered a very refined art to be able to make delicious broth. Cooks were often judged by the quality of their broth. The most sought-after broths are those with a deep rich color yet a light mild flavor. A wide variety of basic stocks can be prepared with all natural ingredients. In most cases, broths can be prepared very simply in a matter of minutes and can be served in a variety of ways to balance seasonal changes. For instance, when served cool or chilled, they help balance the heat of summer. Served hot or thickened with kuzu, noodle broths help keep us warm in the autumn and winter.

Below are recipes for several of the more popular or frequently prepared stocks. These natural, low-fat stocks contain nourishing ingredients such as kombu and shiitake mushrooms, and can serve as a base for your noodle broths, as well as for soups and stews. The recipes do not include seasoning. Depending on how you plan to use the stock, you can season it with tamari soy sauce, miso, sea salt, umeboshi plum, or another natural seasoning. Following the recipes, we explain how to use these stocks in making a variety of delicious noodle in broth dishes.

Noodle Stocks

Kombu Stock (*Ichiban Dashi*)

Kombu, a delicious, mild tasting sea vegetable, is used often in preparing broth or soup stock. In Japan, kombu stock is referred to as *dashi*. Broth made from fresh kombu is known as *ichiban dashi*, or "first time broth."

4–5 cups water
1 strip kombu, 4–5 inches long by 1 inch wide

Take a clean, damp sponge or cloth and gently wipe the surface of both sides of the kombu to remove any light dust, being careful not to scrub too hard, as valuable minerals and natural sugars lie on the surface of the kombu.

Place the water in a pot and add the kombu. Cover the pot and place on a high flame. Bring to a boil. Then reduce the flame to medium-low and simmer the kombu for about 4 to 5 minutes. Remove the cover and take out the kombu. Set it aside for use in other dishes or allow it to dry out completely for use again in soup stock. Stock made from previously used kombu is not quite as flavorful as first time stock but is still very delicious.

The stock is now ready to season.

Second Time Kombu Stock (*Niban Dashi*)

This basic stock is prepared from kombu that was used previously to prepare broth. It is referred to as *niban dashi* or "second time broth."

4–5 cups water
1 leftover strip kombu, 4–5 inches long by 1 inch wide

Place the water and the kombu in a pot and bring to a boil. Cover, reduce the flame to medium-low, and simmer for 15 to 20 minutes. The stock is now ready to season.

Shiitake Mushroom Stock

Shiitake mushrooms grow on logs in partially shaded areas. They are picked and then sun-dried. They grow throughout Japan and in many other Far Eastern countries, as well as in the United States. They make a very flavorful broth when used alone or with kombu or other ingredients. Although high-grade shiitake, known as *donko shiitake*, are the most flavorful, regular or medium grade shiitake mushrooms also make a delicious broth for everyday use. Shiitake mushrooms help balance the intake of animal food and have medicinal qualities.

4–5 cups water
4 shiitake mushrooms (about 1 per person)

Place the shiitake mushrooms in a small bowl and cover with warm water. Soak for about 10 minutes to soften. Remove the shiitake from the soaking water and squeeze out any liquid from the shiitake with your hands. Save the soaking water and use as part of your water measurement. Place the shiitake on a cutting board, and cut away and discard the tip of the stem, which usually has tree bark attached to it. Remove the remaining portion of the stem and slice very thin. Slice the cap of shiitake into thin strips.

Place the sliced shiitake and water in a pot, cover, and bring to a boil. Reduce the flame to medium-low and simmer for about 10 minutes.

The shiitake mushroom stock is now ready to season.

Kombu-Shiitake Stock

This very delicious stock combines shiitake mushrooms and kombu. You can slice the shiitake and kombu after soaking, and cook and eat them along with noodles, or cook them whole in the broth and remove and save them for future use. If you decide to use them again, let them dry out completely before using. You can use them in other dishes or again in broth.

> **4–5 cups water**
> **1 strip kombu, 4–5 inches long by 1 inch wide**
> **4 shiitake mushrooms**

Soak the shiitake mushrooms as described in the previous recipe and remove the tip of the stem. Place the whole shiitake in a pot. Save the soaking water and use as part of the water measurement.

Wipe the kombu with a clean, damp sponge, and place in a small bowl. Cover slightly with cold water and soak for about 3 to 5 minutes. Remove the kombu and place in the pot with the shiitake. Save the soaking water.

Place the shiitake and kombu soaking water and enough fresh water to equal the amount called for above in the pot. Cover the pot, place on a high flame, and bring to a boil. Reduce the flame to medium-low and simmer for 4 to 5 minutes. Remove the cover and take out the kombu, saving it for future use. Cover the pot again and simmer the shiitake for another 5 to 6 minutes. Remove the cover and take out the shiitake, setting them aside for future use.

The stock is now ready to season.

Wakame Stock

Wakame can be used from time to time as a base for noodle broth. Wakame is used less often than kombu for preparing broth. It creates a delicious slightly saltier broth. The wakame can be served along with the noodles.

> **4–5 cups water**
> **1 strip wakame, 4–5 inches long**

Place the wakame in a small bowl, pour cold water over it, and wash. Pour off water. Cover with water again, wash, and pour off water. Then cover the wakame with cold water and soak for 3 to 5 minutes. Remove the wakame, squeeze out the soaking water, and place on a cutting board. If the soaking water tastes salty, discard, otherwise it may be used as part of the water measurement. Slice the wakame into l-inch lengths and place in a pot. Add the water, cover, and place on a high flame. Bring to a boil, reduce the flame to medium-low, and simmer for about 5 minutes. The stock is now ready to season.

Dried Bonito Stock

This is a very delicious stock for those who eat fish or seafood and like a full-bodied, rich tasting broth. Bonito flakes are made from a fish similar to mackerel. The fish is cut into fillets and dried. The dried fish fillets are then shaved using a knife box that looks like a carpenter's plane to produce either long, paper-thin strips or finely shaved flakes. The long, thin strips are commonly used to prepare soup or broth. These strips are called *hana-katsuo* or *kezuri-bushi*. The finely shaved flakes are used mainly for garnish. Either the strips or the flakes can be used in the recipes below. Bonito flakes can be cooked alone or combined with either kombu or kombu and shiitake mushrooms for a variety of different flavored broths.

> **4–5 cups water**
> **2–3 Tbsp bonito flakes**
> **1 strip kombu, 4–5 inches long by 1 inch wide**

Wipe the kombu with a clean, damp sponge, and place in a pot. Add water. Cover, place on a high flame, and bring to a boil. Reduce the flame to medium-low and simmer for 4 to 5 minutes. Remove the kombu and set aside for future use. Place the bonito flakes in the hot water and remove from the stove. Cover the pot again and allow the flakes to sit in the stock for about 1 to 2 minutes. If the flakes are boiled they may become somewhat bitter. Remove the cover and pour the broth through a strainer into another pot to remove the bonito shavings. The stock is now ready to season.

Kombu, Shiitake, and Bonito Stock

In this broth we combine the more yin qualities of shiitake mushrooms with the more yang, or contractive qualities of bonito flakes. The resulting harmony yields a delicious and nourishing broth.

> **4–5 cups water**
> **1 strip kombu, 4–5 inches long by 1 inch wide**
> **4–5 shiitake mushrooms**
> **2–3 Tbsp bonito flakes**

Wipe the kombu dry. Soak the shiitake mushrooms for 10 minutes and remove the woody tip of the stem. Place the kombu, shiitake, and water in a pot. Cover the pot and bring to a boil. Reduce the flame to medium-low. Simmer for 4 minutes and remove the kombu, setting aside for future use. Simmer another 5 to 6 minutes. Remove the shiitake and set aside for future use. Add the bonito flakes, cover, and allow to steep in the water for 1 to 2 minutes. Strain the bonito flakes from the broth as described above. The stock is now ready to season.

Dried Fish Stock

Niboshi, or sun-dried sardines imported from Japan, are also delicious in broth. They come in two varieties: larger dried sardines called *chuba* and smaller ones called *chirimen*. Dried fish can be used alone or in combination with kombu and shiitake mushrooms.

> **4–5 cups water**
> **1/4 cup dried fish**
> **1 strip kombu, 4–5 inches long by 1 inch wide**
> **4 shiitake mushrooms**

Wipe the kombu clean. Soak the shiitake mushrooms and remove stems. Place the kombu, shiitake, and water in a pot. Cover and bring to a boil. Reduce the flame to medium-low and simmer for 4 minutes. Remove the kombu and set aside. Add the dried fish, cover, and simmer for about 6 to 8 minutes. Remove the shiitake and dried fish and set aside. The stock is now ready to season.

Vegetable Stock

During the course of several days you may find that you have accumulated various vegetable roots, stems, tops, or leaves. These can be used to make a delicious vegetable flavored stock. Make sure the ends and pieces of vegetables that you choose for the stock are thoroughly cleaned and that they combine or complement each other well, in order to create a deliciously sweet tasting broth. For the best flavor, be careful not to use a large amount of very strong, sour, or bitter flavored vegetables.

> **4–5 cups water**
> **1–2 cups leftover ends and pieces of fresh vegetables**
> **1 strip kombu, 4–5 inches long by 1 inch wide**

Place the vegetables in a pot as is or tie them up in a cheesecloth sack and place in a pot. Add the kombu and water. Cover and bring to a boil. Reduce the flame to medium-low and simmer for 4 minutes. Remove the kombu and set aside for future use. Cover and continue simmering for another 5 to 10 minutes. Remove the vegetables and discard them. The stock is now ready to season.

Fresh Daikon Stock

This stock is especially nice when you serve tempura or fish on top of noodles or as a base for a fish and pasta soup. The more yin, pungent qualities of daikon help balance the more yang qualities of fish. This stock is usually prepared from the skin of peeled daikon. It can also be made from sliced or finely grated daikon.

> **4–5 cups water**
> **1–2 cups daikon, sliced**

Place the water and daikon in a pot. Cover the pot, bring to a boil, and reduce the flame to medium-low. Simmer for about 5 to 7 minutes. Remove the daikon and use in other dishes. The stock is now ready to season.

Noodle in Broth Recipes

Udon in Broth (*Kake* Udon)

> **2 packages (16 oz) udon**
> **4–5 cups water**

1 strip kombu, 4–5 inches long
2–3 Tbsp tamari soy sauce
1/4 cup scallions, thinly sliced for garnish

Cook the udon as described previously. Rinse under cold water and allow to drain.

Place the water and kombu in a pot and prepare kombu stock as described above. Reduce the flame to medium-low, add the tamari soy sauce, and allow to simmer for 5 minutes. Place the cooked udon in the broth to warm them up. Do not boil them. Place udon in each serving bowl and ladle hot broth over them. Garnish each bowl with 1 or 2 teaspoons of sliced scallions and serve hot.

Soba in Broth (Kake Soba)

2 packages (16 oz) soba (any kind)
1 strip kombu, 4–5 inches long
4–5 cups water
2–3 Tbsp tamari soy sauce
1 sheet nori, for garnish
4–5 Tbsp grated daikon, for garnish
1/4 cup scallions, finely sliced for garnish

Cook the soba as described above. Place in a strainer, rinse with cold water, and allow to drain while you are preparing broth.

Place the kombu and water in a pot and prepare broth as described above. When the stock is ready, season with tamari soy sauce and simmer for about 5 minutes.

Take the sheet of nori and toast it by holding the rough, dull side over a high flame. Rotate the sheet of nori with your hands to evenly toast. The nori will change in color from black or dark green to a light green color when toasted. When completely toasted the entire sheet of nori should be light green in color. To cut the nori, fold it in half lengthwise and tear along the fold. Next, fold each half sheet of nori in half, lengthwise, and again tear along the fold. You should now have 4 equal-sized, long strips of nori. Stack all four strips on top of each other. Take a pair of scissors and cut the long strips into smaller strips about 1 1/2 inches long by 1/4 inch wide. Place the nori strips in a bowl.

Place the drained soba in the hot seasoned broth and allow to sit for 2 to 3 minutes to warm up. Do not boil. Remove the soba and place in each individual serving bowl. Ladle hot broth over each bowl of soba. Next, garnish each bowl of hot soba with 1 tablespoon of grated daikon, 1 to 2 teaspoons of sliced scallions, and sprinkle several strips of nori on top. Serve while hot.

Tokyo-style *Kitsune* Udon

In Japan there is a charming story about the fox and its tremendous liking for deep-fried tofu. The following dish is named *kitsune* or "fox" udon, in honor of the sly fox. Although the many variations of this recipe differ from city to city throughout Japan, they all have one thing in common—deep-fried tofu, the favorite of the fox.

2 packages (16 oz) soba (any type)
4–5 cups water
1 strip kombu, 4–5 inches long
light or dark sesame oil, for deep frying
8–10 slices firm-style tofu, 2 inches wide by 3 inches long by 1/4 inch thick
1–1 1/2 Tbsp mirin (sweet cooking saké; optional seasoning for broth)
2–3 Tbsp tamari soy sauce
1/4 cup scallions, thinly sliced for garnish

Cook, rinse, and drain the soba as described previously.

Place the water and kombu in a pot and prepare stock as described above.

Place 2 to 3 inches of light or dark sesame oil or a combination of the two in a deep-frying pot. Heat up the oil. When hot, place the tofu slices in the hot oil and deep fry until golden brown on all sides. Remove and place on paper towels to drain. Pat the slices with paper towels to remove any excess oil. You can leave the tofu slices whole or slice each piece in half on an angle (for easier eating). Place the tofu in the hot stock and simmer for 2 to 3 minutes.

When the stock is done, add the mirin and tamari soy sauce. Simmer for another 5 minutes. Reduce the flame to low.

Place the soba in the hot broth and heat up, without boiling, for 2 to 3 minutes. Place the soba in each individual serving bowl and ladle hot broth over each serving. Place 2 large slices or 2 half-slices of deep-fried tofu on top of each bowl of soba. Garnish each bowl with 2 to 3 tablespoons of sliced scallions. Serve hot.

As a variation, place 1 teaspoon of grated daikon on top of each bowl of noodles to help balance the oil.

Kyoto-style Kitsune Udon

In Kyoto, during the colder months of the year, you can find this version of "kitsune" or "fox" udon on the menu of many noodle bars. It is prepared with a kuzu thickened broth and garnished with ginger for a nice warming effect.

2 packages (16 oz) udon
4–5 shiitake mushrooms, soaked and stems removed
1 strip kombu, 4–5 inches long
4–5 cups water
light or dark sesame oil
4–5 slices firm-style tofu, 2 inches wide by 3 inches long by 1/2 inch thick
4–5 tsp kuzu
5–6 tsp water, for diluting kuzu
2–3 Tbsp tamari soy sauce
1/4 cup prepackaged finely shaved bonito flakes, for garnish (optional)
1 Tbsp fresh grated ginger, for garnish
1/4 cup scallions, thinly sliced for garnish

Cook the udon as described earlier, place in a strainer, rinse with cold water, and allow to drain.

Place the shiitake mushrooms, kombu, and water in a pot and prepare broth.

Deep fry the tofu slices as described in the above recipes. Place the deep-fried tofu slices on paper towels. Pat the slices with paper towels to remove excess oil. Slice the tofu into strips about 2 inches long by 1/4 inch thick and place the strips in the hot soup stock. Simmer the tofu for 2 to 3 minutes.

Next, place the kuzu in a small bowl or cup, add 5 to 6 teaspoons of water and stir until completely dissolved. Reduce the flame under the stock to low. Add the diluted kuzu to the hot stock, stirring constantly to prevent lumping. When the stock becomes thick and translucent, add the tamari soy sauce and simmer for about 5 minutes longer.

Place the udon in the hot thickened broth and simmer for about 2 to 3 minutes without boiling, just enough to heat the noodles. Place the udon in individual serving bowls and ladle the hot kuzu broth over them. Place several strips of deep-fried tofu on top of each bowl of udon. Garnish each bowl with 2 to 3 teaspoons of bonito flakes, 1/4 teaspoon of grated ginger, and 1 to 2 teaspoons of sliced scallions. Serve hot.

For those who wish to avoid oil, take 1 cake (1 lb) of firm-style tofu and slice it as described above. Just before you season the broth, add the fresh tofu slices, season, and let simmer for 2 to 3 minutes to cook the tofu. Garnish and serve as above.

Udon in Broth with Fried Tempeh

Tempeh, a fermented soybean product, is a traditional staple in Indonesia. It has become increasingly popular in the West and makes a delicious topping for any noodle and broth dish.

> **2 packages (16 oz) udon**
> **1 lb tempeh**
> **1 strip kombu, 4–5 inches long**
> **4–5 shiitake mushrooms, soaked, stems removed, and sliced**
> **4–5 cups water**
> **2–3 Tbsp tamari soy sauce**
> **light or dark sesame oil, for deep frying**
> **5–10 sprigs watercress, washed**
> **4–5 Tbsp grated daikon, for garnish**
> **1/4 cup scallions, thinly sliced for garnish**

Cook, rinse, and drain the udon as described earlier.

Place the kombu, shiitake mushrooms, and water in a pot and prepare the broth. Leave the shiitake in the broth to be served as a garnish on top of the udon. Season the broth with tamari soy sauce and simmer for 5 minutes.

Slice the tempeh into 1/4-inch wide strips or 1-inch cubes and deep fry until golden brown on all sides. Remove, place on a paper towel to drain, and pat with paper towels to remove excess oil.

Place the udon in the hot broth to heat up. Let sit for 2 to 3 minutes without boiling. Place the udon in serving bowls. Place 1 to 2 sprigs of watercress on top of each bowl of udon. Pour hot broth directly over the sprigs of watercress, adding enough broth to slightly cover the watercress. This hot liquid will be sufficient to cook each sprig. Garnish each bowl with several slices of shiitake mushrooms, several strips or cubes of deep-fried tempeh, a teaspoon of grated daikon, and 1 to 2 teaspoons of sliced scallions. Serve while hot.

For those who wish to avoid oil, boil the tempeh slices or cubes for about 20 minutes and season with a little tamari soy sauce. Place the boiled slices on top of the udon. In this case the grated daikon may be omitted.

Soba in Broth with Natto

Natto is made from fermented whole soybeans and is a traditional food of Japan. It has a sticky quality, a slightly cheesy flavor, and a strong fermented fragrance. Many people find it delicious when served with noodles.

> **2 packages (16 oz) soba (any kind)**
> **4–5 Tbsp natto, for garnish**
> **1 strip kombu, 4–5 inches long**
> **4–5 cups water**
> **2–3 Tbsp tamari soy sauce**
> **1 sheet nori**
> **1/4 cup grated daikon, for garnish**
> **4–5 tsp tan sesame seeds, toasted for garnish**
> **1/4 cup scallions, thinly sliced for garnish**

Cook, rinse, and drain the soba.

Place the kombu and water in a pot and prepare the kombu stock. When the stock is done, add the tamari soy sauce, and simmer for 5 minutes.

Place the drained soba in the hot broth. Allow to simmer on a low flame, without boiling, for 2 to 3 minutes to heat up the soba.

While the soba is heating up, the natto may be mixed or chopped. The natto may be placed in a small bowl and whipped, by stirring vigorously with chopsticks, for a few seconds. If you desire a sweeter flavored dish, you may chop the natto. To do this, place the natto on a cutting board. Hold the tip of the knife down on the board, lift the handle, and with quick up-and-down strokes, finely chop the natto. Natto is naturally sticky and a little difficult to handle, but continue until it is finely chopped.

Toast the nori and cut into thin strips. Next, place the soba in individual serving bowls and make a shallow, hollowed out area in the center of each bowl of soba to place the garnishes in.

Place 1 tablespoon of chopped natto in the hollowed area in each bowl of soba. Place a couple of teaspoons of grated daikon on top of the natto. Then sprinkle several strips of toasted nori on top of the grated daikon. Next, sprinkle 1 tablespoon of toasted sesame seeds on top. Ladle hot kombu broth over the soba to almost cover. Then, place 1 to 2 teaspoons of sliced scallions on top of the soba. Serve hot.

Udon in Broth with Natto Tempura

2 packages (16 oz) udon (any kind)
8–10 Tbsp natto
4–5 cups water
1 strip kombu, 4–5 inches long
4–5 shiitake mushrooms
2–3 Tbsp tamari soy sauce
1 tsp kuzu
2 tsp water, for diluting kuzu
1/4 cup carrots, cut into matchsticks
1 sheet nori
light or dark sesame oil, for deep frying
1–1 1/2 tsp grated ginger, for garnish
1/4 cup scallions, thinly sliced for garnish

Cook, rinse, and drain the udon.

Prepare the kombu-shiitake stock. When the stock is done, season with tamari soy sauce and simmer on low heat for 5 minutes. Add the drained udon and simmer for 2 to 3 minutes without boiling.

While the broth is simmering, prepare the natto mixture. Place the natto in a bowl and stir with chopsticks. Then dilute the kuzu with 2 teaspoons of water and add it to the natto. Mix in the diluted kuzu. Add the matchstick carrots. Next, toast the nori and cut into thin strips. Place the nori strips in the bowl with the natto and mix. Heat the sesame oil in a deep-frying pot. Place a tablespoon of the natto mixture in the hot oil and deep fry until golden brown. Remove and place on paper towels to drain. Repeat until all of the natto mixture has been deep fried.

Remove the warm udon and place in individual serving bowls. Ladle the hot broth over the noodles.

Place 2 portions of tempuraed natto and a dab of grated ginger on top of each bowl of udon. Garnish with 1 to 2 teaspoons of sliced scallions. Serve hot.

As a variation, garnish each bowl of udon with 1 teaspoon of grated daikon instead of ginger. For those who wish to avoid oil, place the natto, grated daikon, and toasted nori strips in a bowl, and stir. Place a tablespoon or so of the natto mixture on top of each bowl of udon and garnish with sliced scallions.

Udon or Soba with Vegetable Tempura

Tempura is a traditional way of cooking brought to Japan centuries ago by Portugese traders. Vegetables, fish, or seafood are dipped in batter and deep fried until golden brown. It is a delicious treat and especially wonderful with noodles in broth.

2 packages (16 oz) udon or soba (any kind)
4–5 cups water
1 strip kombu, 4–5 inches long
2–3 Tbsp tamari soy sauce
4–5 slices buttercup squash

    4–5 green string beans
    4–5 medium broccoli spears
    4–5 diagonal slices of carrot
    4–5 mushrooms (natural brown ones or fresh shiitake mushrooms)
    1/4 cup scallions, thinly sliced for garnish
    1/2 cup grated daikon, for garnish
    light or dark sesame oil, for deep frying
Tempura Batter:
    1 cup whole wheat pastry flour
    1 Tbsp kuzu
    2–2 1/2 cups cold water
    1 cup corn flour
    pinch of sea salt

Cook, rinse, and drain the udon or soba.

Prepare the kombu stock and season with tamari soy sauce. Let the stock simmer on a low flame while you prepare the tempura.

Place 1 cup of whole wheat pastry flour on a plate. Roll the sliced vegetables in the flour to coat them. This will help the tempura batter adhere to the vegetables.

Place the kuzu in a bowl. Add a little bit of the above water measurement for the batter to the kuzu and dilute. When completely diluted, add the corn flour, sea salt, and the remaining water. Mix the batter with a wisk and let sit for 2 to 3 minutes.

Heat the sesame oil in a deep-frying pot. Dip one type of vegetable at a time into the batter. When the oil is hot enough, place several pieces of batter-coated vegetables in it and fry until golden brown. Remove the vegetables and place on paper towels to drain. To keep the tempura warm, you may place on a cookie sheet and keep in a 200° F oven until you have deep fried all the vegetables. Repeat until all the vegetables have been deep fried.

Place the drained udon or soba in the hot broth and heat up, without boiling, for 2 to 3 minutes. Place the udon or soba in individual serving bowls. Place 1 piece of each type of tempura on top of each bowl of noodles. Ladle hot broth over the tempura. Garnish with 1 to 2 teaspoons of sliced scallions.

The grated daikon may be served as a garnish on top of the tempura or in a small side dish. The yin, pungent qualities of the daikon help cut through the oil used in the tempura, thus making the dish easier to digest. Serve the noodles hot.

For those who wish to avoid oil, simply boil each type of vegetable separately and place them on top of the noodles. Garnish with chopped scallions and omit the grated daikon.

Udon or Soba with Mixed Vegetable Tempura

This tempura is made by slicing vegetables into thin matchsticks or half-moons, adding all the vegetables to the batter and mixing. The mixed vegetable batter is then placed—a tablespoonful at a time—into the hot oil and deep fried until golden brown. The tempuraed vegetables are then placed on top of a steaming bowl of noodles and broth.

Prepare noodles and broth as described in the above recipe.

Cut 1/3 cup carrots, 1/3 cup burdock, and 1/3 cup buttercup squash into matchsticks. Then cut 1/3 cup onions into half-moons. Prepare tempura batter as described above and add the sliced vegetables to it. Mix thoroughly.

Heat the oil and drop 1 tablespoonful of the mixed vegetable batter into the hot oil. Deep fry until golden brown. Place several pieces of tempura on top of each bowl of noodles. Garnish with chopped scallions and grated daikon and serve hot.

Udon or Soba with Fish and Vegetable Tempura

For this dish, you can use the same ingredients and cooking methods described above. Simply add 4 to 5 pieces of white-meat fish, such as cod, scrod, or haddock. Deep fry the fish last as the flavor of the fish will permeate the vegetables if you fry it before them. Serve as above and include a piece of fish tempura per serving. Serve with a grated daikon garnish.

Udon or Soba with Shrimp Tempura

This dish is prepared in the same way as vegetable tempura. You can omit or use fewer vegetables if you like. Add 5 to 10 shelled and deveined medium or jumbo shrimp to the recipe. Dip the shrimp in the batter and deep fry until golden brown and serve as above with a garnish of grated daikon. For a fancy effect, slit the underside of the shrimp to the tail, being careful not to slice in half. This will prevent the shrimp from curling and help keep them more straight.

Fig. 10

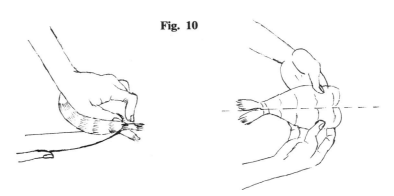

Tanuki Udon or Soba in Broth

Tanuki is the Japanese name for "badger." The name seems to imply that these mythical creatures are fond of this dish, in the way that the fox is thought to be fond of deep-fried tofu. However, this is a modern interpretation. Somehow the word *tanenuki*, meaning that some ingredients are left out of the dish, was changed to *tanuki*. This dish is simply a way of using leftover tempura batter. In it, we place tempura batter itself into hot oil and deep fry it. The result is small morsels of delicious deep-fried batter. These crisp brown morsels of batter are served on top of udon or soba and broth.

2 packages (16 oz) udon or soba (any kind)
4–5 cups water
1 strip kombu, 4–5 inches long
4–5 shiitake mushrooms, soaked and stems removed
2–3 Tbsp tamari soy sauce
light or dark sesame oil, for deep frying
1 cup leftover tempura batter
4–5 lemon wedges, for garnish
1/4 cup parsley, finely minced for garnish

Cook, rinse, and drain the udon or soba.

Prepare the kombu-shiitake stock. When the stock is done, season with tamari soy sauce and simmer for several minutes on a low flame while you prepare the tempura crisps.

Heat up the sesame oil. Place a tablespoon of batter in the hot oil and deep fry until golden brown. It should spread out and form bits of crisp batter. Take a slotted oil spoon and remove the crisp batter morsels. Place them on paper towels to drain. Repeat until all the batter has been deep fried.

Place the cooked udon or soba in the hot broth to heat up and simmer for 2 to 3 minutes. Place the hot noodles in serving bowls. Ladle hot broth over the noodles. Top each bowl of noodles with 1 to 2 tablespoons of crisp batter morsels. Garnish each bowl with 1 lemon wedge and 1 to 2 teaspoons of minced scallions. Serve while hot. Each person may squeeze the lemon over the tempura crisps to help balance the oil.

Ankake (Thick Broth) Udon

Ankake udon is another hearty winter dish, totally vegetarian and oil-free. It is one of the specialty dishes at Ghinga, a popular Japanese-Macrobiotic restaurant in Stockbridge, Massachusetts. The simple kombu broth is thickened with kuzu.

2 packages (16 oz) udon (any kind)
4–5 cups water
1 strip kombu, 4–5 inches long
2–3 Tbsp tamari soy sauce
1/4 cup onions, sliced into thin half-moons
1/4 cup carrots, sliced into thin matchsticks
1/2 cup seitan (wheat meat), sliced into thin strips
1/4 cup snow peas
3 Tbsp kuzu
4 Tbsp water, for diluting kuzu
1 sheet nori, toasted for garnish
2 Tbsp tan sesame seeds, toasted for garnish
1/4 cup scallions, thinly sliced for garnish

Cook, rinse, and drain the udon.

Prepare the kombu stock. After removing the kombu, season with tamari soy sauce. Place the onions, carrots, and seitan in the stock and simmer for 2 to 3 minutes. Add the snow peas. Dilute the kuzu and add to the stock just after adding the snow peas. The kuzu will prevent the snow peas from overcooking.

Place the drained noodles in serving bowls and ladle the hot broth and vegetables over them. Cut the toasted nori into thin strips as described earlier. Garnish each bowl of noodles with several strips of toasted nori, a teaspoon of toasted sesame seeds, and 1 to 2 teaspoons of sliced scallions. Serve while hot.

Udon in Broth with Jinenjo

Jinenjo, or *yama-imo*, is a wild mountain potato from Japan. Unlike the regular potato which is high in potassium, jinenjo is not a member of the nightshade family, is low in potassium, and has a more yang quality. This is a very tasty dish that is also fun to eat due to the sticky quality of the jinenjo.

2 packages (16 oz) udon (any kind)
1–1 1/4 cups jinenjo, grated for garnish
4–5 cups water
1 strip kombu, 4–5 inches long
2–3 Tbsp tamari soy sauce
1 sheet nori, toasted and cut into thin strips for garnish
1/4 cup scallions, thinly sliced for garnish

Cook, rinse, and drain the udon. Prepare the kombu stock as described. When the stock is ready, season with tamari soy sauce and let it simmer for 5 minutes.

Place the cooked udon in the hot broth, reduce the flame to low, and simmer for 2 to 3 minutes without boiling. While noodles are heating up, you can grate the jinenjo on a fine grater. Place the hot udon in serving bowls. Ladle hot broth over each bowl and garnish with 1/4 cup of grated jinenjo, several strips of toasted nori, and 1 to 2 teaspoons of sliced scallions. Serve hot.

Noodles in Broth with Boiled Vegetables and Tofu

2 packages (16 oz) udon, soba, somen, or hiyamugi
4–5 cups water
1 strip kombu, 4–5 inches long
2–3 Tbsp tamari soy sauce
water, for boiling vegetables and tofu
4 leaves Chinese cabbage
4–5 slices firm-style tofu, 2 inches wide by 3 inches long by 1/2 inch thick
4–5 fresh shiitake mushrooms (optional)
4–5 broccoli spears
4–5 red radishes
1/4 cup black sesame seeds, toasted
1/4 cup scallions, thinly sliced for garnish

Cook, rinse, and drain the noodles. Prepare the kombu stock. When the stock is done, season with tamari soy sauce and simmer for 5 minutes.

Place about 1 inch of water in a pot, cover, and bring to a boil. Place the whole Chinese cabbage leaves in the boiling water, cover, and boil for 1 to 1 1/2 minutes. Remove, place in a strainer, and drain. Next, place the tofu in the boiling water, cover, and boil several seconds. Remove, place in a strainer, and drain. Remove the tip of the stem from the shiitake mushrooms and discard. Place the shiitake in the boiling water and boil for 4 to 5 minutes. Remove and drain. Then place the broccoli spears in the boiling water, cover, and simmer for about 1 1/2 minutes or until tender but still bright green. Remove, place in a strainer, and drain. Now slice the red radishes in half and place in the boiling water. Cover and simmer for 1 minute. Remove and drain.

Slice the shiitake into quarters or thin strips. Slice the Chinese cabbage in 1-inch wide strips. Arrange the vegetables on a plate.

Place the cooked noodles in the hot broth, reduce the flame to low, and simmer, without boiling, for 2 to 3 minutes. Place the hot noodles in serving bowls and ladle hot kombu broth over them.

Garnish each bowl with 1 shiitake, 1 broccoli spear, 2 radish halves, several slices of Chinese cabbage, 1 slice of boiled tofu, a few toasted sesame seeds, and 1 to 2 teaspoons of sliced scallions. Serve hot.

Jinenjo Soba in Hot Daikon Broth

Jinenjo soba has a smooth, silky texture and is a real treat.

2 packages (16 oz) jinenjo soba
4–5 cups water
1 strip kombu, 4–5 inches long
1 cup grated daikon
2–3 Tbsp tamari soy sauce
4–5 Tbsp natto, for garnish
1 sheet nori, toasted and cut into thin strips for garnish
1/4 cup scallions, thinly sliced for garnish

Cook, rinse, and drain the jinenjo soba.

Place the water, kombu, and grated daikon in a pot. Cover and bring to a boil. Reduce the flame to medium-low and simmer for 4 to 5 minutes. Remove the kombu and set aside for future use. Season the stock with tamari soy sauce, cover, and simmer for another 5 minutes.

Place the natto in a bowl and stir with chopsticks for several seconds until sticky.

Place the cooked soba in the broth and simmer over a low flame for 2 to 3 minutes, without boiling, just to heat up. Place the soba in serving bowls and ladle hot broth over them.

Garnish each bowl with 1 tablespoon of natto, several strips of toasted nori, and 1 to 2 teaspoons of sliced scallions. Serve while hot.

Soba in Broth with Wasabi

Wasabi is a Japanese horseradish with a hot, spicy taste. It is traditionally served with soba in broth but is also used in making sushi accompanied by raw fish. It has a strong pungent qualities and can be used from time to time by those in normal good health. Wasabi is available in green powdered form in most Oriental and natural food markets. Read the directions on the package when using.

2 packages (16 oz) soba (any kind)
4–5 cups water
1 strip kombu, 4–5 inches long
2 Tbsp mirin
2–3 Tbsp tamari soy sauce
1–1 1/4 tsp wasabi
2 Tbsp tan sesame seeds, toasted for garnish
1 sheet nori, toasted and cut into thin strips for garnish
1/4 cup scallions, thinly sliced for garnish

Cook, rinse, and drain the soba. Prepare the kombu stock as directed. When the broth is ready, add the mirin and tamari soy sauce. Simmer for 5 minutes. Place the cooked soba in the broth, reduce the flame to low, and simmer for 2 to 3 minutes without boiling. Place the soba in serving bowls and ladle hot broth over each serving.

Garnish each bowl with about 1/4 teaspoon of wasabi, 1/3 teaspoon of toasted sesame seeds, a few strips of toasted nori, and 1 to 2 teaspoons of sliced scallions.

Serve hot. Before eating, each person should mix the wasabi into their soba.

Udon in Wakame Broth

2 packages (16 oz) udon (any kind)
4–5 cups water
1 strip wakame, 4–5 inches long
2–3 Tbsp tamari soy sauce
1/2 cup carrots, cut into flowers or matchsticks
1 cup mung bean sprouts
1/4 cup scallions, thinly sliced for garnish

Cook, rinse, and drain the noodles. Prepare the wakame stock as described previously. Season the broth with tamari soy sauce and simmer for 5 minutes. Add the carrot flowers 1 minute before the broth is ready and simmer for 30 seconds. Add the mung bean sprouts and simmer the carrots and bean sprouts for about 1 minute.

Place the cooked udon in individual serving bowls and ladle hot broth, vegetables, and wakame over each bowl. Garnish each bowl with 1 to 2 teaspoons of sliced scallions. Serve hot.

Cha Soba with Steamed Fish

This dish is very simple to prepare and quite delicious. Steaming the fish is a nice change from broiling, baking, deep frying, or pan frying. The steamed fish takes on a pleasant lightness.

> 2 packages (16 oz) cha soba
> 1 1/2–2 lb white-meat fish (cod, haddock, scrod, sole, and so on), washed
> 4–5 cups water
> 1 strip kombu, 4–5 inches long
> 2–3 Tbsp tamari soy sauce
> 2 Tbsp mirin (optional)
> 1/4 cup carrots, cut into flowers for garnish
> 1 bunch watercress, for garnish
> water, for boiling vegetables
> 1/4 cup scallions, thinly sliced for garnish
> 4–5 lemon wedges, for garnish

Cook, rinse, and drain the cha soba. Prepare the kombu stock. When the stock is ready, season with tamari soy sauce and mirin. Simmer for 5 minutes.

Place the soba in individual serving bowls. Pour the kombu broth over the soba and place a fish fillet on top of each bowl. Cover each bowl very tightly with plastic wrap. Place the bowls in a layered bamboo steamer and steam for about 10 minutes until the fish is tender and flakey.

While the soba and fish are steaming, cook the carrot flowers and watercress separately. Place 1/2 inch of water in a pot, cover, and bring to a boil. Remove the cover, place the carrots in the pot, cover again, and boil for 1 minute. Remove and drain. Next, place the watercress in the boiling water and cover. Bring to a boil again and boil for 40 to 45 seconds. Remove the watercress, place in a strainer, and rinse quickly under cold water to stop the cooking action and to set the bright green color. Place the cooked vegetables on a plate.

When the soba and fish are done, remove them from the steamer, and remove and discard the plastic wrap. Garnish each steaming bowl of soba with several sprigs of watercress, several carrot flowers, 1 to 2 teaspoons of sliced scallions, and 1 lemon wedge. Each person can squeeze the lemon wedge over the fish. The more yin qualities of the lemon help to balance the more yang qualities of the fish. Serve hot.

Noodles with Steamed Tofu and Seitan

This is a delicious alternative for those who wish to avoid fish. Follow the recipe for Cha Soba and Steamed Fish above, but instead of placing fish on the noodles, place 2 slices of firm-style tofu (2 inches wide by 3 inches long by 1/4 inch thick) and several strips of precooked seitan (wheat meat) on top of them. Steam as in the above recipe and garnish with the same vegetables. Lemon may be omitted in this case. Any type of noodles or broth may be used in preparing this dish.

Somen with Fresh Shiitake Mushrooms

Although somen are most frequently served cool or chilled, they are also delicious when served in hot kombu or kombu-shiitake broth.

2 packages (16 oz) somen (any kind)
8–10 fresh shiitake mushrooms, stems removed
4–5 cups water
1 strip kombu, 4–5 inches long
2–3 Tbsp tamari soy sauce
8–10 cubes firm-style tofu (l-inch squares)
light or dark sesame oil, for deep frying
water, for cooking vegetables
1 bunch watercress, for garnish
4–5 wedges buttercup squash, 2 inches wide by 3 inches long by 1/4 inch thick, for garnish
4–5 lemon slices, cut into half-moons for garnish
1/4 cup scallions, thinly sliced for garnish

Cook, rinse, and drain the somen. Prepare kombu stock as directed. When the stock is ready, season with tamari soy sauce and simmer for another 5 minutes.

Deep fry the tofu cubes until golden brown, remove, and drain on paper towels. Place the cubes of tofu in the hot broth.

Take the shiitake mushrooms and slice a star into them as illustrated below. Place the shiitake in the broth and simmer for 2 to 3 minutes or so.

Fig. 11

While the broth is simmering, boil the watercress for 45 seconds and then the buttercup squash for 1 to 2 minutes until tender but still firm. Place the cooked vegetables on a plate.

Place the cooked somen in the broth and heat for 1 to 2 minutes without boiling. Remove and place in serving bowls. Ladle hot broth over the somen.

Garnish each bowl with 1 fresh shiitake mushroom, 2 cubes of deep-fried tofu, several sprigs of watercress, 1 slice of buttercup squash, 1 lemon slice, and 1 to 2 teaspoons of sliced scallions. Serve hot.

Harusame (Mung Bean Noodles) with Vegetables in Broth

Harusame are transparent noodles made from mung bean starch flour. They are very light and quite beautiful when served in a broth with vegetables and fresh tofu.

2 packages (6 oz) harusame

4–5 cups water, for broth
1 strip kombu, 4–5 inches long, soaked and sliced into very thin matchsticks
4–5 small or medium shiitake mushrooms, soaked and stems removed
2–3 Tbsp tamari soy sauce
3–4 cups cold water, for soaking harusame
water, for cooking tofu and vegetables
1/2 lb soft-style tofu
5 Chinese cabbage leaves
1/4 cup carrots, cut into flowers
5 scallions
1 sheet nori, toasted for garnish

Place the water, kombu, and shiitake mushrooms in a pot. Cover and bring to a boil. Reduce the flame to medium-low and simmer for about 10 minutes or so. When the stock is done, season with tamari soy sauce. Reduce the flame to low and simmer for another 5 minutes.

While the stock is cooking, place the harusame in a bowl and pour cold water over them. Soak for about 10 minutes. Remove and drain when soft.

Place 1 inch of water in a pot, cover, and bring to a boil. Slice the tofu into 1-inch cubes and place in the boiling water. Cover and simmer for 1 to 2 minutes. Remove and place on a plate. Next, place the whole Chinese cabbage leaves in the boiling water. Cover and boil for 1 minute. Remove, rinse quickly under cold water, and drain. Stack the Chinese cabbage leaves on top of each other on a cutting board. Roll or form into a cylinder with your hands. Slice the Chinese cabbage into 1- to 1 1/2-inch long rounds and place them on a platter. Place the carrot flowers in the boiling water, cover, and simmer for about 1 minute. Remove and place on the plate with the other vegetables. Finally, take the scallions and slice off the hairy root section and most of the upper green portion. Save these for use in other dishes. You should now have 5 pieces of scallion about 3 inches long. Place the scallion pieces in the boiling water, cover, and simmer for 30 seconds. Remove and place on the plate.

Place the harusame in each serving bowl. Add, in an attractive arrangement, 2 to 3 pieces of tofu, 1 round portion of Chinese cabbage, 3 to 4 carrot flowers, and 1 piece of scallion, to each bowl. Ladle hot kombu-shiitake broth over the harusame and vegetables.

Cut the toasted nori into thin strips and garnish each bowl with several strips. Serve hot.

Instead of plain boiled tofu, you may deep fry tofu cubes, sliced tempeh, or seitan strips, for a heartier flavor. You may also place boiled, poached, or fried fish or other seafood in this dish.

Somen in Onion Broth

2 packages (16 oz) somen
1 strip kombu, 4–5 inches long, soaked
4 shiitake mushrooms, soaked and stems removed
4–5 cups water
2 cups onions, sliced into half-moons

    1 cup whole wheat bread cubes, for croutons
    light or dark sesame oil, for deep frying (optional)
    water, for blanching carrots
    2 Tbsp carrots, cut into matchsticks
    2–3 Tbsp tamari soy sauce
    1 1/2 Tbsp parsley, minced for garnish

Cook, rinse, and drain the somen.

Roll the kombu into a log shaped cylinder and slice into very thin strips. Place on a plate. Slice the shiitake mushrooms and place on a plate.

Place enough water on the bottom of a pot to just cover and bring to a boil. Add the onions and water sauté them until almost translucent. Add the kombu, shiitake, and remaining water measurement for broth. Cover and bring to a boil. Reduce the flame to medium-low and simmer for about 20 to 25 minutes.

While the stock is simmering, deep fry the bread cubes until golden brown, remove, place on paper towels, and allow to drain. You may dry roast the bread in a skillet or in the oven as described earlier, if you wish to avoid oil.

Place a small amount of water in a saucepan, cover, bring to a boil, and blanch the carrots for 45 to 50 seconds. Remove the carrots and place on a plate.

When the onion stock is ready, season with tamari soy sauce and simmer for another 5 minutes. Place the somen in the broth, reduce the flame to low, and simmer for 2 to 3 minutes to heat up.

Place the somen in serving bowls, ladle hot onion broth over them, and garnish with several croutons, several pieces of matchstick carrots, and 1 teaspoon of minced parsley. Serve while hot.

Summer Soba in Chilled Broth

In Japan they have a wonderful tradition of serving noodles in a chilled broth during the hot summer months. Chilled noodles are very cooling and apealing when hot food seems unappetizing.

    2 packages (16 oz) soba (any kind)
    4–5 cups water
    1 strip kombu, 4–5 inches long
    2–3 Tbsp tamari soy sauce
    1/4 cup grated daikon, for garnish
    1/4 cup tan sesame seeds, roasted for garnish
    1 sheet nori, toasted and cut into thin strips for garnish
    4–5 tsp bonito flakes, for garnish (optional)
    1/4 cup scallions, thinly sliced for garnish

Cook the soba, rinse, and drain. Prepare the kombu stock. When it is ready, season with tamari soy sauce and simmer for 5 minutes. Place the broth in the refrigerator and allow to chill. Remove the broth.

Place the soba in serving bowls. Ladle chilled broth over each bowl of soba. Garnish with 2 teaspoons of grated daikon, 2 teaspoons of roasted sesame seeds, a few strips of toasted nori, 1 teaspoon of bonito flakes, and 1 to 2 teaspoons of sliced scallions.

Cha Soba and Tofu in Chilled Broth

> 2 packages (16 oz) cha soba
> 1/2 lb soft-style tofu
> 4–5 cups water
> 1 strip kombu, 4–5 inches long
> 4–5 shiitake mushrooms, soaked and stems removed
> 2–3 Tbsp tamari soy sauce
> 1 tsp grated ginger, for garnish
> 1 sheet nori, toasted and cut into strips for garnish
> 4–5 tsp bonito flakes, for garnish (optional)
> 1/4 cup scallions, thinly sliced for garnish

Cook, rinse, and drain the cha soba. Prepare the kombu-shiitake stock, leaving the whole shiitake in the stock to be served with the cha soba. When the stock is ready, season with tamari soy sauce and simmer for 5 minutes. Place the broth in the refrigerator and allow to chill. Remove the chilled broth.

Place the cha soba in serving bowls and ladle chilled broth over them.

Cut the tofu into 4 to 5 equal-sized slices and place one slice on top of each bowl of cha soba (you may boil the tofu for 1 to 2 minutes if desired). Garnish each bowl of cha soba with a dab of grated ginger, several strips of toasted nori, 1 teaspoon of bonito flakes, and 1 to 2 teaspoons of sliced scallions, and serve.

Ume-Yakko Soba

> 2 packages (16 oz) soba (any kind)
> 1 umeboshi plum
> 1 lb soft-style tofu
> 4–5 cups water
> 1 strip kombu, 4–5 inches long
> 4 shiitake mushrooms, soaked and stems removed
> 2–3 Tbsp tamari soy sauce
> 4–5 tsp chopped red shiso leaves or 4–5 whole green shiso leaves
> 4–5 Tbsp bonito flakes (optional)
> 4–5 Tbsp grated daikon
> 4–5 tsp scallions, thinly sliced for garnish

Cook, rinse, and drain the soba. Prepare the kombu-shiitake stock, removing the kombu and shiitake when the stock is ready. Season the stock with tamari soy sauce and simmer for 5 minutes. Place the broth in the refrigerator and allow to chill. Remove the broth.

Slice the tofu into 4 to 5 equal-sized thick slices. Place the soba in serving bowls and ladle the broth over the soba. Place a slice of tofu on each bowl of soba. Next, place the red or green shiso leaves on top of the raw tofu. Place a small piece of umeboshi on top of the shiso. Place 1 tablespoon of bonito flakes, 1 tablespoon of grated daikon, and 1 to 2 teaspoons of sliced scallions on top of the other garnishes. Serve.

Summer Somen with Natto in Chilled Broth

> **2 packages (16 oz) somen**
> **1/2 cup natto**
> **4–5 cups water**
> **1 strip kombu, 4–5 inches long**
> **2–3 Tbsp tamari soy sauce**
> **1/4 cup grated daikon**
> **1/4 cup scallions, thinly sliced for garnish**
> **1 sheet nori, toasted and cut into thin strips for garnish**

Cook, rinse, and drain the somen. Prepare the kombu broth and chill as described above. Place the somen in serving bowls and ladle the chilled broth over them. Garnish each bowl with 2 tablespoons of natto (you may chop the natto first), 1 to 2 teaspoons of grated daikon, 1 to 2 teaspoons of sliced scallions, and several strips of toasted nori. Serve.

Hiyamugi with Lemon and Watercress in Chilled Broth

> **2 packages (16 oz) hiyamugi**
> **4–5 lemon wedges, for garnish**
> **1 bunch watercress**
> **4–5 cups water**
> **1 strip kombu, 4–5 inches long**
> **2–3 Tbsp tamari soy sauce**
> **water, for boiling watercress**
> **1/4 cup black sesame seeds, toasted for garnish**
> **1/4 cup scallions, thinly sliced for garnish**

Cook, rinse, and drain the hiyamugi. Prepare the kombu broth and allow to chill.

Place 1/2 inch of water in a pot, cover, and bring to a boil. Add the watercress, cover, and bring to a boil again. Cook for 40 seconds, remove, and rinse under cold water. Allow to drain.

Place the hiyamugi in serving bowls and ladle the chilled broth over each serving. Garnish each bowl with several sprigs of watercress, 1 lemon wedge, and 1 to 2 teaspoons of black sesame seeds and sliced scallions. Each person may squeeze lemon juice over the hiyamugi before eating for a delightful and refreshing flavor. Serve.

Udon with Fresh Steamed Fish Cakes

The Japanese name for these delicious cakes of steamed fish paste is *kamaboko*. Now, however, it is very difficult to find good quality, natural fish cakes in Japan, as the modern varieties usually contain eggs and artificial dyes. Therefore, when you order noodles in a restaurant, it is better to avoid eating the fish cakes. However, it is possible to make natural, chemical-free fish cakes at home. Below is a recipe for totally natural kamaboko you are sure to enjoy.

Fish Cakes (Kamaboko)
  1/2 lb cod, haddock, scrod, or sole (without skin or bones)
  1 strip kombu, 3 inches long, dusted
  1/2 cup water, for soaking kombu
  1 tsp sea salt
  3 Tbsp mirin
  2 Tbsp kuzu
  1/4 cup unbleached white flour
  light sesame oil

Place the kombu in a small bowl and cover with 1/2 cup of water. Soak for 25 to 30 minutes. Remove the kombu and set aside for use in another dish.

Chop the fish into small pieces and place, a few pieces at a time, in a blender. Purée the fish until it becomes a thick paste. Remove the fish paste from the blender and place it in a bowl. Add sea salt and mirin to the paste. Place the kuzu in a small cup, add 2 tablespoons of the kombu soaking water, and dilute. Add the diluted kuzu to the fish paste. Mix well with a spoon.

Place the flour in the bowl of kombu water and mix vigorously with a wood wisk or spoon to remove lumps. Pour the flour-kombu mixture into the bowl of fish paste and mix thoroughly. Divide the paste in half, in order to make 2 loaves of fish cakes.

Take a small bread pan (3 inches by 6 inches) or a small casserole dish and oil the bottom with light sesame oil. Line the bottom of the pan with foil wrap. Place the fish paste on top of the foil, and form into an oblong cake about 2 inches wide by 5 inches long, and about 1 1/2 to 2 inches high (you may pull the foil up around the edges of the paste to hold it in place). Take another glass or metal casserole dish and fill it half full with boiling water. Place the pan with the fish paste in the middle of the water-filled casserole dish. Repeat to form 2 loaves of fish cakes.

Bake the fish cake loaves in a 250°F oven for 55 to 60 minutes or until they are firm to the touch. Turn the oven off, and without opening the oven door, allow the loaves to sit for 10 minutes. Remove and glaze with the following:

Glaze
  2 tsp brown rice syrup
  1/4 tsp light sesame oil
  2 tsp water
  1–2 drops tamari soy sauce

Place the above ingredients in a bowl and mix thoroughly. Brush the steam-baked loaves with the glaze. Lift the fish cake-filled foil wrap out of the pan and place directly under the broiler. Broil the loaves for about 5 to 7 minutes to brown the top. Remove and allow to cool to room temperature. Remove the loaves from the foil wrap and slice into several 1/4-inch thick pieces.

Noodles in Broth
> **2 packages (16 oz) udon (any kind)**
> **4–5 cups water**
> **1 strip kombu, 4–5 inches long**
> **2–3 Tbsp tamari soy sauce**
> **1/4 cup scallions, thinly sliced for garnish**

Cook, rinse, and drain the udon. Prepare kombu broth while the fish cakes are steaming. Place the cooked udon in the hot broth and heat up for 2 to 3 minutes without boiling. Remove the udon and place in serving bowls. Ladle hot broth over the udon.

Place several pieces of steamed fish cake slices on top of each serving of udon. Garnish with sliced scallions and serve hot.

Soba with Deep-fried Fish Balls

Fish Balls (14–16 balls)
> **1/2 lb cod, haddock, scrod, or sole (without skin or bones)**
> **1/4 cup unbleached white or whole wheat flour**
> **1 tsp sea salt**
> **3 Tbsp mirin (optional)**
> **2 scallions, thinly sliced**
> **4 Tbsp carrots, finely diced**
> **4 Tbsp celery, finely diced**
> **2 tsp black sesame seeds, washed**
> **2 Tbsp kuzu**
> **2 Tbsp water, for diluting kuzu**
> **1/2 cup whole wheat flour, to roll fish balls in**
> **light or dark sesame oil, for deep frying**

Cut the fish into small pieces and purée, adding a little at a time to a blender until the fish is a thick, smooth paste. Remove the fish paste and place in a mixing bowl. Add 1/4 cup of unbleached white or whole wheat flour, sea salt, mirin, sliced scallions, carrots, celery, and black sesame seeds. Dilute the kuzu in water and add to the mixing bowl. Mix all ingredients in the bowl until smooth.

Place 1/2 cup of flour in a small bowl. Form the fish paste into small balls about the size of a ping pong ball. Roll the balls in the flour to coat them evenly, and then deep fry until golden brown. Remove, place on paper towels, and allow to drain.

Soba in Broth
> **2 packages (16 oz) soba (any kind)**
> **4–5 cups water**
> **1 strip kombu, 4–5 inches long**
> **4–5 shiitake mushrooms, soaked and stems removed**
> **2–3 Tbsp tamari soy sauce**
> **1 Tbsp grated ginger**
> **1/4 cup scallions, thinly sliced for garnish**

Cook, rinse, and drain the soba. Prepare the kombu-shiitake broth, leaving the whole mushrooms in the broth to be served with the soba. Place the cooked soba in the hot broth and heat up for 2 to 3 minutes without boiling. Remove the soba and place in serving bowls. Ladle hot broth over the soba.

Place 2 to 3 fish balls in each bowl of soba and garnish each bowl with 1/4 to 1/3 teaspoon of grated ginger and 1 to 2 teaspoons of sliced scallions. Serve while hot.

Deep-fried Rice Noodles in Broth

1 package (8 oz) rice noodles, uncooked
light or dark sesame oil, for deep frying
4–5 cups water
1 strip kombu, 4–5 inches long
8–10 medium shrimp, shelled and deveined (optional)
8–10 green string beans or snow peas, stems and strings removed
1/2 cup tofu, cut into l-inch cubes
2 cups Chinese cabbage, sliced into l-inch pieces
2–3 Tbsp tamari soy sauce
1 tsp ginger juice
1/4 cup scallions, thinly sliced for garnish

Heat up oil. To test if the oil is hot enough, break a small piece of noodle off and drop it into the oil. If the noodle immediately puffs up and floats to the surface, the oil is hot enough. If the noodle stays on the bottom of the pot and takes several seconds to rise, the oil is too cold. Do not allow the oil to smoke. (If the oil smokes it is too hot.) Drop the entire bundle of rice noodles into the hot oil, or first break them in half or thirds, and deep fry until puffed up and golden brown. Remove, place on paper towels, and drain. Break up into pieces.

Place the water and kombu in a pot, cover, and simmer for 4 minutes. Remove the kombu and set aside for future use. Place the shrimp in the stock and simmer for 1 minute. Add the string beans (if using snow peas add at the end). Cook for 1 to 2 minutes. Add the tofu and Chinese cabbage and simmer for 30 seconds. Add the tamari soy sauce to season and simmer for another 4 to 5 minutes on a very low flame. Add the ginger juice.

Place 1/4 cup or so of deep-fried rice noodles in each serving bowl and ladle the broth, vegetables, shrimp, and tofu over them. Garnish with sliced scallions. Serve hot.

Quick Ramen in Broth

Ramen noodles are a traditional Chinese dish in which either udon or soba are deep fried in animal fat and served in broth. Dried natural ramen from Japan are now available in natural food stores. These natural ramen come in individual servings and include small packets of seasoned tamari soy sauce or miso broth. They cook very quickly and are great for those on the go. For those who wish to avoid spices, add your own puréed miso or tamari soy sauce to the ramen and cooking water instead of using the preseasoned broth that comes with the ramen.

2 packages instant ramen (udon, whole wheat noodles, or soba)
2 packages instant broth (included in package)
5 cups water
1 sheet nori, toasted and cut into thin strips
2–3 Tbsp scallions, thinly sliced for garnish

Place water in a pot, cover, and bring to a boil. Add the instant ramen and cook for about 3 minutes. Add the instant broth. Stir, reduce the flame to low, and simmer for 1 to 2 minutes. Place in serving bowls and garnish with several strips of toasted nori and sliced scallions.

As a variation, add thinly sliced vegetables when you put the ramen in the boiling water, or add cubed tofu when you add the instant broth. You can also garnish your ramen with roasted sesame seeds, sliced scallions, and toasted nori. You can also garnish with chopped parsley, chives, or celery instead of sliced scallions.

Chapter 5: Noodle and Pasta Soups

Hundreds of nourishing noodle and pasta soups can be made simply by varying the type and amount of vegetables, noodles or pasta, and seasoning that you use. In this chapter, we explain how to use both Oriental and Western varieties of noodles and pasta in hearty soups and stews flavored with such healthful seasonings as miso, sea salt, and umeboshi plums. All of the soups in this chapter are low in saturated fat and cholesterol, high in complex carbohydrates and fiber, and based on natural ingredients. We hope you enjoy them as much as we do.

Udon Miso Soup

Udon are delicious when served in a light miso broth at breakfast or lunch, especially during the cool times of year. Although udon are specified in this recipe, any kind of noodle or pasta may be substituted.

> **1 package (8 oz) udon (any kind), cooked**
> **4–5 cups water**
> **1/2 cup wakame, soaked and sliced**
> **1 cup daikon, sliced into thin quarters**
> **1/2 cup celery, sliced on a thin diagonal**
> **4–5 tsp barley miso**
> **5–6 tsp water or soup stock, for puréeing miso**
> **1/4 cup scallions, thinly sliced for garnish**

Place the water in a pot, cover, and bring to a boil. Place the wakame in the boiling water, cover, and reduce the flame to medium. Simmer for about 3 to 4 minutes. Add the daikon and celery, cover, and simmer for another 2 to 3 minutes. Reduce the flame to very low, so that the water is not boiling. Add the udon. Purée the miso and add to the soup stock. Cover and simmer for 2 to 3 minutes without boiling. Place in individual serving bowls and garnish each with 1 to 2 teaspoons of sliced scallions. Serve hot.

White Miso Soup with Somen and Croutons

In this recipe, the wonderful sweet flavor of cooked onions combines with the rich flavor of deep-fried croutons to produce a delicious and nourishing soup.

> **1 package (8 oz) somen (any kind), cooked**
> **1 cup bread cubes, for making croutons**
> **4–5 cups water**
> **2 cups onions, sliced into thin half-moons**
> **1 strip kombu, 4–5 inches long, soaked and sliced into very thin matchsticks**
> **4–5 shiitake mushrooms, soaked, tip of stems removed, and thinly sliced**
> **1/2 cup carrots, sliced into thin matchsticks**

light or dark sesame oil, for deep frying croutons (optional)
4–5 tsp white miso
1/4 cup parsley, minced for garnish

Place enough water in the bottom of a pot to just cover it. Bring to a boil. Add the onions and water sauté for 3 to 4 minutes or until the onions are translucent. Add the water, kombu, and shiitake mushrooms. Cover and bring to a boil over a high flame. Reduce the flame to medium-low and simmer for about 20 minutes or until the onions are very tender. Add the carrots, cover, and simmer for 1 to 2 minutes. Reduce the flame to very low, so that the stock does not boil.

Deep fry the croutons until golden brown, place on paper towels, and allow to drain. If you wish to avoid oil, you may pan fry, or bake, without oil, as described earlier.

Purée the white miso with a little soup stock or cold water. Add the miso to the stock. Then add the somen and simmer, without boiling, over a low flame for 2 to 3 minutes. Place in individual serving bowls and garnish each bowl with minced parsley.

Instead of white miso, you can use mellow barley or yellow miso for a different flavor. Other whole grain noodles may be used in place of somen.

Grated Daikon and Natto Miso Soup with Noodles

1 package (8 oz) soba, somen, or udon, cooked
1 cup grated daikon
1 cup natto
4–5 cups water
1 strip kombu, 4–5 inches long, soaked
4–5 tsp barley miso
1 sheet nori, toasted and cut into thin strips
1/4 cup scallions, thinly sliced for garnish

Place the water, kombu, and kombu soaking water in a pot. Cover and bring to a boil. Reduce the flame to medium-low and simmer for 3 to 4 minutes. Remove the kombu and set aside. Add the grated daikon, cover, and simmer for 1 to 2 minutes. Reduce the flame to very low.

Purée the barley miso. Add the natto to the stock. Then add the puréed miso. Place the cooked noodles in the miso soup and simmer for 2 to 3 minutes without boiling. Remove and place in individual serving bowls. Garnish each bowl with several toasted nori strips and sliced scallions. Serve hot.

As a variation, garnish with bonito flakes for a wonderful smoked flavor.

Soba and Tofu Miso Soup

In most recipes for kombu stock the kombu is usually simmered for several minutes before the broth is seasoned. In this recipe, the kombu is presoaked for several hours. This causes the stock to have a very light, subtle flavor that helps balance the more yang quality of soba.

1 package (8 oz) soba (any kind), cooked
1 lb soft-style tofu, cubed
4–5 cups water
1 strip kombu, 6–8 inches long
4–5 carrot flower slices, for garnish
1 bunch watercress
4–5 tsp barley miso
1/3 cup grated daikon
1 sheet nori, toasted and cut into strips
1/4 cup scallions, thinly sliced for garnish

Place the water and kombu in a glass bowl and soak for 6 to 8 hours or overnight. Remove the kombu and set aside. Place the kombu water in a pot, cover, and bring to a boil.

Place 1/2 inch of water in a pot, cover, and bring to a boil. Add the carrot flowers, cover, and simmer for 1 minute. Remove and place on a plate. Now add the watercress, cover, bring to a boil again, and simmer for 45 seconds. Remove the watercress, place in a strainer, and quickly rinse with cold water. Squeeze the watercress with your hands to remove excess liquid and place on a cutting board. Slice into 1- to 2-inch lengths and put on the plate with the carrot flowers.

Reduce the flame under the kombu stock to very low. Purée the miso and add it to the stock. Add the tofu and soba. Cover and simmer for 2 to 3 minutes without boiling.

Remove and place in individual serving bowls. Garnish each bowl with several pieces of tofu, 1 to 2 sections of chopped watercress, 1 carrot flower, 1 teaspoon of grated daikon, several strips of toasted nori, and 1 teaspoon of sliced scallions. Serve hot.

Puréed Cauliflower Miso Soup with Pasta

1 small head cauliflower
1/3 package (4–6 oz) small whole grain pastina (soup pasta), cooked
4–5 cups water
1 strip kombu, 4–5 inches long
4–5 slices dried tofu, soaked and sliced into 1/4-inch thick strips
2–3 Tbsp white or yellow miso, puréed
4 Tbsp water or soup stock, for puréeing miso
1/4 cup scallions, parsley, or chives, thinly sliced for garnish

Place the water and kombu in a pot, cover, and bring to a boil. Cut the cauliflower into small pieces and place in the boiling water. Cover, bring to a boil, and reduce the flame to medium-low. Simmer for 3 to 4 minutes and remove the kombu. Set the kombu aside for future use. Cover and simmer the cauliflower in the soup stock for about 15 to 20 minutes or until very tender.

Place a hand food mill over a clean pot and pour the stock and cauliflower into the mill. Purée the cauliflower into the pot. Place the pot over a medium-low flame, add the slices of dried tofu, cover, and simmer for 5 to 7 minutes. Reduce the flame to low and add the puréed miso. Place the cooked pastina in the pot and allow to simmer for 2 to 3 minutes without boiling.

Place in individual serving bowls and garnish with sliced scallions, parsley, or chives. Serve hot.

Puréed Broccoli Miso Soup with Pasta

> 1 medium head of broccoli, finely chopped
> 8 oz small whole grain pastina, cooked
> 4–5 cups water
> 2–3 Tbsp mellow barley miso, puréed
> 1 sheet nori, toasted and cut into thin strips for garnish
> 1 cup bread cubes, oven- or pan-fried, for crouton garnish

Place the water and broccoli in a pot, cover, and bring to a boil. Reduce the flame to medium-low and simmer for 15 to 20 minutes until the broccoli is very tender. Purée in a hand food mill as above. Place on a low flame and add the pastina and puréed miso. Cover and simmer for another 2 to 3 minutes without boiling. Remove, place in serving bowls, and garnish each bowl with several toasted nori strips and croutons. Serve hot.

Macaroni Miso Soup

> 8 oz whole grain elbow macaroni, cooked
> 4–5 cups water
> 1/4 cup wakame, soaked and sliced
> 1/4 cup onions, diced
> 1/4 cup celery, diced
> 1/4 cup carrots, diced
> 1/4 cup burdock, diced
> 2–3 Tbsp barley miso, puréed
> 1/4 cup scallions, thinly sliced for garnish

Place the water and sliced wakame in a pot. Cover and bring to a boil. Reduce the flame to medium-low and simmer for 3 to 4 minutes. Add the onions, celery, carrots, and burdock, cover, and simmer for 5 to 7 minutes. Reduce the flame to low. Add the cooked macaroni and the puréed miso. Simmer for 2 to 3 minutes without boiling. Place in individual serving bowls and garnish with sliced scallions. Serve hot.

Mixed Bean and Pasta Miso Soup

This rich miso-pasta soup is wonderful in late summer or early autumn.

> 8 oz whole grain ziti, elbows, or rigatoni, cooked
> 1/4 cup kidney beans, washed and soaked
> 1/4 cup navy beans, washed and soaked
> 1/4 cup pinto beans, washed and soaked

> 4–5 cups water
> 1 strip kombu, 2–3 inches long, dusted
> 1/4 cup onions, diced
> 1/4 cup sweet corn, removed from cob
> 1/4 cup green string beans, sliced into 1/2-inch lengths
> 2–3 Tbsp barley miso, puréed
> 1/4 cup scallions, parsley, or chives, thinly sliced for garnish

Discard the soaking water from the beans. Place the beans in a pressure cooker with fresh water. Add the kombu. Place the cover on the cooker and bring up to pressure on a high flame. Reduce the flame to medium-low and cook for 50 minutes. Remove from the flame and allow the pressure to come down.

Place the onions, corn, and string beans in the uncovered pressure cooker. Cover the pressure cooker with a regular lid (not the pressure cooker lid), bring to a boil, and reduce the flame to medium-low. Simmer the vegetables for 5 to 7 minutes. Add the cooked pasta and puréed miso. Reduce the flame to low. Simmer for 2 to 3 minutes without boiling. Place in individual serving bowls and garnish each bowl with sliced scallions, parsley, or chives. Serve hot.

Corn Ribbon Miso Soup

> 8 oz corn ribbons, cooked
> 4–5 cups water
> 1 strip kombu, 4–5 inches long
> 1/4 cup onions, diced
> 1/4 cup celery, diced
> 1/2 cup sweet corn, removed from cob
> 1/4 cup carrots, cut into matchsticks
> 2–3 tsp barley miso, puréed
> 1/4 cup scallions, thinly sliced for garnish

Place the water and kombu in a pot, cover, and bring to a boil. Reduce the flame to medium-low and simmer for 3 to 4 minutes. Remove the kombu and set aside. Add the onions, celery, sweet corn, and carrots. Cover and simmer for 3 to 4 minutes. Reduce the flame to low and add the corn ribbons and puréed miso. Simmer for 2 to 3 minutes without boiling. Place in serving bowls and garnish with sliced scallions. Serve hot.

Udon and Bonito Flake Miso Soup

> 1 package (8 oz) udon (any kind), cooked
> 2–3 Tbsp bonito flakes
> 4–5 cups water
> 1 strip kombu, 4–5 inches long, dusted
> 1 cup Chinse cabbage, sliced into l-inch wide pieces
> 2–3 Tbsp barley miso, puréed
> 1/4 cup scallions, thinly sliced for garnish

Prepare the kombu stock. When done, remove the kombu and set aside. Place the bonito flakes in the stock and simmer over a low flame for 3 to 4 minutes. Strain the stock through a strainer to remove the bonito flakes. Place the pot of stock over a medium flame, add the Chinese cabbage, cover, and simmer for 1 to 2 minutes. Reduce the flame to low and add the puréed miso and cooked udon. Simmer for 2 to 3 minutes without boiling. Place in serving bowls and garnish each bowl with sliced scallions. Serve hot.

Fish and Pasta Miso Soup

> 1/2 lb fresh white-meat fish (cod, scrod, haddock, and so on)
> 1 cup whole grain elbows, small shells, or other small pasta, cooked
> 1 strip kombu, 4–5 inches long, soaked and diced
> 3 shiitake mushrooms, soaked, stems removed, and diced
> 1/4 cup onions, diced
> 1/4 cup carrots, diced
> 2 Tbsp celery, diced
> 2 Tbsp burdock, diced
> 1/4 cup green peas or green beans, diced
> 1/4 cup sweet corn, removed from cob
> 4–5 cups water
> 2–3 Tbsp barley miso, puréed
> 1 tsp grated ginger
> 1/4 cup scallions, thinly sliced for garnish

Layer the vegetables in a pot as follows: First place the kombu on the bottom of the pot. On top of the kombu place the shiitake mushrooms, onions, carrots, celery, burdock, green peas or green beans, and fresh sweet corn. Add the water, cover, and bring to a boil. Reduce the flame to medium-low and simmer for several minutes until the vegetables are tender. Place the fish and cooked pasta on top of the vegetables, cover, and simmer for 5 minutes or so until the fish is done. Reduce the flame to very low, add the puréed miso, and simmer for another 2 to 3 minutes. Remove and place in serving bowls. Garnish each bowl with a dab of grated ginger and sliced scallions. Serve hot.

Instead of fish, you may add cubes of dried tofu or tempeh, or cubes of deep-fried tofu, at the beginning of the recipe, or use the above ingredients without the fish.

Minestrone

For those who wish to avoid nightshades, this recipe explains how to use umeboshi vinegar to create a slightly sour flavor similar to that of tomatoes. Umeboshi vinegar makes a delicious minestrone.

> 2 cups whole grain elbows, small shells, or other small soup pasta, cooked
> 1 strip kombu, 2–3 inches long, soaked and diced
> 1/4 cup kidney beans, soaked 6–8 hours
> 1/4 cup navy beans, soaked 6–8 hours

1/4 cup lentils
6 cups water
1/4 cup onions, diced
1/4 cup green string beans, chopped in l-inch lengths
2 Tbsp celery, diced
1/4 cup carrots, diced
1/4 cup sweet corn, removed from cob
1/4 cup leeks, finely chopped
3 Tbsp umeboshi vinegar
2 tsp tamari soy sauce
1/4 cup chives, scallions, or parsley, finely minced for garnish

Place the kombu, kidney beans, navy beans, and lentils in a pot. Add the water, cover, and bring to a boil. Reduce the flame to medium-low and simmer for about 1 1/2 to 2 hours or until the beans are tender. Add the onions, string beans, celery, carrots, sweet corn, and leeks. Cover and simmer for 5 to 7 minutes until the vegetables are tender. Add the cooked pasta, umeboshi vinegar, and tamari soy sauce. Cover and simmer for about 4 to 5 minutes. Remove, place in serving bowls, and garnish each bowl with minced chives, scallions, or parsley. Serve hot.

Lentil, Barley, and Pasta Soup

1/4 cup green lentils
1/4 cup barley, soaked 6–8 hours
2 cups whole grain pasta, shells, ziti, elbows, and so on, cooked
5 cups water
1/4 cup onions, diced
1/4 cup celery, diced
1/4 cup mushrooms, sliced
1/4 cup carrots, diced
1/4 cup yellow wax beans, sliced into l-inch lengths
1/4 tsp sea salt
1 Tbsp umeboshi vinegar
2 Tbsp parsley, minced for garnish

Place the barley, lentils, and water in a pot. Cover and bring to a boil. Reduce the flame to medium-low and simmer for 1 hour. Add the onions, celery, mushrooms, carrots, and yellow wax beans. Cover and simmer for another 5 minutes. Add the sea salt, umeboshi vinegar, and cooked pasta. Cover and simmer for another 7 to 10 minutes. Remove and place in serving bowls. Garnish each bowl with minced parsley. Serve hot.

Creamy Onion and Pasta Soup

3 cups onions, minced
1 cup thin spaghetti, broken into l-inch lengths and cooked
4–5 cups water
1 strip kombu, 1–2 inches long, soaked and sliced into thin matchsticks

2 Tbsp corn oil
1/4 cup mushrooms, diced
1/4 cup celery, diced
3–4 Tbsp unbleached white flour
2 Tbsp bonito flakes, small ground variety (optional)
1/4 tsp sea salt
1 Tbsp parsley, minced
1/4 cup scallions or chives, finely chopped for garnish

Place the water and kombu in a pot, cover, and bring to a boil. Reduce the flame to low and simmer for 10 minutes.

Place the corn oil in a skillet and sauté the onions, mushrooms, and celery for 2 to 3 minutes. Add the flour and sauté for 1 to 2 minutes. Place the sautéed ingredients in a pot. Add the bonito flakes. Add the kombu stock, a little at a time, stirring constantly to prevent lumping. Add the sea salt. Cover and simmer over a low flame for about 10 minutes. Add the cooked spaghetti and parsley and simmer for 2 to 3 minutes. Remove, place in serving bowls, and garnish each bowl with chopped scallions or chives. Serve hot.

Fish and Rice Noodle Soup

1/2 lb cod or haddock (without bones), cubed
2 cups rice noodles, cooked
5 cups water
1 strip kombu, 1–2 inches long, soaked and diced
1/2 lb firm-style tofu, cubed
light or dark sesame oil, for deep frying
1/4 tsp sea salt
1 tsp parsley, minced
1/4 cup scallions, finely chopped for garnish
1 sheet nori, toasted and cut into strips for garnish

Place the water and kombu in a pot. Cover and bring to a boil. Reduce the flame to medium-low and simmer for 5 to 7 minutes.

Deep fry the tofu until golden brown, remove, and drain on paper towels. Place the tofu in the pot with the kombu. Cover and simmer for 2 to 3 minutes. Add the fish and sea salt. Simmer for 4 to 5 minutes. Add the cooked rice noodles and parsley. Cover and simmer for 1 to 2 minutes.

Remove, place in serving bowls, and garnish with chopped scallions and toasted nori strips. Serve hot.

Pasta Soup with Greens

1 cup whole grain alphabet noodles or other small soup pasta, cooked
5 cups water
1 strip kombu, 1–2 inches long, soaked and finely diced
1 1/2 lb firm-style tofu, cubed and deep-fried
1/4 tsp sea salt

3 cups bok choy, finely chopped
2–3 Tbsp kuzu, diluted
1/2 cup croutons, oven- or pan-fried
1/4 cup scallions, chives, or parsley, finely chopped for garnish
4–5 half-moon slices of lemon, for garnish

Prepare the kombu stock. When the stock is done, remove the kombu and set aside. Place the deep-fried tofu cubes in the stock, cover, and simmer on a medium-low flame for 2 to 3 minutes. Add the sea salt and simmer for another 10 minutes. Add the bok choy and the cooked pasta. Cover and simmer for 1 minute. Add the diluted kuzu, stirring constantly to prevent lumping. Remove and place in serving bowls. Garnish each bowl with several croutons, chopped scallions, chives, or parsley, and lemon slices. Serve hot.

Clam and Pasta Soup

1 cup clams, shucked and diced
1 cup clam juice
2 cups whole grain shells, cooked
2 tsp light sesame oil
1 cup mushrooms, thinly sliced
1/2 cup onions, finely minced
1/4 cup celery, diced
4 cups water
2 Tbsp tamari soy sauce
3 Tbsp parsley, finely minced

Place the light sesame oil in a pot and heat up. Add the mushrooms and sauté for 1 minute. Add the onions and celery and sauté for another minute. Add the clams, water, and clam juice. Cover and bring to a boil. Reduce the flame to low and simmer for 4 to 5 minutes. Add the tamari soy sauce and simmer for 3 minutes. Add the cooked pasta and simmer for another 2 to 3 minutes. Add the parsley and place in individual serving bowls. Serve hot.

Pinto Bean and Pasta Soup

1 cup pinto beans, cooked
1 cup small whole grain soup pasta, cooked
2 tsp dark sesame oil
1/2 cup onions, diced
1/2 cup carrots, diced
1/4 cup celery, diced
4–5 cups water
1/4 tsp sea salt
1 cup leeks sliced in 1/2-inch lengths
1/4 cup celery leaves, chopped for garnish

Place the dark sesame oil in a pot and heat up. Add the onions and sauté for 1 to 2 minutes. Add the pinto beans, carrots, celery, and water. Cover and bring to a boil. Reduce the flame to low and simmer for 1 to 2 minutes. Add the sea salt and cook for about 10 minutes. Add the cooked pasta and leeks. Cover and simmer for another 5 to 7 minutes. Remove, place in serving bowls, and garnish with chopped celery leaves. Serve hot.

Split Pea and Pasta Soup

1 cup split peas
1 cup whole grain elbows, shells, or other small pasta, cooked
1/2 cup onions, diced
1/4 cup celery, diced
1/2 cup carrots, quartered and sliced
1/4 cup wakame, soaked and sliced
1 cup seitan, sliced in strips or cubed
5 cups water
1/4 tsp sea salt
1/4 cup scallions, thinly sliced for garnish

Place the onions, celery, carrots, wakame, seitan, split peas, and water in a pot. Bring to a boil, cover, and reduce the flame to medium-low. Simmer for 1 hour or until the peas become very soft and creamy. Add the sea salt and simmer for another 7 minutes. Add the cooked pasta and simmer for another 3 minutes. Place in serving bowls and garnish each bowl with sliced scallions. Serve hot.

Lentil and Pasta Soup

1 cup green lentils
1 cup whole grain elbows or shells, cooked
1 cup onions, diced
1/2 cup carrots, diced
1/4 cup celery, diced
5 cups water
1/4–1/2 tsp sea salt
1 cup bok choy, sliced into l-inch pieces
1/2 cup green string beans, diced
1/4 cup parsley, minced for garnish

Place the onions, carrots, celery, lentils, and water in a pot. Cover and bring to a boil. Reduce the flame to medium-low and simmer for about 1 hour. Add the sea salt. Cover and simmer for another 10 to 12 minutes. Add the bok choy, green string beans, and cooked pasta. Simmer for another 2 to 3 minutes. Place in serving bowls and garnish with minced parsley. Serve hot.

Navy Bean and Pasta Soup

The bonito flakes and fu in this recipe give the soup a mild smoked flavor reminiscent of old-fashioned bean soup.

1 1/2 cups navy beans, soaked 6–8 hours (discard soaking water)
1 cup whole grain elbows, shells, or other small soup pasta, cooked
1 strip kombu, 1–1 1/2 inches long, soaked and diced
5–6 cups water
1/2 cup onions, diced
1/4 cup celery, diced
1 cup sweet corn, removed from cob
1/2 cup round fu, soaked and sliced in 1/2-inch cubes
1–2 Tbsp bonito flakes (prepackaged variety used for garnish)
1/4–1/2 tsp sea salt
1/4 cup chives, scallions, or parsley, finely sliced for garnish

Place the kombu, navy beans, and water in a pot. Cover and bring to a boil. Reduce the flame to medium-low and simmer for 1 1/2 hours or until the beans are about 80 percent done. Add the onions, celery, sweet corn, fu, bonito flakes, and sea salt. Cover and simmer for another 20 minutes or until the beans are very soft. Add the cooked pasta and simmer for another 5 minutes or so. Place in serving bowls and garnish with sliced chives, scallions, or parsley. Serve.

Vegetable and Pasta Soup

2 cups corn ribbons, cooked
5 cups water
1 strip kombu, 2 inches long, soaked and diced
2 Tbsp bonito flakes
pinch of sea salt
1/2 cup onions, diced
1 cup jinenjo, diced
1/4 cup green peas, shelled
1/4 cup daikon, diced
1/2 cup carrots, cut into flowers
1 cup tofu cubes, deep-fried or fresh
2–3 Tbsp tamari soy sauce
1 cup watercress, sliced into 1-inch lengths
1/4 cup celery leaves, finely chopped for garnish

Place the water, kombu, and bonito flakes in a pot and prepare the stock. Remove the kombu and bonito flakes. Add the sea salt, onions, jinenjo, green peas, daikon, carrots, and deep-fried or fresh tofu. Cover and bring to a boil. Reduce the flame to medium-low and simmer for 5 to 7 minutes. Add the tamari soy sauce and simmer for 2 to 3 minutes. Add the cooked corn ribbons and simmer for 1 to 2 minutes. Then add the watercress, cover, and simmer for about 1 minute. Place in serving bowls and garnish with chopped celery leaves. Serve hot.

Seitan and Somen Soup

  1 cup seitan, cut into thin strips
  1 package (8 oz) somen, broken into 2-inch lengths and cooked
  2 tsp dark sesame oil, for sautéing
  8–10 small mushrooms, halved
  8–10 small shallots or small white onions, peeled and left whole
  1/2 cup carrots, cut into irregular shapes
  1/4 cup yellow wax beans, sliced into 1-inch lengths
  1/2 cup green peas
  5 cups water
  2 Tbsp tamari soy sauce
  1/2 cup scallions, sliced into 1-inch lengths

Place the dark sesame oil in a pot and heat up. Add the mushrooms and shallots or white onions. Sauté for 1 to 2 minutes. Add the carrots, yellow wax beans, and green peas. Add the water and seitan strips. Cover and bring to a boil. Reduce the flame to medium-low and simmer for about 5 to 7 minutes or until the shallots and carrots are tender. Add the tamari soy sauce and simmer for another 3 minutes. Add the cooked somen and sliced scallions. Cover and simmer for 1 to 2 minutes. Place in serving bowls and serve hot.

Cream of Broccoli and Pasta Soup

  2 cups broccoli flowerettes, boiled 1 minute (use water from boiling broccoli as part
    of the water measurement)
  1 cup shells or other small soup pasta, cooked
  5 cups water
  1 strip kombu, 2–3 inches long
  2 Tbsp corn oil
  1 clove garlic, minced (optional)
  1/2 cup onions, minced
  4–5 Tbsp unbleached white flour
  1/4–1/2 tsp sea salt
  1 bay leaf
  1/4 cup carrots, cut into matchsticks and blanched for garnish
  1–2 tsp parsley, finely chopped for garnish

Prepare the kombu stock. Remove the kombu and set aside. Place the corn oil in a pot and heat up. Add the garlic and onions. Sauté for 1 to 2 minutes. Place the flour in the pot and mix in thoroughly with the sautéed vegetables. Slowly pour the kombu stock into the pot with the vegetables, stirring constantly to prevent lumping. When the soup becomes thick and creamy, add the sea salt and the bay leaf, reduce the flame to very low, and simmer for about 10 minutes. Remove and discard the bay leaf. Add the cooked broccoli and pasta. Simmer for 2 to 3 minutes. Place in serving bowls and garnish with carrot matchsticks and chopped parsley. Serve hot.

  As a variation, use cauliflower instead of broccoli. You can add chunks of low-fat, white-meat fish such as cod, haddock, or scrod to the soup.

Pasta and Fish Dumpling Soup

    1/2 lb white-meat fish
1 cup whole grain shells or other small soup pasta, cooked
1 tsp onions, minced
1 tsp parsley, minced
1 tsp carrots, minced
3 Tbsp whole wheat flour
2 Tbsp water
5 cups water
1/4–1/2 tsp sea salt
1 cup Chinese cabbage or bok choy, sliced into l-inch pieces
1 Tbsp dulse, soaked and sliced
1/4 cup scallions, thinly sliced for garnish

Chop the fish into very small pieces. Place in a suribachi and purée until fairly smooth. Place the onions, parsley, carrots, and whole wheat flour in the suribachi. Mix with the fish. Add 2 tablespoons of water and mix. Take a tablespoonful of the fish mixture and form it into small balls (about the size of a ping pong ball) with your hands. Repeat until all of the mixture is used up.

    Place the water and sea salt in a pot. Cover and bring to a boil. Add the fish dumplings and simmer for about 4 to 5 minutes. Add the Chinese cabbage or bok choy and simmer for about 1 to 2 minutes. Reduce the flame to low and add the dulse and cooked pasta. Simmer for 1 to 2 minutes. Place in serving bowls and garnish each bowl with sliced scallions. Serve hot.

Alphabet Soup

    2 cups whole wheat alphabet pasta, cooked
4–5 cups water
1 strip kombu, 2–3 inches long
4–5 shiitake mushrooms, soaked and stems removed
1/4 cup onions, diced
1/4 cup celery, diced
1/4 cup carrots, cut into matchsticks
1/2 cup tofu, cut into l-inch cubes
2–3 Tbsp tamari soy sauce or miso
1 sheet nori, toasted and cut into thin strips
1/4 cup scallions, thinly sliced for garnish

Prepare the kombu-shiitake stock. When done, remove the kombu and shiitake and set aside. Add the onions, celery, carrots, and tofu. Cover and simmer for 1 to 2 minutes. Season with tamari soy sauce or miso. If using tamari soy sauce, simmer for another 3 to 4 minutes. If using miso, simmer for 2 to 3 minutes. Place in serving bowls and garnish each bowl with several strips of toasted nori and a pinch of sliced scallions.

Chapter 6: Fried Noodles and Pasta

Fried noodles and pasta are a delicious and nourishing treat. They are quick and easy to make and can include a wide variety of whole natural ingredients, such as fresh organic vegetables, soybean foods like tofu and tempeh, whole wheat seitan, beans, and sometimes fish and seafood. They can be made with or without oil. In the recipes that follow, we present a wide variety of healthful fried noodle and pasta dishes. Some of the dishes in this chapter use ingredients that are normally reserved for special occasions. If you have changed your diet for health reasons and are unsure about using some of these special ingredients, check first with a macrobiotic counselor. Or you can simply omit any ingredients that you may be unsure about using. The dish will still be delicious and satisfying.

Winter Soba with Vegetables

This fried noodle dish is most delicious in the autumn and winter.

> **2 packages (16 oz) soba (any kind), cooked**
> **1 Tbsp dark sesame oil**
> **1 cup onions, sliced in thin half-moons**
> **1/4 cup burdock, sliced into thin matchsticks**
> **1/2 cup carrots, sliced into thin matchsticks**
> **1/2 cup cabbage, shredded**
> **1–2 Tbsp tamari soy sauce**
> **1/4 cup scallions, thinly sliced**

Place the dark sesame oil in a skillet and heat up. Add the onions and sauté for 1 to 2 minutes. Add the burdock and sauté for 1 to 2 minutes. Add the carrots and sauté for 1 to 2 minutes. Add the cabbage and sauté for another minute or so. Reduce the flame to low and place the cooked soba on top of the vegetables. Cover and cook for 5 to 7 minutes until the noodles are hot. Add the tamari soy sauce, mix the vegetables and soba, cover, and cook for another 3 to 4 minutes. Add the scallions, cover, and cook another minute or so. Serve hot.

Spring/Summer Soba with Vegetables

This dish is lighter than the one above and especially good in warm weather.

> **2 packages (16 oz) soba (any kind), cooked**
> **1 Tbsp light or dark sesame oil**
> **1–2 Tbsp tamari soy sauce**
> **1/2 cup scallions, thinly sliced**
> **1/4 cup tan sesame seeds, toasted**

1 tsp fresh ginger juice
1/2 cup nori, toasted and cut into strips

Place the sesame oil in a skillet and heat up. Add the soba and stir continuously for 1 to 2 minutes. Add the tamari soy sauce and scallions. Cover, reduce the flame to low, and cook the scallions for about 1 to 2 minutes. Remove the cover. Add the toasted sesame seeds, ginger juice, and nori strips. Mix well, cover, and cook for 1 more minute. Serve hot.

Winter Udon with Vegetables

This hearty fried udon is especially nourishing in cool weather.

2 packages (16 oz) udon (any kind), cooked
1 Tbsp dark sesame oil
1 cup onions, sliced into thin half-moons
1 cup mushrooms, thinly sliced
1/2 cup carrots, cut into thin matchsticks
1/2 cup daikon, sliced into thick matchsticks
1 cup Chinese cabbage, sliced into 1-inch squares
1/4 cup scallions, thinly sliced
1 tsp fresh ginger juice
1–2 Tbsp tamari soy sauce

Place the dark sesame oil in a skillet and heat up. Add the onions and sauté for 1 to 2 minutes. Next, add the mushrooms and sauté for 1 minute. Add the carrots and daikon and sauté for 1 to 2 minutes. Place the Chinese cabbage on top of the other vegetables but do not mix. Place the cooked udon on top of the vegetables. Cover, reduce the flame to low, and cook for about 5 to 7 minutes until the noodles are hot. Add the scallions and sprinkle the ginger juice and tamari soy sauce over the udon. Cover and cook for another 3 to 4 minutes. Mix and serve hot.

Spring/Summer Udon with Vegetables

This simple, light udon dish is wonderful during warmer weather.

2 packages (16 oz) udon (any kind), cooked
1 Tbsp light or dark sesame oil
1–2 Tbsp tamari soy sauce
1 cup scallions or chives, thinly sliced

Place the sesame oil in a skillet and heat up. Add the udon and tamari soy sauce. Cover, reduce the flame to low, and cook for about 4 to 5 minutes or until the noodles are hot. Add the scallions. Serve hot.

Quick Stir-fried Udon or Soba

      2 packages (16 oz) udon or soba, cooked
      1 Tbsp light or dark sesame oil
      1 cup mushrooms, thinly sliced
      1 cup scallions, thinly sliced
      1–2 Tbsp tamari soy sauce
      1 tsp fresh ginger juice
      2 Tbsp tan sesame seeds, roasted
      1/2 cup nori, toasted and cut into strips

Place the sesame oil in a skillet and heat up. Add the mushrooms and sauté for 1 minute. Add the scallions, udon, tamari soy sauce, ginger juice, and roasted sesame seeds. Mix and sauté, stirring over a high flame until the scallions are cooked and the noodles are hot. Place in serving bowls or plates and garnish with the toasted nori strips.

Water-sautéed Noodles with Vegetables

Those who wish to limit their intake of oil may find this oil-free noodle dish quite delicious. Feel free to use vegetables other than those suggested in the recipe. You may also add tofu, tempeh, seitan, or even beans to the dish.

      2 packages (16 oz) udon, somen, or soba, cooked
      water
      1/2 cup onions, sliced into thin half-moons
      1/2 cup carrots, sliced into thin matchsticks
      1/2 cup leeks, sliced into thin rounds
      1–2 Tbsp tamari soy sauce

Place enough water in a skillet to just barely cover the bottom. Bring to a boil. Add the onions and water sauté for 1 to 2 minutes. Add the carrots and sauté for another 1 to 2 minutes. Add the leeks, but do not sauté. Place the cooked noodles on top of the vegetables. Add the tamari soy sauce, cover, reduce the flame to low, and simmer for about 5 to 7 minutes or until the noodles are hot. Mix and serve hot.

Ramen with Vegetables

Although natural ramen comes prepackaged with an instant miso or tamari soy sauce broth, it is not necessary to always cook them in the broth. You can cook the ramen in boiling water for 2 to 3 minutes, remove, and drain. You can then pan fry them (either whole or sliced in half) as in the following recipe.

      3 packages (9.3 oz) instant ramen, cooked
      1 Tbsp light or dark sesame oil
      1/2 cup carrots, sliced into thin matchsticks
      1/4 cup summer squash, quartered and thinly sliced

1 cup kale, sliced into 1/4-inch strips
1–2 Tbsp tamari soy sauce
1/4 cup scallions or chives, thinly sliced

Place the sesame oil in a skillet and heat up. Add the carrots and sauté for 1 to 2 minutes. Add the summer squash and kale. Sauté for 1 minute. Place the ramen on top of the vegetables. Reduce the flame to low, add the tamari soy sauce, cover, and cook for about 5 minutes until the noodles are warm. Add the scallions or chives, cover, and cook for 1 minute longer. Mix thoroughly and cook for another 30 seconds or so. Serve hot.

Stir-fried Ramen with Tofu and Vegetables

3 packages (9.3 oz) ramen, cooked
1/2 lb tofu, sliced into l-inch cubes
1 Tbsp light or dark sesame oil
1/4 cup onions, sliced into thin half-moons
1/2 cup carrots, sliced into thin matchsticks
1/2 cup green string beans, sliced on long, thin diagonals
1/4 cup almonds, roasted and slivered
1/2 cup mung bean sprouts, rinsed and drained
1/2 cup scallions, sliced into 2-inch lengths
1–2 Tbsp tamari soy sauce

Place the sesame oil in a wok and heat up. Add the onions and sauté for 1 minute. Add the carrots and string beans. Sauté for 1 to 2 minutes. Add the slivered almonds and tofu cubes. Sauté for another minute. Add the mung bean sprouts and sauté for 1 minute. Then add the scallions, ramen, and tamari soy sauce. Sauté for another 3 to 4 minutes, stirring constantly, until all ingredients are hot. Remove and place on serving plates or in bowls. Serve hot.

Hiyamugi with Vegetables

2 packages (16 oz) hiyamugi, cooked
1 Tbsp light sesame oil
1 cup onions, sliced into 1/2-inch thick wedges
1/2 cup cauliflower flowerettes
1 cup broccoli flowerettes
1/4 cup carrots, sliced into thin diagonals
1/4 cup scallions, thinly sliced
1–2 Tbsp tamari soy sauce

Place the light sesame oil in a skillet and heat up. Add the onions and sauté for 1 to 2 minutes. Add the cauliflower and sauté for 2 minutes. Next, add the broccoli and carrots and sauté for 2 minutes. Place the hiyamugi on top of the vegetables. Reduce the flame to low, cover, and cook for about 5 minutes. Place the scallions on top of the hiyamugi and add the tamari soy sauce. Mix and cover. Cook for another 1 to 2 minutes or until the hiyamugi and vegetables are hot and tender. Serve hot.

Noodles with Seitan

2 packages (16 oz) udon, soba, or somen, cooked
2 cups seitan, sliced into thin strips
1 Tbsp dark or light sesame oil
1/2 cup onions, sliced into half-moons
1 cup mushrooms, quartered
1–2 Tbsp tamari soy sauce
1 cup snow peas, stems removed and sliced in half

Place the sesame oil in a skillet and heat up. Add the onions and sauté for 1 to 2 minutes. Add the mushrooms and sauté for another 1 to 2 minutes. Place the seitan and noodles on top of the vegetables but do not mix. Cover, reduce the flame to low, and cook for about 5 to 7 minutes. Sprinkle the tamari soy sauce over the noodles. Set the snow peas on top of the noodles. Cover and simmer for 2 to 3 minutes or until the snow peas are tender but still slightly crisp and bright green in color. Mix the noodles, seitan, and vegetables. Serve hot.

Udon with Tofu and Vegetables

2 packages (16 oz) udon, cooked
1 lb firm-style tofu, sliced into l-inch cubes
1 Tbsp dark or light sesame oil
1 cup onions, sliced into half-moons
1/2 cup carrots, sliced into thin half-diagonals
1/4 cup yellow summer squash, quartered and thinly sliced
1–2 Tbsp tamari soy sauce
1/4 cup scallions, thinly sliced for garnish

Place the sesame oil in a skillet and heat up. Add the onions and sauté for 1 to 2 minutes. Then layer the carrots, yellow summer squash, and tofu on top of the onions. Place the cooked udon on top of the tofu. Cover the skillet, reduce the flame to low, and cook for about 5 to 7 minutes or until the noodles are hot. Sprinkle the tamari soy sauce over the udon. Add the scallions, cover, and cook for another 1 to 2 minutes. Mix and serve hot.

Soba with Tofu and Mushrooms

2 packages (16 oz) soba, cooked
1 lb firm-style tofu, sliced into l-inch cubes
1 cup mushrooms, quartered
1 Tbsp dark or light sesame oil
1–2 Tbsp tamari soy sauce
1/2 cup scallions, thinly sliced

Place the sesame oil in a skillet and heat up. Add the mushrooms and sauté for 1 to 2 minutes. Add the tofu and half the amount of tamari soy sauce called for above. Sauté for 1 to 2 minutes. Place the soba and remaining tamari soy sauce in the skillet.

Reduce the flame to low, cover, and cook for 4 to 5 minutes or until the noodles are hot. Sprinkle the scallions on top of the soba, cover, and cook for another 1 to 2 minutes until bright green. Mix and serve hot.

Udon with Tempeh and Sauerkraut

2 packages (16 oz) udon, cooked
1 lb tempeh, sliced into strips 1/4 inch thick by 2 inches long
1/2 cup sauerkraut, juice squeezed out and chopped
1 Tbsp dark or light sesame oil
water
1 cup cabbage, shredded
1/2 cup carrots, sliced into matchsticks
1–2 Tbsp tamari soy sauce
2 Tbsp parsley, finely chopped

Place the sesame oil in a skillet and heat up. Add the tempeh strips and fry until golden brown on each side. Add enough water to half cover the tempeh. Cover, bring to a boil, reduce the flame to medium-low, and simmer for about 10 to 15 minutes. Remove the cover and cook off most of the water, leaving just enough to cover the bottom. Layer the sauerkraut, cabbage, and carrots on top of the tempeh. Set the cooked udon on top of the vegetables. Cover, reduce the flame to low, and cook for about 5 to 7 minutes until the noodles are hot. Sprinkle the tamari soy sauce over the udon and add the chopped parsley. Cover and cook for another 1 to 2 minutes. Mix and serve hot.

Somen with Tempeh and Vegetables

2 packages (16 oz) somen, cooked
1 lb tempeh, sliced into l-inch cubes
1 Tbsp dark or light sesame oil
water
1/2 cup carrots, cut into flowers
1–2 Tbsp tamari soy sauce
1 cup scallions, thinly sliced

Place the sesame oil in a skillet and heat up. Add the tempeh and sauté for 2 to 3 minutes until golden brown on all sides. Add enough water to almost half cover the tempeh. Cover, bring to a boil, reduce the flame to medium-low, and simmer for about 10 to 15 minutes. Remove the cover, turn the flame up high, and cook off most of the remaining liquid. Leave just enough water to cover the bottom of the skillet. Place the carrot flowers and somen on top of the cooked tempeh, cover, and reduce the flame to low. Cook for about 5 minutes until the noodles are hot. Sprinkle the tamari soy sauce and the scallions on top of the somen. Cover and cook for another 2 minutes or so until the scallions are cooked. Mix and serve hot.

Somen with Seitan and Sweet Corn

2 packages (16 oz) somen, cooked
1 cup seitan, sliced into 1/2-inch cubes
1 cup sweet corn, removed from cob
1 Tbsp dark or light sesame oil
1 cup green peas, removed from shell
1–2 Tbsp tamari soy sauce
1 sheet nori, toasted and cut into thin strips for garnish
2 Tbsp scallions, thinly sliced for garnish

Place the sesame oil in a skillet and heat up. Add the sweet corn, green peas, and seitan cubes. Sauté for 1 minute. Place the cooked somen on top of the seitan and vegetables. Reduce the flame to low, cover, and cook for 5 minutes or until the noodles are hot. Sprinkle the tamari soy sauce over the somen, cover, and cook for another 2 minutes or so. Mix and place on serving plates or bowls. Garnish each serving with a few strips of toasted nori and sliced scallions. Serve hot.

Udon with Vegetables and Dried Tofu

2 packages (16 oz) udon, cooked
1 cup dried tofu, soaked and sliced into 1/4-inch strips
1 Tbsp dark or light sesame oil
1 cup burdock, shaved or sliced into thin matchsticks
2–3 Tbsp water
1 cup carrots, cut into matchsticks
1–2 Tbsp tamari soy sauce
1 tsp fresh ginger juice
2 Tbsp sesame seeds, toasted
1/4 cup scallions, thinly sliced

Place the sesame oil in a skillet and heat up. Add the burdock and sauté for 2 to 3 minutes. Add 2 to 3 tablespoons of water. Layer the carrots, dried tofu, and cooked udon on top of the burdock. Cover, reduce the flame to low, and cook for about 5 to 7 minutes until the burdock is tender and the noodles are hot. Sprinkle the tamari soy sauce, ginger juice, toasted sesame seeds, and sliced scallions over the udon. Cover and cook for another 2 minutes or so until the scallions are done. Mix and serve hot.

Soba with Natto

2 packages (16 oz) soba, cooked
1 cup natto
1 Tbsp dark or light sesame oil
1 cup scallions, thinly sliced
1–2 Tbsp tamari soy sauce
1 sheet nori, toasted and cut into thin strips
1/2 cup grated daikon, for garnish

Place the sesame oil in a skillet and heat up. Add the cooked soba and sauté for 2 to 3 minutes, stirring constantly. Add the natto and scallions. Sprinkle the tamari soy sauce over the soba, mix, and sauté for another 2 to 3 minutes. Place in serving bowls and garnish with several strips of toasted nori and 1 tablespoon of grated daikon. Serve hot.

Soba with Shrimp and Vegetables

> 2 packages (16 oz) soba, cooked
> 8 oz medium shrimp, shelled, deveined, and cut into 1/4-inch thick pieces
> 1 Tbsp dark or light sesame oil
> 1 cup onions, sliced into 1/4-inch thick half-moons
> 1/4 cup celery, sliced into thin diagonals
> 1/2 cup carrots, cut into matchsticks
> 1–2 Tbsp tamari soy sauce
> 1/2 cup scallions, thinly sliced
> 1/4 cup grated daikon, for garnish

Place the sesame oil in a skillet and heat up. Add the onions and sauté for 1 to 2 minutes. Add the celery, shrimp, and carrots. Sauté for 2 minutes. Place the cooked soba on top of the shrimp and vegetables. Reduce the flame to low, cover, and cook for about 5 to 7 minutes until the noodles are hot. Sprinkle the tamari soy sauce over the soba, cover, and cook for another 2 minutes. Mix, place in serving bowls, and garnish with sliced scallions. Place 2 to 3 teaspoons of grated daikon on each plate as a garnish.

Udon with Shrimp and Vegetables

> 2 packages (16 oz) udon, cooked
> 8 oz medium shrimp, shelled, deveined, and chopped into 1/4-inch thick pieces
> 1 Tbsp light or dark sesame oil
> 1/2 cup fresh shiitake mushrooms, stems removed and sliced into thin strips
> 1/4 cup celery, sliced into thin diagonals
> 1/2 cup carrots, cut into matchsticks
> 8 oz mung bean sprouts, rinsed
> 1–2 Tbsp tamari soy sauce
> 1/2 cup snow peas, stems removed and sliced in half on a diagonal

Place the sesame oil in a skillet and heat up. Add the shiitake mushrooms and sauté for 1 minute. Add the celery, carrots, shrimp, and mung bean sprouts. Sauté for 1 to 2 minutes. Place the cooked udon on top of the vegetables. Cover and reduce the flame to low. Cook for about 5 minutes until the noodles are hot. Sprinkle tamari soy sauce over the udon and place the snow peas on top. Cover and cook for 2 minutes. Mix the udon and vegetables. Serve hot.

Stir-fried Noodles with Shrimp and Scallops

2 packages (16 oz) udon, soba, or somen, cooked
8 oz medium shrimp, shelled, deveined, and sliced into 1/4-inch pieces
8 oz bay scallops
1 Tbsp light or dark sesame oil
1/2 cup onions, sliced into 1/4-inch half-moons
1 cup small broccoli flowerettes
1/2 cup mushrooms, quartered
1 cup Chinese cabbage, sliced into 1-inch pieces
1/4 cup carrots, cut into matchsticks
1–2 Tbsp tamari soy sauce

Place the sesame oil in a skillet and heat up. Add the onions and sauté for 1 minute. Add the broccoli, mushrooms, and shrimp. Sauté for 1 to 2 minutes. Place the noodles on top of the vegetables. Place the Chinese cabbage and carrot matchsticks on top of the noodles. Cover and reduce the flame to low. Cook for 5 to 7 minutes until the noodles are hot. Sprinkle the tamari soy sauce over the noodles, mix with the vegetables, and cover. Cook for another 2 to 3 minutes. Serve hot.

Chinese Stir-fried Noodles with Vegetables

2 packages (16 oz) natural rice noodles, cooked
1 Tbsp light or dark sesame oil
1 cup onions, sliced into 1/4-inch thick half-moons
1/2 cup mushrooms, quartered
1/2 cup cauliflower, sliced into small flowerettes
1/2 cup carrots, sliced into thick matchsticks
1/4 cup celery, sliced diagonally
1 cup broccoli flowerettes
1/2 cup green string beans, stems removed and sliced into 2-inch lengths
2 cups water
1 1/2 Tbsp kuzu, diluted
1–2 Tbsp tamari soy sauce
2 tsp fresh ginger juice

Place the sesame oil in a wok and heat up. Add the onions and mushrooms. Sauté for 1 minute. Add the cauliflower, carrots, and celery. Sauté for 2 minutes. Add the broccoli and string beans. Sauté for 1 to 2 minutes. Add the water to the wok. Mix in the diluted kuzu, stirring constantly to prevent lumping. When translucent, add the tamari soy sauce, ginger juice, and rice noodles. Mix thoroughly and cook another 2 to 3 minutes to heat the rice noodles. Serve hot.

Simple Stir-fried Soba or Udon

2 packages (16 oz) soba or udon, cooked
1 Tbsp light or dark sesame oil
1 lb firm-style tofu, sliced into l-inch cubes

1 cup scallions, sliced into 1-inch lengths
1–2 Tbsp tamari soy sauce

Place the sesame oil in a wok or skillet and heat up. Add the tofu and sauté for 1 to 2 minutes. Add the scallions and cooked soba or udon. Add the tamari soy sauce and sauté for 3 to 5 minutes until the noodles are hot. Place in serving bowls and serve hot.

Tofu and Vegetable Chow Mein

1 package (8 oz) udon or rice noodles, cooked and drained
1/2 lb firm-style tofu, sliced into 1-inch cubes
sesame oil, for deep frying
4 cups water
1 strip kombu, 2–3 inches long
1 cup onions, sliced into 1/2-inch thick wedges
1/2 cup mushrooms, quartered
1/2 cup carrots, sliced into thick matchsticks
1/4 cup celery, sliced in thick diagonals
1 cup broccoli flowerettes
3–4 Tbsp kuzu, diluted
1–2 Tbsp tamari soy sauce

Heat up the sesame oil and deep fry the noodles, a small amount at a time, until they are golden brown. Remove the noodles and place on paper towels to drain.

Place the water and kombu in a pot. Cover and bring to a boil. Reduce the flame to medium-low and simmer the kombu for 2 to 3 minutes. Remove the kombu and set aside.

Turn the flame up high and bring the kombu stock to a boil. Add the onions, mushrooms, carrots, celery, and broccoli. Reduce the flame to medium-low, cover, and simmer for 2 minutes. Add the tofu and simmer another minute. Reduce the flame to low, add the diluted kuzu, stirring constantly to prevent lumping, until the liquid becomes thick and translucent. Add the tamari soy sauce and simmer for 1 to 2 minutes.

Place the deep-fried noodles in individual serving bowls and ladle the vegetable-kuzu broth over them. Serve hot.

For a different flavor, add tempeh cubes or strips instead of tofu.

Seitan and Vegetable Chow Mein

1 package (8 oz) udon or rice noodles, cooked and drained
3 cups seitan, cut into 1-inch cubes or thin strips
sesame oil, for deep frying
4 cups water
4 shiitake mushrooms, stems removed and thinly sliced
1 cup mung bean sprouts, rinsed
1 cup mustard greens, sliced into 1-inch pieces

1 cup Chinese cabbage, sliced into l-inch pieces
1/2 cup celery, sliced into thin diagonals
3-4 Tbsp kuzu, diluted
1–2 Tbsp tamari soy sauce
2 tsp fresh ginger juice
1/4 cup scallions, thinly sliced for garnish

Deep fry the noodles as described in the above recipe and place on paper towels to drain.

Place the water and shiitake mushrooms in a pot, cover, and bring to a boil. Reduce the flame to medium-low and simmer for about 5 to 7 minutes. Add the seitan, mung bean sprouts, mustard greens, Chinese cabbage, and celery. Cover and simmer for 1 minute. Add the diluted kuzu, stirring constantly to prevent lumping. When the sauce becomes thick and translucent, add the tamari soy sauce and ginger juice. Simmer, uncovered, for another 2 minutes.

Place the deep-fried noodles in individual serving bowls and ladle vegetable-seitan-kuzu sauce over them. Garnish with chopped scallions and serve hot.

Shrimp and Vegetable Chow Mein

1 package (8 oz) udon or rice noodles, cooked and drained
1 lb medium shrimp, shelled and deveined
sesame oil, for deep frying
5 cups kombu-shiitake stock (p. 63)
1 cup carrots, cut into matchsticks
1 bunch scallions, sliced into 2-inch lengths
1 cup mung bean sprouts, rinsed
1 cup snow peas, stems removed
3–4 Tbsp kuzu, diluted
1–2 Tbsp tamari soy sauce
2 tsp fresh ginger juice

Deep fry the noodles until golden brown and drain on paper towels.

Place the kombu-shiitake stock in a pot, cover, and bring to a boil. Add the shrimp and carrots. Cook for 1 to 2 minutes. Add the scallions, mung bean sprouts, and snow peas, cover, and simmer for 1 minute. Add the diluted kuzu, stirring constantly, until the sauce becomes thick and translucent. Add the tamari soy sauce and ginger juice. Simmer for another 1 to 2 minutes.

Place the deep-fried noodles in serving bowls and ladle the shrimp-vegetable sauce over them. Serve hot.

Deep-fried Udon with Sweet and Sour Seitan

1 package (8 oz) udon, cooked, drained, and deep-fried
2 cups seitan, sliced into thin strips
4 cups kombu stock (p. 62)
1/2 cup onions, sliced into 1/4-inch thick wedges

1/2 cup mushrooms, quartered
1 cup green string beans, sliced in half
1 cup broccoli flowerettes
1 cup summer squash, sliced into 1/4-inch thick half-moons
1/4 cup brown rice vinegar
1/2 cup barley malt or brown rice syrup
4 Tbsp kuzu, diluted
1–2 Tbsp tamari soy sauce
1 tsp ginger juice
1/4 cup scallions, thinly sliced for garnish

Place the kombu stock in a pot, cover, and bring to a boil. Add the onions and mushrooms. Cover and simmer for 1 minute. Add the string beans and broccoli. Cover and simmer for 1 minute. Add the summer squash and seitan. Add the brown rice vinegar and barley malt or brown rice syrup. Stir in. Add diluted kuzu, stirring constantly, until the sauce is thick and translucent. Add the tamari soy sauce and ginger juice and simmer for another 1 to 2 minutes.

Place the deep-fried udon in serving bowls and ladle the seitan-vegetable sauce over them. Garnish each bowl with sliced scallions and serve hot.

Deep-fried Somen with Sweet and Sour Tofu

1 package (8 oz) somen, cooked, drained, and deep-fried
1 lb firm-style tofu, sliced into 1-inch cubes
4 cups kombu stock (p. 62)
1 cup onions, sliced into thin half-moons
1 cup carrots, cut into matchsticks
1 cup celery, sliced into thin diagonals
1 cup scallions, sliced into 2-inch lengths
1/4 cup sweet brown rice vinegar
1/2 cup brown rice syrup
4 Tbsp kuzu, diluted
1–2 Tbsp tamari soy sauce
2 Tbsp tan sesame seeds, toasted

Place the kombu stock in a pot, cover, and bring to a boil. Add the onions, carrots, and celery. Cover and simmer for 1 to 2 minutes. Add the tofu and scallions. Simmer for 1 minute. Stir in the sweet brown rice vinegar and brown rice syrup. Add the diluted kuzu, stirring constantly, until the sauce becomes thick and translucent. Add the tamari soy sauce and simmer for another 1 to 2 minutes.

Place the somen in serving bowls and ladle the tofu-vegetable sauce over them. Sprinkle a few toasted tan sesame seeds over each bowl for garnish. Serve hot.

Tempeh can be substituted for tofu for a different flavor. When using tempeh, add it to the kombu stock at the beginning and simmer for about 15 minutes before adding vegetables. Tempeh needs to be cooked longer than tofu.

Whole Wheat Spaghetti with Vegetables

1 lb whole wheat spaghetti, cooked
1 Tbsp dark sesame oil
1 cup carrots, cut into matchsticks
1–2 Tbsp tamari soy sauce
1 cup scallions, thinly sliced
1 Tbsp tan sesame seeds, toasted

Heat the dark sesame oil in a skillet. Add the carrots and place the spaghetti on top. Cover and reduce the flame to low. Cook until carrots are almost tender. Add the tamari soy sauce and sliced scallions. Cover again and cook for another 2 to 3 more minutes. Mix the cooked spaghetti and vegetables thoroughly and place in a serving dish. Mix toasted tan sesame seeds throughout or sprinkle them on top and serve hot.

Whole Wheat Shells with Tofu and Vegetables

1 lb whole wheat shells, cooked
1 lb firm-style tofu
1 Tbsp dark or light sesame oil
1 cup onions, sliced into thin half-moons
1/4 cup celery, sliced on a thin diagonal
1/2 cup carrots, cut into matchsticks
1 cup sweet corn, removed from cob
1–2 Tbsp tamari soy sauce
1/4 cup parsley, finely chopped

Place the sesame oil in a skillet and heat up. Add the onions and sauté for 1 to 2 minutes. Layer the celery, carrots, and sweet corn on top of the onions. Crumble the tofu with your hands so that it falls on top of the vegetables. Place the cooked shells on top of the tofu. Cover, reduce the flame to low, and cook for 5 minutes. Sprinkle the tamari soy sauce over the shells and place the chopped parsley on top of the shells. Cover and cook for another 2 to 3 minutes. Mix thoroughly and place in serving dishes. Serve hot.

Elbow Macaroni with Mushrooms

1 lb whole grain elbows, cooked
1 cup mushrooms, quartered
1 Tbsp light or dark sesame oil
1 cup scallions, sliced into 1-inch lengths
1–2 Tbsp tamari soy sauce
1 sheet nori, toasted and cut into thin strips

Place the sesame oil in a skillet and heat up. Add the mushrooms and sauté for 2 minutes. Add the scallions and elbows. Mix thoroughly and add the tamari soy sauce and toasted nori strips. Sauté for 2 to 3 minutes or until the elbows are hot and the scallions are tender but still bright green in color. Serve hot.

Corn Ribbons with Pinto Beans and Sweet Corn

    1 lb corn ribbons, cooked
    2 cups pinto beans, cooked
    1 cup sweet corn, removed from cob
    1 Tbsp light or dark sesame oil
    1 cup onions, diced
    1–2 Tbsp tamari soy sauce
    2 Tbsp parsley, chives, or scallions, finely chopped for garnish

Place the sesame oil in a skillet and heat up. Add the onions and sauté for 2 to 3 minutes. Add the sweet corn and pinto beans. Mix and sauté for 1 to 2 minutes. Place the corn ribbons on top of the pinto beans and vegetables. Sprinkle the tamari soy sauce over the corn ribbons. Cover and reduce the flame to low. Cook for about 5 minutes until the corn ribbons are hot. Mix thoroughly, place in serving dishes, and garnish with chopped parsley, chives, or scallions. Serve hot.

Kasha Varnitchkes (Pasta with Whole Buckwheat)

    2 cups whole wheat or Jerusalem artichoke shells or elbows, cooked
    1 cup buckwheat groats, washed
    2 cups water
    pinch of sea salt
    2 Tbsp light sesame oil
    1/2 cup onions, diced
    1 cup cabbage, shredded
    1–2 Tbsp tamari soy sauce
    1/4 cup parsley, finely chopped

Place the water and pinch of sea salt in a saucepan. Cover and bring to a boil. Add the buckwheat groats, cover, and reduce the flame to medium-low. Simmer for 20 minutes. Remove the buckwheat groats and place in a bowl. Fluff for several minutes with a wooden spoon to cool off.

    Heat the light sesame oil in the skillet and add the diced onions. Sauté for 1 to 2 minutes. Add the cabbage and sauté for 1 to 2 minutes. Add the pasta and mix. Add the cooked buckwheat groats and mix. Sprinkle the tamari soy sauce over the buckwheat groats and pasta. Cover, reduce the flame to low, and cook for another 5 to 7 minutes until hot. Mix in the chopped parsley and cook for 1 to 2 minutes. Remove and place in serving dishes. Serve hot.

Kasha Varnitchkes with Tempeh and Sauerkraut

    2 cups elbows, shells, bows, or other small pasta, cooked
    1 cup buckwheat groats
    1 lb tempeh, sliced into l-inch cubes

    1/2 cup sauerkraut, minced
    2 cups water
    pinch of sea salt
    2 Tbsp light or dark sesame oil
    1/2 cup water
    1–2 Tbsp tamari soy sauce
    1/4 cup parsley, finely chopped

Place the water and sea salt in a saucepan, cover, and bring to a boil. Add the buck-wheat groats, cover, reduce the flame to medium-low, and simmer for 20 minutes. Remove, place in a bowl, and fluff with a wooden spoon to cool off.

Place the sesame oil in a skillet and heat up. Add the tempeh and fry until golden brown on all sides. Add water and place the chopped sauerkraut on top of the tempeh. Bring the water to a boil, cover, and reduce the flame to medium-low. Cook for 10 to 15 minutes. Remove the cover, turn the flame up high, and cook off most of the re-maining liquid. Add the buckwheat groats and cooked pasta. Mix thoroughly, sprinkle the tamari soy sauce over ingredients, and cover. Reduce the flame to low and cook for about 5 to 7 minutes until hot. Mix in the chopped parsley, cover, and cook for an-other 1 to 2 minutes. Place in serving dishes and serve hot.

Pan-fried Spaghetti Pizza

This special treat yields 2 pies (8 slices). You can omit the olives if you wish.

    6 oz thin spaghetti or somen, cooked
    5 Tbsp corn oil
    1/2 cup onions, diced
    1 1/2 cups mushrooms, thinly sliced
    2–3 tsp tamari soy source
    1 lb brown rice mochi, coarsely grated (like cheese) on a box grater
    1/2 cup seitan, sliced into thin strips
    1/2 cup black olives, sliced into thin rounds
  Tofu Cream:
    1/2 lb firm-style tofu, drained
    1/4 cup scallions, finely chopped
    2 Tbsp umeboshi vinegar
    2 Tbsp water

To make tofu cream, place the tofu, scallions, umeboshi vinegar, and water in a blander and purée until smooth and creamy. Remove and place in a small bowl.

Place 1 tablespoon of corn oil in a skillet and heat up. Add the onions and mush-rooms. Sauté for 2 to 3 minutes. Season with tamari soy sauce. Sauté for another min-ute or so. Remove and place in a small bowl.

Heat 2 tablespoons of corn oil in a skillet or on a griddle. Spread the oil around to evenly coat the surface. Cover the bottom of the skillet with half of the grated mochi. Spread half of the cooked spaghetti evenly over the mochi. Reduce the flame to medium-low. Spread half of the sautéed vegetables and seitan over the spaghetti.

Next, spoon half of the tofu cream over the vegetables and spread it around. Place half of the sliced olives on top of the tofu cream. Turn up the flame slightly to brown the bottom of the mochi until it becomes crisp. (The total pan-frying time is approximately 10 minutes.)

Using a spatula, loosen the mochi from the skillet. It should move very easily. Tip the skillet slightly and let the pizza slide on to a baking sheet. Place the pizza under the broiler and broil for about 5 minutes to thoroughly cook the tofu cream.

Remove the pizza from the oven, slice into quarters, and place on serving plates. To make another pizza, repeat the above process with the remaining ingredients. Cook, slice, and serve as above.

Mochi and Spaghetti Pancakes

This recipe yield 5 medium-sized pancakes. They are delicious with or without the olives.

> 1 1/2 lbs brown rice mochi, coarsely grated on a box grater
> 6 oz thin spaghetti, cooked
> 5 Tbsp corn oil
> 1 cup onions, diced
> 1 1/2 cups mushrooms, thinly sliced
> 1/2 cup carrots, coarsely grated on a box grater
> 2–3 Tbsp tamari soy sauce
> 1/2 cup tofu cream (see above recipe)
> 1/2 cup black olives, sliced into thin rounds

Place 1 tablespoon of corn oil in a skillet and heat up. Add the onions, mushrooms, and carrots. Sauté for 2 to 3 minutes. Add the tamari soy sauce. Sauté for another minute or so. Remove and place in a small bowl.

Heat up 1 tablespoon of corn oil in a skillet and spread around evenly. Place about 4 tablespoons of grated mochi evenly in the middle of the skillet, forming a circle about 4 inches in diameter. Place a small handful of cooked spaghetti on top. Reduce the flame to medium-low. Evenly spread about 3 tablespoons of sautéed vegetables on top of the spaghetti. Spread about 3 tablespoons of tofu cream on top. Place a tablespoon of black olives on top of the tofu cream. Next, sprinkle another 3 tablespoons of grated mochi on top of the olives. Cover the pan and cook for about 4 minutes. Remove the cover and gently flip the pancake over. Cover and cook the other side for about 5 minutes. Both sides of the pancake should be slightly browned and crisp. If not, turn the flame up to high and brown both sides. Remove and place on serving plates.

Repeat the above process until you use up the remaining ingredients. You should now have 5 spaghetti pancakes.

Pan-fried Macaroni and Corn Fritters

This recipe for deep-fried macaroni and corn treats yields 18 fritters.

> 1 cup elbow macaroni, cooked
> 1 cup sweet corn, removed from cob
> 1/2 cup whole wheat pastry flour
> 1/4 cup corn flour
> pinch of sea salt
> 1/4 cup onions, minced
> 1/2 cup mushrooms, finely diced
> 3/4 cup water
> 1 tsp kuzu, diluted in 2 tsp water
> corn oil, for frying

Place flours, sea salt, and vegetables in a bowl and mix thoroughly. Add the water and mix. Add the dileted kuzu and cooked macaroni. Mix well.

Place 2 to 3 tablespoons of corn oil in a skillet and heat up. Take a tablespoon and fill it full with the batter. Place the batter in the hot skillet and press down slightly with the spoon to flatten. A 10- to 12-inch skillet can fry about 5 to 6 fritters at a time. Fry the fritters until golden brown, turn over with a spatula, and fry the reverse side until golden brown. Remove and continue frying until all ingredients are used. Place on a serving platter. Serve as is, with a couple of drops of tamari soy sauce, or a tamari-ginger dip sauce (see recipe below).

Deep-fried Macaroni and Corn Fritters

This variation of the above recipe produces light and crisp fritters that are similar to tempura. The recipe yields 18 fritters.

> 1 cup whole grain elbow macaroni, cooked
> 1 cup sweet corn, removed from cob
> 1/2 cup whole wheat pastry flour
> 1/4 cup corn flour
> 1/2 cup brown rice mochi, coarsely grated
> 1/2 cup mushrooms, diced
> 1/4 cup onions, diced
> 1/4 cup parsley, minced
> pinch of sea salt
> 3/4 cup water
> 1 tsp kuzu, diluted in 2 tsp water
> light or dark sesame oil, for deep frying

Place the flours, grated mochi, vegetables, and sea salt in a mixing bowl and mix thoroughly. Add the water, cooked macaroni, and diluted kuzu. Mix again thoroughly.

Heat sesame oil in a deep-frying pot and drop the batter, a tablespoonful at a time, into the hot oil. Deep fry until golden brown. Remove, place on paper towels to drain, and serve with one of the dip sauce below. Repeat until all the batter has been deep fried.

As a variation, serve the fritters with a mushroom-kuzu sauce, or in a plain kombu-daikon broth, instead of with dip sauce.

Tamari-Ginger Dip Sauce
1 cup kombu stock (p. 62)
1/4 cup tamari soy sauce
1 tsp grated ginger

Tamari-Daikon Dip Sauce
1 cup kombu stock
1/4 cup tamari soy sauce
1/4 cup grated daikon

Place the kombu stock and tamari soy sauce in a saucepan and heat up. Turn the flame off, add the grated ginger or daikon, and place in small dishes (about 3 to 4 tablespoons per dish).

Somen Tempura

1 package (8 oz) somen, cooked
1/2 cup whole wheat pastry flour
1/4 cup corn flour
pinch of sea salt
3/4 cup water
1 tsp kuzu, diluted in 2 tsp water
light or dark sesame oil, for deep frying

Place the flours and sea salt in a mixing bowl and mix. Add water and diluted kuzu and mix thoroughly. Mix in the cooked somen.

Pick up a small amount of batter-coated somen with chopsticks or a wooden fork and place it in the hot oil. Deep fry until golden brown. Remove and place on paper towels to drain. Repeat until all noodles are cooked. Serve in a kombu-based broth as a soup, or with one of the above dip sauces as tempura.

Udon Pancakes

1 1/2 cups udon, cooked and chopped in 2-inch lengths
1 1/2 cups whole wheat flour
1 cup whole wheat pastry flour
1/4 tsp sea salt
2 tsp corn oil
2 cups water
1/2 cup cabbage, shredded
1/4 cup onions, diced
1/2 lb medium shrimp, shelled, deveined, and chopped
2–3 Tbsp celery, diced
2–3 Tbsp carrots, coarsely grated on a box grater
corn oil, for frying

Place the flours, sea salt, corn oil, and water in a bowl and mix thoroughly. Cover with a damp towels, place in a warm place, and let sit overnight to ferment slightly, similar to sourdough.

Place the udon, cabbage, onions, shrimp, celery, and carrots in the batter. Mix thoroughly.

Oil a griddle or skillet and heat up. When hot, ladle the batter on to the griddle and pan fry as you would pancakes. Brown on one side, and when bubbles start to form on the top, flip it over with a spatula, and fry the other side until golden brown. Repeat until all the batter is used up.

The pancakes may be eaten as is, with a dip sauce sprinkled over them, or with your favorite low-fat, natural sauce or gravy.

Fried Noodle Dough

1/2 lb fresh whole grain pasta dough (any kind)
light or dark sesame oil, for deep frying

Prepare the pasta dough (see Chapter 9 for instructions) and roll out. With a knife or pasta wheel cut the dough into 2- to 3-inch long strips about 1/4 to 1/2 inch wide or into fancy bows (see Chapter 9).

Heat up the sesame oil. When hot, place several pieces of pasta in the pot and deep fry until golden brown. Remove and place on paper towels to drain.

Continue deep frying until all the dough has been used up.

The deep-fried strips may be eaten as is for a snack, placed in a broth for soup, or served with one of the previously described dip sauce.

Deep-fried Canneloni

In Chapter 9 we explain how to make noodles and pasta at home. Please refer to that chapter for instructions on making fresh canneloni dough. The recipe yields 8 to 10 deep-fried canneloni.

8–10 pieces fresh, whole grain canneloni dough, about 5 inches by 4 inches, cooked
1 1/2 cups tofu, seitan, or fish stuffing (see pp. 146 and 147 for ravioli stuffing recipes)
1/2 cup fresh whole wheat bread crumbs
1/2 cup brown rice mochi, finely grated on a flat grater
1 cup whole wheat pastry flour
1 cup water
pinch of sea salt
light or dark sesame oil, for deep frying

Spoon the filling on to the canneloni dough and roll up as described in Chapter 9. Set aside for several minutes. Mix the whole wheat bread crumbs and grated mochi in a mixing bowl. Take another mixing bowl and combine the whole wheat pastry flour, water, and sea salt. Mix thoroughly to remove any lumps.

Heat the sesame oil in a deep-frying pot (about 375° F). Dip the canneloni in the pastry batter and then roll each one in the mixture of bread crumbs and grated mochi. Deep fry the stuffed canneloni for about 3 minutes or until golden brown. Remove and place on paper towels to drain. Repeat until all canneloni are deep fried. Serve as is with slices of lemon, which can be squeezed over the canneloni, or sprinkle a little tamari-ginger sauce over each one.

Deep-fried Ravioli with Sauce

> 16–20 fresh homemade ravioli (see Chapter 9)
> light or dark sesame oil, for deep frying
> 4–5 lemon wedges
> 4–5 small watercress or parsley sprigs.

Heat the sesame oil to about 375° F and deep fry the ravioli until golden brown. Remove and place on paper towels to drain. Repeat until all the ravioli have been deep fried. Place 4 pieces on each serving plate. Garnish each with a lemon wedge and a sprig of watercress or parsley. You may also serve the ravioli in broth.

Deep-fried Wonton with Sauce

> 16–20 fresh, homemade, filled wontons (use eggless egg roll wrappers in Chapter 9)
> light or dark sesame oil, for deep frying
> 1/2 cup tamari-ginger or tamari-daikon dip sauce (p. 118)
> 1 parsley sprig

Prepare eggless egg roll wrappers as described in Chapter 9. Fill with any of the ravioli stuffings presented on pages 146 and 147. Deep fry the wontons until golden brown. Remove and place on paper towels to drain. Repeat until all wontons have been deep fried. Place wontons on a serving platter with a small bowl of dip sauce in the center. Garnish the platter with a parsley sprig and serve.

Deep-fried Tagliatelle with Onion Tempura

> 1/2 lb freshly made tagliatelle (see Chapter 9)
> 1 large Spanish onion, sliced into thin rings
> light or dark sesame oil, for deep frying
> 1 cup whole wheat pastry flour
> 1 cup water
> pinch of sea salt
> 1 tsp kuzu, diluted in 2 tsp water

Heat up the sesame oil and deep fry the tagliatelle until golden brown. Remove and drain on paper towels.

Mix the flour, water, sea salt, and diluted kuzu. Separate the rounds of onion into rings. Roll the rings in just enough flour to coat them. Dip the onion rings into the batter and deep fry until golden brown. Remove and place on paper towels to drain. Repeat until all onions have been deep fried. Place deep-fried tagliatelle and onion rings on each serving plate. Serve with a tamari-daikon or tamari-ginger dip sauce, or with broth poured over the pasta and onion rings. Garnish and serve.

Deep-fried Somen and Chestnut Stuffed Shrimp Balls

These are attractive hors d'oeuvres and are wonderful at parties or special dinners. The recipe yields approximately 12 stuffed shrimp balls.

> **5 oz (about 2 cups) somen**
> **2 lb large shrimp, shelled, deveined, and tails removed**
> **1 strip kombu, 4 inches long, dusted**
> **1/2 cup water**
> **1/2 cup unbleached white or whole wheat pastry flour**
> **1/4 tsp sea salt**
> **1 Tbsp mirin (optional)**
> **1 Tbsp kuzu, diluted in 1 Tbsp water**
> **light or dark sesame oil, for deep frying**
> *Chestnut Filling:*
> **8–10 whole dried or fresh chestnuts**
> **1 1/2 cups water for dried chestnuts or 2 cups water for fresh chestnuts**
> **small pinch of sea salt (for dried chestnuts)**
> **2 Tbsp brown rice syrup**
> **1 tsp tamari soy sauce**

Place the kombu in a bowl and cover with 1/2 cup of water. Soak for about 1/2 hour. Remove the kombu and set aside for future use. Mix in the flour thoroughly and set aside for several minutes.

While the kombu is soaking, prepare the chestnut filling. If using dried chestnuts, first wash them and then dry roast in a skillet for 2 to 3 minutes. Place in a pressure cooker with water and pinch of sea salt. Pressure cook for about 40 to 50 minutes. Allow pressure to come down and remove the cover. Add brown rice syrup and tamari soy sauce. Simmer the chestnuts, uncovered, for about 10 minutes over a medium flame. Remove and place in a bowl.

If using fresh chestnuts, wash the chestnuts. Place 1 cup of water in a saucepan and bring to a boil. Boil the fresh chestnuts for about 2 to 4 minutes. Remove and discard water. With a paring knife, cut a long shallow slice through the skin of each chestnut and remove the shell.

Place the peeled chestnuts in a saucepan with 1 cup of water, cover, and bring to a boil. Reduce the flame to medium-low and simmer for about 25 minutes. Remove the cover and add the brown rice syrup and tamari soy sauce. Simmer, uncovered, for another 20 minutes. Remove the chestnuts and place in a bowl.

Purée the shrimp in a blender, 1 or 2 at a time. Add the sea salt, mirin, and diluted kuzu. Purée again. Remove the purée from the blender and combine with the kombu soaking water and flour mixture. Mix very well. Divide the mixture into 12 equal-sized portions and roll into balls.

Break the somen into 1-inch long pieces and place them in a small bowl. Take a ball of shrimp purée and flatten it slightly to form a patty. Place a cooked chestnut in the center of the purée. Form into a ball again, this time with the chestnut in the center, and the shrimp purée completely covering it. Repeat the process until all of the chestnuts have been covered in shrimp purée.

Roll the balls in the broken pieces of somen, so that they are completely covered. Repeat until all balls are coated with somen pieces. Heat 3 inches or more dark sesame oil to about 375° F in a deep-frying pot. Deep fry 2 to 3 balls in the pot at a time, until they are golden brown. Remove and place on paper towels to drain. Repeat until they have all been deep-fried.

Place 1 to 2 balls on each person's plate. Make an X in the top of each ball with a paring knife and gently spread the cut area open, revealing the chestnut inside.

Deep-fried Somen and Chestnut Stuffed Squash Balls

This is a vegetarian alternative to the previous recipe. The squash has a very satisfying naturally sweet flavor. The recipe yields 12 deep-fried balls.

5 oz dry somen, broken into 1/2-inch lengths
12 dried or fresh chestnuts, cooked as described in the previous recipe
1/2 medium-sized buttercup squash or Hokkaido pumpkin
1/2 cup water
1/4 cup pastry flour
1/4 tsp sea salt
light or dark sesame oil, for deep frying

Cut the squash in half. Remove the seeds and skin. Cut the squash into wedges 1 inch thick. Place in a saucepan. Add water to cover and cook about 10 minutes until tender. Place in a suribachi and purée. Mix thoroughly with the flour and sea salt. Moisten your hands and mold the squash mixture into 12 balls about the size of a ping pong ball. Place a cooked chestnut inside each squash ball and completely cover with the squash mixture.

Roll the balls in the broken pieces of somen. Repeat until they are all covered. Heat the deep-frying sesame oil to about 375° F and deep fry 2 to 3 balls at a time until golden brown. Remove and place on paper towels to drain. Repeat until they have all been deep fried.

Place 2 to 3 balls per person on serving dishes. Make an X in the top of each ball with a paring knife. Spread the cut area open to reveal the chestnut inside.

Chapter 7: Pasta East / Pasta West

In this chapter we present a variety of special noodle and pasta dishes from around the world. Included are recipes for noodle sukiyaki and other one-dish specialties from Japan; meat, dairy, and nightshade-free adaptations of such classic Italian favorites as lasagne, spaghetti (with whole wheat seitan balls), and ravioli, along with several traditional northern and eastern European noodle dishes that have been converted into nutritious, low-fat entrées.

The dishes in this chapter are recommended for enjoyment on special occasions, such as parties and special dinners that you prepare for company. Persons who have changed their diets because of health reasons may need to wait until normal health is established before including some of these dishes in their diets. If you are not sure about the appropriateness of any of the dishes or ingredients in this chapter, please check with a macrobiotic teacher or educational center. Also please feel free to omit any ingredient you are not sure about. If you wish to avoid garlic, for example, simply omit it from the recipe. Olive oil, which is more suited to a warm Mediterranean climate, can be enjoyed once in a while by those in normal health. However, if you wish to avoid using it, simply use high-quality sesame oil wherever olive oil is called for.

Zaru Soba (Soba in a Basket)

Zaru soba is a traditional dish served with a slightly chilled dipping sauce, making it a refreshing dish on hot and humid summer days. The word *zaru* means "basket made of bamboo." Special bamboo boxes with a slotted mat, similar to a sushi mat, are used for serving zaru soba. The dipping sauce that accompanies the soba in Japan varies from region to region and reflects local custom.

> **1 lb soba (any kind)**
> **4 cups kombu stock (p. 62)**
> **1/2 cup tamari soy sauce**
> **3 Tbsp mirin (optional)**
> **1/2 cup bonito flakes (optional)**
> **1 sheet nori, toasted and cut into thin strips**
> **1 tsp wasabi**
> **1/4 cup scallions, thinly sliced**

Cook, rinse, and drain the soba. Place in 4 to 5 baskets or bowls.

Place the kombu stock, tamari soy sauce, and mirin in a saucepan and place on a medium-high flame. Bring almost to a boil. Add the bonito flakes and turn the flame off. Let sit for about 15 seconds or so. Strain out the bonito flakes and discard. Let the dip sauce cool to room temperature or place in a refrigerator to chill slightly. Place equal amounts of dip sauce in small serving bowls.

Sprinkle several pieces of toated nori strips over each serving of soba. Place a small amount of wasabi and a teaspoon of sliced scallions in small dishes. (Wasabi can be omitted if desired.)

Mix wasabi and scallions into dip sauce. Pick up the soba with chopsticks or a fork and place in the dip sauce before eating.

Cha Soba with Daikon Dip Sauce

    1 lb cha soba
    4 cups kombu stock (p. 62)
    1/2 cup tamari soy sauce
    3 Tbsp mirin (optional)
    1/2 cup bonito flakes
    1/4 cup daikon, finely grated
    1 sheet nori, toasted and cut into thin strips
    1/4 cup scallions, thinly sliced
    1/4 cup tan sesame seeds, toasted

Cook, rinse, and drain the cha soba. Place the cooked cha soba in baskets or bowls.

Place the kombu stock, tamari soy sauce, and mirin in a saucepan and bring almost to a boil over a medium-high flame. Add the bonito flakes and turn the flame off. Let sit for about 15 seconds. Strain and discard the bonito flakes. Let the dip sauce cool to room temperature, or place in a refrigerator to chill slightly. Place equal amounts of dip sauce in small bowls. Mix about 2 to 3 teaspoons of grated daikon in each serving.

Garnish each serving of cha soba with several strips of toasted nori strips. Before dipping the cha soba, mix sliced scallions and a teaspoon of toasted tan sesame seeds into dip sauce. Use the dip sauce as described in the recipe above.

Nabeyaki Udon

Nabeyaki is another traditional dish from Japan in which udon or soba are cooked and served in special earthenware casserole and garnished with vegetables and other foods. The earthenware casseroles are called *nabe*. The ingredients used in nabeyaki are similar to those used in sukiyaki. However, sukiyaki is usually served in a cast iron skillet rather than an earthenware casserole. Below are several delicious versions of nabeyaki.

    1/2 lb udon (any kind), cooked al dente
    5–6 cups kombu stock(p. 62)
    4–5 shiitake mushrooms, soaked, stems removed, and with a star cut into each cap
    4–5 daikon rounds, 1/2 inch thick
    4–5 pieces carrots, sliced on a long diagonal
    1–2 Tbsp tamari soy sauce
    1 lb firm-style tofu, cubed
    1 bunch watercress
    2 cups Chinese cabbage, sliced into l-inch wide diagonals

Place the kombu stock in a saucepan and add the shiitake mushrooms and daikon rounds. Cover and bring to a boil. Reduce the flame to medium-low and simmer for about 15 minutes or until the daikon is tender. Remove the daikon and shiitake and place on a plate. Place the carrot slices in the stock and simmer for 2 minutes until tender. Remove the carrot slices and place on the plate with the shiitake and daikon. Season the stock with tamari soy sauce and simmer for 4 to 5 minutes while you arrange each nabe as instructed below.

Divide the cooked udon into 4 to 5 equal portions and place each in an individual nabe. Place equal amounts of shiitake, daikon, carrot slices, uncooked tofu cubes, uncooked watercress, and uncooked Chinese cabbage on top of each serving of udon. Ladle about 1 1/2 to 2 cups of kombu broth over the ingredients in each nabe.

Put the lid on each nabe, place each on a medium flame, and bring to a boil. Simmer for 4 to 5 minutes until the tofu is cooked and the watercress and Chinese cabbage are bright green in color. Remove from the flame and serve.

Nabeyaki Soba with Deep-fried Tofu

> 1/2 lb soba, cooked al dente
> 1 lb firm-style tofu, sliced into 8–10 equal slices (about 1/4 inch thick), deep-fried until golden brown, and drained
> 5–6 cups kombu stock (p. 62)
> 4–5 shiitake mushrooms, soaked, stems removed, and with a star cut into each cap
> 4–5 slices carrot, cut on a long diagonal
> 4–5 broccoli spears
> 1–2 Tbsp tamari soy sauce
> 4–5 red radishes with greens
> 1 bunch scallions, sliced into 2-inch lengths

Place the kombu stock in a saucepan and add the shiitake mushrooms. Cover and bring to a boil. Reduce the flame to medium and simmer for 10 minutes. Remove the shiitake and place on a plate. Place the carrot slices in the stock and simmer for 2 minutes. Remove and place on the plate with the shiitake. Place the broccoli spears in the stock, cover, and simmer for 1 1/2 to 2 minutes. Remove and place on a plate with other vegetables. Season the stock with tamari soy sauce and add the deep-fried tofu slices. Simmer for 4 to 5 minutes. Remove the tofu slices and place on the plate with the vegetables. Reduce the flame to low and simmer the broth until you have arranged the soba and vegetables in the nabe.

Place equal amounts of soba in the bottom of each nabe. Take an equal amount of vegetables, deep-fried tofu slices, uncooked red radishes, and raw scallions and arrange them attractively on top of the soba. Ladle 1 1/2 to 2 cups of kombu broth over each serving.

Place each nabe on a medium flame, cover, and simmer for 4 to 5 minutes until hot and until the scallions are tender but still bright green in color. Serve immediately.

Harusame *Yosenabe* with Seafood and Vegetables

Yosenabe is a variation of nabe-style cooking. The word itself means "everything gathering." The ingredients are cooked separately in advance and then placed in the nabe for just 1 to 2 minutes with kombu stock. A portable butane burner can be used to heat the broth. In Japan they have special heating units built into their dining tables for these dishes.

Although the recipe calls for harusame, or mung bean thread noodles, you can substitute any other whole grain Japanese noodles in this dish. In this recipe, the broth is left unseasoned because the dish is served with a seasoned dip sauce. However, if you wish, you can season the broth and omit the dip sauce. Those with vegetarian preferences can also omit the seafood and use vegetable quality proteins such as tofu, deep-fried tofu, tempeh, fu, or seitan slices instead. Feel free to experiment and be creative with the recipes in this book.

> 3–4 oz harusame
> 4 cups kombu stock (p. 62)
> 4–5 shiitake mushrooms, soaked, stems removed, and with a star cut into each cap
> 1 cup water, for boiling seafood
> 8–10 medium or large shrimp, shelled and deveined
> 1/2 lb codfish, cut into l-inch pieces (without bones)
> 8–10 shucked clams
> 1/2 lb cooked lobster, cut into l-inch pieces
> 1 cup water, for boiling vegetables and tofu
> 6–7 whole Chinese cabbage leaves
> 1/2 lb firm-style tofu, sliced into l-inch cubes
> 1 carrot, sliced into thin diagonals
> 1 bunch scallions, sliced into 2-inch long pieces
> *Daikon and Lemon Dip Sauce:*
> 1/2 cup daikon, finely grated
> 2–3 Tbsp fresh squeezed lemon juice
> 1/2 cup water
> 2 Tbsp tamari soy sauce
> 2–3 Tbsp scallions, finely sliced

Place the harusame in a bowl, cover with cold water, and soak for about 30 minutes. Then remove the harusame and slice into pieces 5 inches long. Arrange the pieces on a platter.

While the harusame are soaking, place the kombu stock in a pot with the shiitake mushrooms. Cover, bring to a boil, and reduce the flame to medium-low. Simmer the shiitake for about 15 minutes. Remove and place on the serving platter with the harusame.

While the kombu broth is cooking, place 1 cup of water in a saucepan and bring to a boil. Add the shrimp, codfish, and clams. Boil for about 30 seconds. Remove, place in a strainer, and rinse under cold water. Place the seafood and precooked lobster on a large serving platter.

Place 1 cup of water in a saucepan, cover, and bring to a boil. Place the whole Chinese cabbage leaves in the boiling water, cover, and cook for 1 minute. Remove, place in a strainer, and rinse under cold water. Remove and squeeze out excess water. Take 3 to 4 leaves and stack them on top of each other on a sushi mat. Roll the leaves up into a log shape, as if you were making sushi, and slice into l-inch lengths. Repeat until all the leaves have been rolled and sliced. Arrange the cabbage rolls on the platter with the seafood.

Place the tofu cubes in the boiling water and simmer for 1 minute. Rinse and place on the platter with the other ingredients. Then, place the carrots in the boiling water, cover, and simmer for 1 minute. Rinse and place on the platter with the other ingredients. Then place the scallion slices in the boiling water and simmer for 10 seconds. Rinse and place on the platter.

Combine the water, tamari soy sauce, and lemon juice in a small saucepan to make dip sauce. Place over a medium flame. Add the grated daikon and simmer for 1 minute. Turn the flame off and add the sliced scallions. Place the dipping sauce in small serving bowls for each person.

All the ingredients should now be attractively arranged on a large serving platter. To make serving easier or more accessible, you may divide the ingredients into equal amounts and place them on small individual serving plates.

To cook the yosenabe ingredients, place the unseasoned kombu stock in a large nabe and place the nabe over a butane burner. Bring to a boil. Reduce the flame to medium-low, so that the broth constantly, but gently simmers.

Each person can select the foods he or she wishes to eat, place them in the nabe, and warm them in the hot kombu stock for about 1 to 2 minutes. The ingredients are then individually removed and dipped in dip sauce before eating.

Udon and Vegetable Sukiyaki

Although sukiyaki is widely known around the world, it appeared only recently in Japanese cooking. It was not known until around 1860, at which time meat and fowl started to become more common in the diets of some people in Japan. Before the westernization of Japan, beef was not a part of the Japanese diet. Buddhism prohibited the eating of four-legged animals and this influence generally kept the Japanese from eating meat until the modern era.

Sukiyaki dishes originally included animal food but have now been adapted to vegetarian tastes. Tofu, tempeh, seitan, or fu can be substituted for animal foods. Noodles can also be included in sukiyaki. You can prepare sukiyaki in a cast iron skillet large enough to hold food for several people, or in several small cast iron skillets that are served to each person. A wide variety of ingredients can be included in sukiyaki and the dish is usually cooked over a butane burner at the table. The uncooked ingredients are arranged on a large platter or on individual plates. Each person then selects the items he or she wishes to eat and then places them in the skillet to cook. If you do not have a butane setup, you may cook the ingredients at the stove and then serve the skillet at the table.

> **4–6 oz udon, cooked al dente**
> **4–5 fresh shiitake mushrooms, stems removed and boiled in 1 cup water and 1 Tbsp tamari soy sauce for 10–15 minutes**
> **4–5 slices Hokkaido pumpkin or buttercup squash, about 1/4 inch thick**

4–5 slices butternut or yellow summer squash, about 1/4 inch thick
1/2 cup carrots, sliced on a thin diagonal
4–5 daikon rounds, about 1/4 inch thick, boiled for 40 minutes over a medium-low flame until tender
1 medium Spanish onion, sliced into 1/4-inch thick rings or rounds
5–6 Chinese cabbage leaves, sliced into l-inch diagonal pieces
1 bunch scallions, sliced into 2-inch lengths
4–5 slices seitan, cooked
4–5 slices deep-fried tofu or tempeh, cooked for 4–5 minutes in water lightly seasoned with tamari soy sauce (to remove excess oil and give the slices a slightly salty flavor)
1 lb firm-style tofu, sliced into l-inch cubes
4–5 cups kombu stock (p. 62)
1–2 Tbsp tamari soy sauce
1 cup tamari-ginger, tamari-daikon (p. 118), or lemon-daikon dip sauce (p.126), served in small bowls

Arrange udon, vegetables, seitan, deep-fried tofu, and fresh tofu on a large platter. Place 2 cast iron skillets (about 10 to 12 inches in diameter) on the stove or portable butane cooking units at the table. Place equal amounts of kombu stock in each skillet and season with tamari soy sauce. Turn the flame to high and bring to a boil.

Arrange the ingredients, with the exception of the Chinese cabbage, udon, fresh tofu cubes, and scallions, attractively in the skillets. Cover and bring to a boil. Reduce the flame to medium-low and simmer until the squash and carrots are almost tender. Move the ingredients to the sides of the skillets and place the udon, Chinese cabbage, scallions, and fresh tofu in the center. Cover and simmer for 2 to 3 minutes or until the Chinese cabbage and scallions are done and bright green in color. Remove the cover and reduce the flame under the skillets to very low, just enough to keep the ingredients warm. Your guests can then help themselves from the skillets and dip their foods in the individual bowls of dip sauce.

Somen and Seafood Sukiyaki

8 oz somen, cooked al dente
8–10 large shrimp, shelled and deveined
8–10 cod fillets, about 2-inch square
8–10 fresh shiitake mushrooms, stems removed
8–10 slices carrots, cut on a thin diagonal
2 cups Chinese cabbage, sliced on a l-inch thick diagonal
1 bunch scallions, sliced into 2-inch lengths
1/2 lb firm-style tofu, sliced into l-inch cubes
4–5 cups kombu-shiitake stock (p. 63)
1–2 Tbsp tamari soy sauce
1 cup tamari-ginger or tamari-daikon dip sauce (p. 118), placed in individual serving bowls

Arrange all ingredients on a large serving platter and place on the table.
Place 2 medium-sized cast iron skillets over portable butane burners at the table.

You may also cook the sukiyaki on the stove and then place it on the table when serving. Place the kombu-shiitake stock in each skillet and season with tamari soy sauce. Bring to a boil over a high flame.

Place the shiitake mushrooms and seafood in the skillets, cover, and bring to a boil. Reduce the flame to medium and simmer for 3 to 5 minutes until almost done. Then arrange all of the other ingredients attractively in the skillets. Cover and simmer for 2 to 3 minutes or until the carrots, Chinese cabbage, and scallions are done and brightly colored. Remove the cover and reduce the flame to very low, just enough to keep the ingredients warm. Each person may then select the foods he or she wishes to eat from the skillets and place in the dip sauce before eating.

Steamed Noodles with Tofu

    8 oz udon or soba, cooked al dente
    2 cups kombu stock (p. 62)
    2 lb soft-style tofu
    1 Tbsp tamari soy sauce
    4–5 slices firm-style tofu, 1/2 inch thick, deep-fried and sliced into strips
    1 bunch watercress, sliced into l-inch lengths
    1/4 cup almonds, slivered

Place the cooked udon or soba in a nabe and add 1/2 cup of kombu stock.

Place the soft-style tofu, remaining kombu stock, and tamari soy sauce in a blender and purée to a smooth, creamy consistency.

Place the deep-fried tofu strips, watercress, and slivered almonds evenly on top of the noodles. Then place the tofu purée evenly over the noodles and other ingredients so that you completely cover them. Cover the nabe and bring to a boil over a high flame. Reduce the flame to low and simmer until the tofu cream becomes firm. Remove from the flame and serve.

Noodle Miso Stew

    8 oz udon, soba, or somen, cooked
    4–5 daikon rounds, 1/4–1/2 inch thick
    1 carrot, sliced on a 1/4-inch thick diagonal
    1/2 cup buttercup or butternut squash, sliced into l-inch cubes
    4–5 cups kombu stock (p. 62)
    2–3 tsp white, yellow, or barley miso, puréed
    1 bunch watercress, sliced into l-inch lengths
    1/4 cup scallions, thinly sliced

Place the daikon, carrots, and squash in a pot. Add the kombu stock and bring to a boil. Reduce the flame to medium-low, cover, and simmer for about 25 to 30 minutes.

Add the puréed miso and mix in. Place the noodles and watercress in the pot, cover, and simmer for about 2 to 4 minutes without boiling. Place in individual serving bowls and garnish each bowl with sliced scallions. Serve hot.

Chinese-style Noodles with Vegetables and Kuzu Sauce

> 8 oz udon or somen, cooked
> 1–2 tsp light or dark sesame oil
> 1 medium onion, sliced into half-moons
> 4 shiitake mushrooms, soaked, stems removed, and thinly sliced
> 1 cup celery, thinly sliced on a diagonal
> 4–5 cups water or kombu stock (p. 62)
> 1 cup firm-style tofu, cut into l-inch cubes
> 1–1 1/2 cups Chinese cabbage, sliced on a 1/2-inch thick diagonal
> 1/2 lb snow peas, thinly sliced on a diagonal
> 4 Tbsp kuzu, diluted in 5 Tbsp water
> 1–2 Tbsp tamari soy sauce
> 1 tsp fresh ginger juice
> 1/4 cup scallions, thinly sliced

Place the sesame oil in a pot and heat up. Add the onions and shiitake mushrooms. Sauté for 2 to 3 minutes. Add the celery and sauté for 1 to 2 minutes. Add the water or kombu stock and bring to a boil. Reduce the flame to medium-low, cover, and simmer for about 5 minutes. Add the tofu, Chinese cabbage, and snow peas. Cover and simmer for 1 to 2 minutes. Add the diluted kuzu, mixing constantly to prevent lumping. Add the tamari soy sauce and ginger juice. Reduce the flame to low and simmer for 1 to 2 minutes. Place the noodles in individual serving bowls and ladle the sauce over them. Garnish each bowl with sliced scallions and serve hot.

Baked Noodles with Tempura

> 8 oz udon or soba, cooked al dente
> light or dark sesame oil, for making tempura
> 2–3 fresh mushrooms, stems removed and quartered
> 1 carrot, sliced on a thin diagonal
> 5–6 broccoli flowerettes
> 5–6 slices burdock, sliced on a thin diagonal
> 1 medium onion, sliced into half-moons
> 2 cups whole wheat tempura batter (p. 72)
> 2 cups kombu-tamari broth (p. 72)
> 1 tsp ginger juice
> tamari soy sauce

Heat the sesame oil in a tempura pot. When the oil is hot, dip the vegetables, several pieces at a time, into the batter, and deep fry until golden brown. Remove and drain on paper towels. Repeat until all vegetables have been deep fried.

Layer the cooked noodles and tempuraed vegetables in a casserole dish until all ingredients are used up. Mix the kombu-tamari broth and ginger juice and pour over the noodles and vegetables. Sprinkle a few drops of tamari soy sauce over the noodles. Cover the casserole dish and bake at 375° F for 30 to 35 minutes. Remove the cover and bake for another 5 to 10 minutes. The batter on the vegetables will become soft and melt, giving the dish a very delicious flavor. Serve hot.

Soba Hand-rolled Sushi

In this delicious dish, cooked soba are wrapped in toasted nori, rolled, and cut into bite-sized pieces. It is served along with a tasty dip sauce.

> **8 oz jinenjo soba, cooked al dente**
> **4–5 sheets nori, toasted**
> **4–5 slices firm-style tofu, 1/4–1/2 inch thick, deep-fried until golden brown and**
> **cooked in 1 cup of water seasoned with 1 Tbsp tamari soy sauce**
> **4–5 whole raw scallions**
> *Kombu-Bonito Dip Sauce:*
> **1 cup kombu stock (p. 62)**
> **1–1 1/2 Tbsp tamari soy sauce**
> **1–2 Tbsp finely ground bonito flakes**

After cooking, spread the soba on a clean dry dish towel in order to drain.

Place a bamboo sushi mat (sudare) on your cutting board. Place a sheet of nori on the mat with the smooth shiny side down. Spread the cooked noodles evenly across the width of the sheet of nori, so that they are about 1/4 inch thick on the sheet. Leave about 1 to 1 1/2 inches at the upper end of the nori uncovered by noodles. Trim any noodles that may be hanging over the edges of the nori with a knife.

Cut the deep-fried tofu slices lengthwise into 1/2-inch strips and squeeze out excess liquid from cooking. Place several strips end to end in a straight line across the width of the center of the soba. Place a raw scallion on top of the tofu strips.

Use the bamboo mat to roll the nori and soba up into a log-shaped roll. Stop rolling when you get to the uncovered area at the far end of the nori. Moisten the area slightly with a little water and continue rolling. You should now have a log- or cylinder-shaped roll. Wrap the mat completely around the roll and gently squeeze to seal the nori together. Remove the roll from the sushi mat and place it on the cutting board.

Slice the roll in half, making 2 equal-sized pieces. Then slice each half in half and each quarter in half, which will give you 8 equal-sized pieces of soba hand-rolled sushi. Repeat the above process until all the ingredients are used up. To serve, place the cut pieces on a serving platter or individual plates with the soba ends facing up.

Place the kombu stock and tamari soy sauce in a saucepan and heat up. Remove from the flame and add the bonito flakes. Let the broth cool to room temperature. Place in small serving bowls for each person. For those who wish to avoid fish, serve with a tamari-ginger or tamari-daikon dip sauce.

Udon or Somen Hand-rolled Sushi

Other types of noodles, especially udon or somen, can also be used to make hand-rolled sushi. Simply cook the noodles and roll up as above. You may use strips of cooked carrots, cooked watercress, cooked whole scallions, natto, or other ingredients in the roll instead of deep-fried tofu. Serve with any of the dip sauces described in this chapter.

Noodles au Gratin

8 oz soba or udon, cooked al dente
1 1/2 Tbsp light or dark sesame oil
1/2 cup onions, sliced into half-moons
1/2 cup carrots, cut into matchsticks
1/2 cup Brussels sprouts, sliced in half or quarters
5 Tbsp whole wheat pastry flour
3 cups water
tamari soy sauce
1/2 cup seitan, sliced into l-inch cubes or thin strips
1/4 cup scallions, thinly sliced

Place the sesame oil in a skillet and heat up. Add the onions and sauté for 2 to 3 minutes. Add the carrots and Brussels sprouts. Sauté for another 2 to 3 minutes. Add the flour to the skillet, stirring constantly to evenly coat the vegetables with flour. Slowly add water to the skillet, stirring constantly to prevent lumping. Stir until the sauce becomes thick and smooth. Season to taste with a little tamari soy sauce. Mix in the seitan and stir.

Place the cooked noodles in a lightly oiled casserole dish and pour the vegetable sauce over them. Cover the casserole dish and bake at 400° to 425°F for about 15 minutes. Remove the cover and brown the top slightly for about 5 minutes. Remove from the oven and garnish with sliced scallions. Serve hot.

French Onion Noodle Soup with Mochi

8 oz whole grain shells or homemade bow ties (see Chapter 9), cooked
2 cups onions, sliced into thin half-moons
1/2 cup brown rice mochi, grated
1–2 tsp light or dark sesame oil
4–5 cups water
4–5 shiitake mushrooms, soaked, stems removed, and thinly sliced
1 strip kombu, dusted, soaked 3–5 minutes, and sliced into very thin matchsticks
1–2 Tbsp tamari soy sauce
1/2 cup whole wheat croutons, pan-, oven-, or deep-fried
1/4 cup parsley, chives, or scallions, finely chopped

Heat the sesame oil in a pot. Add the onions and sauté for several minutes until they become translucent. Add the water, shiitake mushrooms, and kombu. Cover and bring to a boil. Reduce the flame to medium-low and simmer for about 25 minutes or so. Season with tamari soy sauce and simmer for another 5 minutes.

Place the cooked noodles in individual earthenware soup dishes. Ladle the hot soup over the noodles. Add the croutons. Sprinkle the grated mochi evenly over each bowl to cover the top.

Place the soup bowls in a 425°F oven and cook for several minutes until the mochi on top of the soup melts. Remove the bowls from the oven and garnish each with either chopped parsley, chives, or scallions. Serve hot.

Fresh Tuna Fettucine Casserole

8 oz whole grain Jerusalem artichoke fettucine, cooked al dente
1 lb fresh tuna chunks or fillet, washed
2 cups water
1–2 tsp corn oil
1/2 lb mushrooms, stems removed and sliced or diced
3–4 Tbsp unbleached white or whole wheat pastry flour
2 cups plain soy milk (optional; water may be used instead)
1/2 tsp sea salt

Place the tuna in a saucepan with 2 cups of water, cover, and bring to a boil. Reduce the flame to medium-low and simmer for about 5 minutes or until tender and flaky. Remove the tuna and place on a plate. Reserve the water from cooking the tuna.

Heat the corn oil in a skillet and add the sliced mushrooms. Sauté for 3 to 4 minutes. Add the flour and sauté for 1 to 2 minutes. Gradually add the 2 cups of tuna cooking water and the 2 cups of soy milk, stirring constantly. Bring to a boil and continue stirring until the sauce becomes thick and creamy. Add the cooked tuna and mix in. Add the sea salt. Mix in, cover, and reduce the flame to low. Simmer for about 2 to 3 minutes.

Place a layer of fettucine in a baking or casserole dish and ladle some of the sauce over it. Place another layer of fettucine, followed by another layer of sauce in the dish. Continue until all the fettucine and sauce are in the baking dish.

Preheat the oven to 450° F. Place the casserole in the oven and bake for about 10 to 15 minutes until the top is slightly browned and the fettucine are very hot. Remove and serve.

Creamed Cod and Fettucine

8 oz whole grain Jerusalem artichoke fettucine, cooked al dente
1 lb fresh cod fillets (without bones), washed
1–2 Tbsp corn oil
1/2 cup onions, diced
3–4 Tbsp unbleached white or whole wheat pastry flour
2 cups water
2 cups plain soy milk (optional; water can be used instead)
1/2 tsp sea salt
1/4 cup parsley, finely chopped

Heat the corn oil in a skillet. Add the onions and sauté for 2 to 3 minutes. Add the flour, stirring constantly. Sauté for 1 to 2 minutes longer. Slowly add the 2 cups of water and 2 cups of soy milk (or 4 cups of water), stirring constantly to prevent lumping. Continue stirring until the sauce becomes thick and creamy. Add the sea salt and parsley. Mix thoroughly. Place the cod fillet in the sauce, cover, and cook for about 2 minutes. Remove from the flame.

Preheat the oven to 450° to 475° F. Place the cooked fettucine in a casserole or baking dish. Pour the fish and sauce over the fettucine. Do not mix. Bake for about 15 minutes or until slightly browned. Remove from the oven and serve.

Creamy Vegetable and Mushroom Sauce over Pasta

> 8 oz whole grain pasta (any type), cooked al dente
> 1 lb fresh mushrooms, stems removed and sliced or quartered
> 1–2 Tbsp corn oil
> 3–4 Tbsp unbleached white or whole wheat pastry flour
> 2 cups water
> 2 cups plain soy milk (optional; water can be used instead)
> 1 cup carrots, cut into matchsticks
> 2 cups fresh green peas, removed from pods
> 1/2 tsp sea salt
> 2 Tbsp parsley, finely chopped

Place the corn oil in a skillet and heat up. Sauté the mushrooms for 2 to 3 minutes. Add the flour and sauté for another 1 to 2 minutes. Add the water and soy milk, stirring constantly until the sauce becomes thick and creamy. Place the carrots, green peas, and sea salt in the skillet, and mix. Cover, reduce the flame to low, and simmer until the green peas are tender. Remove from the flame, mix in the chopped parsley, and serve over the hot, drained pasta.

Polish Noodles and Cabbage

> 8 oz whole grain fettucine or other wide pasta, cooked al dente
> 3–4 cups cabbage, finely shredded
> 1–2 Tbsp corn oil
> 1 cup onions, diced
> 1/2 cup seitan, diced
> 1/4 tsp sea salt
> 1/2–1 tsp caraway seeds (optional)
> 1/2–1 cup plain soy milk (optional; water can be used instead)

Place the corn oil in a skillet and heat up. Add the onions and sauté for 4 to 5 minutes. Add the cabbage and sauté for another 5 to 7 minutes until tender. Add the diced seitan, sea salt, and optional caraway seeds. Mix well. Stir in the noodles and add the soy milk. Reduce the flame to low and simmer for about 5 minutes or so, stirring often. Serve hot.

Seitan Stroganoff

> 8 oz homemade whole grain green noodles or fettucine (see Chapter 9), cooked
> 1–1 1/2 lb fresh seitan, cooked and cut into 1/2-inch thick slices
> 2 Tbsp corn oil
> 1/4 cup onions, minced
> 1 lb fresh mushrooms, stems removed and sliced
> 2 Tbsp unbleached white or whole wheat pastry flour
> 2 cups plain soy milk (optional; water can be used instead)
> sea salt
> 4–6 sprigs parsley

Heat the corn oil in a skillet. Add the onions and mushrooms. Sauté for 2 to 3 minutes. Add the seitan slices and sauté for 3 to 4 minutes. Add the flour and mix in thoroughly. Slowly add the soy milk stirring constantly to prevent lumping. When the sauce is thick and creamy, season to taste with a little sea salt. Reduce the flame to low, cover, and simmer for several minutes. Serve over homemade green noodles or fettucine. Garnish each plate with a sprig of parsley. Serve hot.

Seitan and Vegetable Kuzu Sauce over Pasta

> 8 oz whole grain udon, fettucine, or homemade bow ties, cooked
> 1 lb fresh seitan, cooked and sliced into strips or cubes
> 1–2 tsp light or dark sesame oil
> 1/4 cup mushrooms, stems removed and quartered
> 1/4 cup onions, sliced into half-moons
> 1/4 cup celery, sliced on a thin diagonal
> 1/4 cup carrots, cut into matchsticks
> 2 cups water
> 1 cup broccoli flowerettes
> 1–1 1/2 Tbsp kuzu, diluted in 2 Tbsp water
> 1–2 Tbsp tamari soy sauce
> 2 Tbsp scallions, thinly sliced for garnish

Place the sesame oil in a pot and heat up. Add the mushrooms and onions. Sauté for 1 to 2 minutes. Add the celery and carrots. Sauté for 1 to 2 minutes. Add the water, cover, and bring to a boil. Add the broccoli, cover, and reduce the flame to medium-low. Simmer and cook for about 2 minutes until the broccoli is tender but still slightly crisp and bright green in color. Reduce the flame to low, add the seitan, and stir in the diluted kuzu, stirring constantly to prevent lumping. Season with tamari soy sauce to taste and simmer for 1 more minute. Serve over the noodles and garnish each serving with chopped scallions.

You can substitute fresh or deep-fried tofu or tempeh for seitan in this dish. Add deep-fried tofu, or fresh or deep-fried tempeh before you add the broccoli and cook for about 3 to 4 minutes. Fresh tofu can be added at the same time you add the broccoli.

For variety, include a bunch of sliced scallions or large leek. Cook as above. Sliced mushrooms can also be included for variety.

Linguine with Fresh White Clam Sauce No. 1

> 1 lb whole grain linguine or udon, cooked al dente
> 1 quart shucked clams, cut into small pieces
> 2 cups fresh clam juice
> 2 Tbsp extra-virgin olive oil
> 1 clove garlic, minced (optional)
> 2 small onions or shallots, diced
> 1 1/2 cups water
> sea salt
> 2 Tbsp parsley, finely chopped

Heat up the olive oil in a skillet. Add the optional garlic and sauté for 1 minute. Add the onions or shallots and sauté for 3 to 4 minutes until the onions or shallots are soft and translucent. Add the water and clam juice. Season to taste with a little sea salt. Cover, reduce the flame to low, and simmer for several minutes. Add the clams and chopped parsley to the sauce. Remove from the flame. Place the cooked pasta in individual serving bowls and ladle the clam sauce over each serving. Serve with fresh sourdough garlic bread below.

Fresh Sourdough Bread
> **1 small or medium loaf sourdough Italian or French peasant bread or other sourdough wheat bread**
> **olive oil**
> **garlic, minced**

Cut the loaf of bread into slices 1/2 inch thick, leaving the bottom of the loaf uncut so that the slices hold together and stand up straight. Sprinkle a little olive oil and minced garlic between each slice of bread. Place on a cookie sheet and warm up in a 350° F oven for about 7 to 10 minutes. Remove and serve hot.

Linguine with Fresh White Clam Sauce No. 2

This milder version of the above recipe is for those who wish to avoid garlic.

> **1 lb linguine or udon, cooked al dente**
> **1 quart shucked clams, chopped into small pieces**
> **2 cups fresh clam juice**
> **2 Tbsp light sesame oil**
> **2 small onions or shallots, diced**
> **1 1/2 cups water**
> **2 tsp tamari soy sauce**
> **2 Tbsp parsley, finely chopped**

Heat the light sesame oil in a skillet. Add the onions or shallots and sauté for 3 to 4 minutes until tender and translucent. Add the water and clam juice. Season to taste with tamari soy sauce. Cover, reduce the flame to medium-low, and simmer for 5 minutes. Add the clams and parsley. Mix and turn the flame off. Place pasta in serving bowls and ladle the clam sauce over it. Serve hot with the delicious onion bread below.

French Onion Sourdough Bread
> **1 small or medium loaf Italian or French peasant sourdough bread or other whole wheat bread**
> **onion, minced**
> **corn oil**

Slice the bread as in the recipe above and sprinkle minced onion and a little corn oil between each slice. Bake and serve as above.

Linguine with Shrimp and Italian Broccoli

> 1 lb whole grain linguine, udon, spaghetti, or spaghettini, cooked al dente
> 1 medium or large shrimp, shelled, deveined, and sliced into 1/4–1/2-inch pieces
> 1/2 bunch Italian broccoli (rabé or rappini) flowerettes, cooked 1–2 minutes until
>   tender
> 2 Tbsp extra-virgin olive oil
> 1 clove garlic, minced (optional)
> 1 cup water
> sea salt
> 2 Tbsp parsley, finely chopped

Heat the olive oil in a skillet. Add the garlic and sauté for 1 to 2 minutes without burning. Add the shrimp and sauté for 1 minute. Add the water, cover, and bring to a boil. Reduce the flame to low and season to taste with sea salt. Cover and simmer for 3 to 5 minutes longer. Add the parsley and turn off the flame. Place the pasta in serving bowls. Place the broccoli on top of each serving and ladle the shrimp sauce over the pasta. Serve hot.

Tofu Stuffed Shells

> 1 dozen large whole wheat stuffing shells, cooked al dente
> 1 lb firm-style tofu, mashed in a suribachi
> 1 tsp light or dark sesame oil
> 1/2 cup green string beans, very thinly sliced
> 1/2 cup sweet corn, removed from cob
> 2 Tbsp umeboshi vinegar
> 2 tsp tamari soy sauce

Heat the sesame oil in a skillet. Add the green string beans and sweet corn and sauté for 1 to 2 minutes. Remove and mix together with the mashed tofu. Place the umeboshi vinegar and tamari soy sauce in the suribachi and mix thoroughly with the tofu and vegetables. Stuff each shell with the tofu stuffing and place in a baking dish. Cover with one of the previous creamy mushroom sauces or kuzu sauces. Bake for 20 to 25 minutes at 350° F until hot. Remove and serve.

Baked Whole Wheat Shells with Fish Stuffing

> 1 dozen whole wheat stuffing shells, cooked al dente
> 1 lb cod (without bones), washed, chopped into small pieces, and steamed or boiled
>   3–4 minutes
> 2–3 tsp whole wheat pastry flour
> 1/4 tsp sea salt
> 1/4 cup celery, finely diced
> 2 Tbsp carrots, diced

Place the cooked cod in a suribachi and mash until it becomes a smooth paste. Mix in the flour, sea salt, celery, and carrots. Stuff each shell with the fish stuffing and place in a baking dish. Cover the stuffed shells with the creamy vegetable and mushroom sauce (p. 134). Bake for about 20 to 25 minutes in a 350°F oven. Remove and serve hot.

Pasta Fagioli (Pasta and Beans)

Umeboshi vinegar gives this dish a flavor like that of tomatoes.

> **2 cups whole grain elbows, shells, or other small pasta, cooked al dente**
> **1 cup navy beans, soaked 6–8 hours**
> **1/2 cup kidney beans, soaked 6–8 hours**
> **1 strip kombu, 1–2 inches long, dusted**
> **4 cups water**
> **1/2 tsp sea salt**
> **1 Tbsp extra-virgin olive oil**
> **1–2 tsp umeboshi vinegar**

Place the kombu, navy beans, kidney beans, and water in a pressure cooker. Cover, place on a high flame, and bring up to pressure. Reduce the flame to medium-low and cook for 50 to 55 minutes. Remove from the flame and allow the pressure to come down. Remove the cover and place the pot over a medium flame. Add the cooked pasta, sea salt, olive oil, and umeboshi vinegar. Bring to a boil, reduce the flame to low, and simmer for about 15 minutes or so. Serve hot.

Baked Beans and Pasta

> **2 cups whole grain elbows or shells, cooked al dente**
> **2 cups navy beans, soaked 6–8 hours**
> **1 strip kombu, 2 inches long, dusted**
> **3 1/2–4 cups water**
> **1 cup onions, finely diced**
> **1/4 cup finely ground bonito flakes (optional)**
> **2 tsp miso mustard**
> **1/2 tsp sea salt**
> **1/2 cup brown rice syrup or barley malt**

Place the kombu, navy beans, and water in a pressure cooker and cook for 45 minutes. Remove from the flame and allow the pressure to come down. Remove the cover. Place the cooked pasta, onions, bonito flakes, miso mustard, sea salt, and brown rice syrup or barley malt in the pot and mix thoroughly with the beans.

Pour the mixture into a 12-by-8-inch baking dish. Preheat the oven to 400° F and cover the baking dish. Bake for about 25 to 30 minutes until the onions are tender. Remove the cover and bake several more minutes to brown the top of the beans. Remove and serve hot.

Baked Macaroni and Mochi

> 1 lb whole grain elbow macaroni, cooked al dente
> 1 cup mochi, grated
> 4 tsp corn oil
> 1/2 cup onions, finely minced
> 3–4 Tbsp unbleached white flour
> 2 cups plain soy milk (optional; water can be used instead)
> 1/8 tsp sea salt
> 1 cup whole wheat bread crumbs
> tamari soy sauce

Heat 2 teaspoons of corn oil in a skillet and sauté the onions for 1 to 2 minutes. Add the flour, mix in, and sauté for another minute or so. Add the soy milk (or an equivalent amount of water), stirring constantly to prevent lumping. Continue stirring until the sauce becomes thick, smooth, and creamy. Add the sea salt and simmer for another 2 to 3 minutes.

Place the other 2 teaspoons of corn oil in a skillet and heat up. Place the bread crumbs in the skillet and sauté for 1 to 2 minutes. Sprinkle a little tamari soy sauce on the sautéed bread crumbs, mix, and place in a small bowl.

Place the cooked pasta in a baking dish and pour the sauce over it. Mix in the sauce. Sprinkle the grated mochi evenly over the top of the pasta. Then sprinkle the sautéed bread crumbs on top of the mochi.

Bake in a 350° F oven for about 25 to 30 minutes until the pasta is hot, the mochi melts, and the top is slightly browned. Remove and serve hot.

Fish and Pasta Pie

This recipe yields 6 to 8 pieces of pie.

> 1 lb cod, haddock, scrod, or tuna (without bones), washed and cut into l-inch chunks
> 2 cups whole grain elbows, shells, or other small pasta, cooked al dente
> 1 Tbsp sesame or corn oil
> 1/2 cup onions, diced
> 1/2 lb mushrooms, quartered
> 1/2 cup celery, halved and sliced into 1/4-inch thick diagonals
> 1 cup green peas, removed from shell
> 1/2 cup carrots, quartered
> 1 cup Brussels sprouts, quartered
> 4 Tbsp unbleached white flour or pastry flour (or 3 Tbsp diluted kuzu)
> 3 cups water or plain soy milk
> 1 Tbsp tamari soy sauce
> *Basic Wheat Pastry Dough:*
> 4 cups whole wheat pastry flour
> 1/4 tsp sea salt
> 1/4 cup corn oil
> 3/4–1 cup water

Heat the sesame or corn oil in a skillet. Add the onions and mushrooms. Sauté for 2 to 3 minutes. Add the celery, green peas, carrots, and Brussels sprouts. Sauté for 3 to 4 minutes. Add the flour and sauté for 1 to 2 minutes. Slowly stir the water or soy milk into the dish. Continue stirring until the sauce becomes thick and creamy. Add the cooked pasta and fish chunks to the sauce, cover, reduce the flame to medium-low, and simmer for 2 to 3 minutes. Season with tamari soy sauce. Mix and simmer for 1 to 2 minutes.

Place the whole wheat pastry flour and sea salt in a mixing bowl. Mix thoroughly. Add the corn oil. Sift the corn oil into the flour with your hands, by rubbing them back and forth through the flour. Add the water, gradually, to form a ball of dough. Knead the dough for 1 minute or so. Place in the refrigerator for 10 to 20 minutes.

Divide the dough in half. Lightly flour a table or cutting board and roll out one-half of the dough. Place the crust in 10- to 12-inch pie plate. Trim the edges of the crust with a paring knife and press the edges with a fork or your thumbs. Poke several holes in the bottom of the crust with a fork.

Preheat the oven to 350° to 375° F and bake the bottom crust for 10 minutes. Remove the pie plate. Place the fish and pasta filling in the crust.

Roll out the remaining half of the pie crust. With a little water, moisten the rim of the partially baked pie crust. Place the top crust on top of the pie plate. Press down to seal the bottom and top crust together with a fork or your thumbs. Then use a fork or paring knife to poke several holes in the center of the crust.

Bake for another 25 to 30 minutes until the crust is golden brown. Remove, let cool slightly, slice, and serve.

Seitan and Pasta Pie

Use the same recipe as above, except substitute 1 pound of cooked seitan for the fish. Cook as above. Roll out the pastry dough and bake as above.

Bean and Pasta Pie

Prepare a bean and pasta filling according to the recipe for Pasta Fagioli (p. 138). Then prepare pie crust as described above. Bake the bottom crust for 10 minutes and then fill it with pasta fagioli. Place the top crust on and bake as above.

Schinkenfleckerln

In this traditional Austrian dish we use whole wheat fu and bonito flakes in place of meat. This low-fat alternative is quite delicious.

> **2 cups whole grain shells, bow ties, or other small pasta, cooked al dente**
> **1 Tbsp corn oil**
> **1 cup round fu, soaked 10 minutes and sliced into l-inch pieces (squeeze out excessive water)**
> **1 cup plain soy milk or water**
> **1 Tbsp kuzu, diluted**

1/4 cup finely ground bonito flakes
1–2 tsp tamari soy sauce or 1/4 tsp sea salt

Heat up the corn oil in a skillet and sauté the fu for 1 to 2 minutes. Add the soy milk or water. Stir in the diluted kuzu and bring to a boil, stirring constantly to prevent lumping. Add the bonito flakes and tamari soy sauce or sea salt. Mix in the cooked pasta.

Place the mixture in a baking dish and bake at 350° to 375° F for 35 to 45 minutes until browned. Remove and serve hot.

French Pasta and Vegetable Soup (au Pistou)

1–1 1/2 cups whole grain elbows, shells, or other small pasta, cooked al dente
1 cup kidney beans, soaked 6–8 hours
1/2 cup navy or northern beans, soaked 6–8 hours
6 cups water
1/2 cup onions, diced
1/4 cup celery, diced
1/4 cup carrots, diced
1/4 cup green string beans, sliced into 1/2-inch lengths
1/4 cup yellow wax beans, sliced into 1/2-inch lengths
1–2 tsp extra-virgin olive oil
1–2 Tbsp umeboshi vinegar
1/2 clove garlic, minced (optional)

Pressure cook the kidney beans and navy or northern beans for 50 to 55 minutes in 6 cups of water. Remove from the flame and allow the pressure to come down. Remove the cover. Add the onions, celery, carrots, green string beans, yellow wax beans, olive oil, umeboshi vinegar, and optional garlic. Cover and bring to a boil. Reduce the flame to medium-low and simmer until the vegetables are tender. Add the cooked pasta and simmer for another 3 to 5 minutes. Ladle into individual serving bowls and serve hot.

Low-fat Goulash

1 cup whole grain elbows, shells, or other small pasta, cooked al dente
3 Tbsp corn oil
2 lbs fresh seitan, cubed or ground in a hand food mill
2 cups onions, diced
3 cups water
1 cup kidney beans, cooked and puréed
1 Tbsp umeboshi vinegar

Heat the corn oil in a pot. Add the seitan and sauté for 4 to 5 minutes. Add the onions and sauté for another 1 to 2 minutes. Add the water, puréed kidney beans, and umeboshi vinegar. Cover, bring to a boil, and reduce the flame to medium-low. Simmer for about 15 minutes. Add the cooked pasta, cover, and simmer for another 10 to 15 minutes. Remove, place in serving bowls, and serve hot.

Chili with Pasta

    1 1/2 cups whole grain elbows, shells, or other small pasta, cooked al dente
    1 cup kidney beans, soaked 6–8 hours
    1/4 cup bulgur, rinsed
    4–5 cups water, for rinsing bulgur
    1 strip kombu, 1 inch long, dusted
    1–2 tsp sesame oil (optional)
    1/2 cup onions, diced
    2–3 tsp barley miso, puréed

Place the kidney beans, bulgur, bulgur rinsing water, and kombu in a pressure cooker and cook for 50 minutes. Remove from the flame and bring down the pressure. Remove the cover.

    Heat the sesame oil in a skillet, add the onions, and sauté for 3 to 4 minutes. Add the sautéed onions to the kidney beans.

    Season the kidney beans with miso, cover, and simmer for about 4 to 5 minutes. Add the cooked pasta and simmer for another 10 minutes. Place in serving bowls and serve hot.

Seitan and Vegetable Lasagne

    5–6 whole grain lasagne noodles, cooked al dente
    2 lb seitan, sliced into strips or cubed
    4 cups water
    1/2 cup onions, diced
    1/2 cup carrots, diced
    1/4 cup celery, diced
    1/2 cup green peas, removed from shell
    1/2 cup mushrooms, quartered
    3–4 Tbsp kuzu, diluted
    1–2 Tbsp tamari soy sauce
    1–2 Tbsp parsley, finely chopped
    light sesame oil

Place the water in a pot, cover, and bring to a boil. Add the onions, carrots, celery, green peas, and mushrooms. Cover and simmer for 3 to 4 minutes. Reduce the flame to low and add the diluted kuzu, stirring constantly to prevent lumping. When the kuzu becomes thick and translucent, add the tamari soy sauce and cooked seitan. Cook for another 1 minute. Turn the flame off and mix in the chopped parsley.

    Lightly oil the sides and bottom of an oblong baking dish or glass bread pan. Place a layer of lasagne in the bottom. Ladle a third of the seitan and vegetable sauce over the lasagne. Repeat twice, so that the last third of the seitan and vegetable sauce becomes the top layer. Preheat the oven to 350° to 375° F and bake the lasagne for 25 to 30 minutes or until hot and the sauce is bubbling. Remove from the oven, allow to cool slightly, and slice into 4 to 6 pieces. Serve hot.

Lasagne with Tofu Cream and Black Olives

    5–6 oz (about 6 pieces) whole grain lasagne noodles, cooked al dente
    1 lb firm-style tofu
    1 cup black olives, sliced in thin rounds
    6 scallions, finely chopped
    3–4 Tbsp umeboshi vinegar
    1/2 cup water
    1 Tbsp light sesame oil
    1 cup onions, diced
    1/2 lb mushrooms, stems removed and sliced
    1 cup brown rice mochi, grated

Place the scallions, tofu, umeboshi vinegar, and water in a blender. Purée until smooth and creamy. Remove and place in a bowl.

Heat the light sesame oil in a skillet. Sauté the onions and mushrooms for 3 to 4 minutes. Remove and place in a bowl.

Take an oblong lasagne baking dish or a glass bread pan and lightly oil the bottom and sides with sesame oil. Preheat the oven to 350° to 375° F. Cover the bottom of the baking dish with a layer of lasagne. Spread a layer of tofu cream over the lasagne. Then spread a layer of sautéed vegetables and a few black olives on top. Repeat with another layer of lasagne, tofu cream, and vegetables until all the ingredients have been used up. (The top layer should be tofu cream.) Sprinkle the grated mochi and several slices of olive on the top layer of tofu cream. Bake for about 30 minutes or so until noodles are very hot, the tofu cream is firm, and the mochi has melted and slightly browned. Remove, slice into 4 to 6 pieces, and serve hot.

Fish and Vegetable Lasagne

    5–6 oz (about 6 pieces) whole grain lasagne noodles, cooked al dente
    1 lb cod or haddock fillets (without bones), washed and cut into l-inch pieces
    1 Tbsp light sesame or corn oil
    1/2 cup onions, diced
    4–5 Tbsp unbleached white or whole wheat pastry flour
    2 cups water
    2 cups plain soy milk or water
    1/2 cup celery, diced
    1/2 cup green peas, removed from shell
    1/2 cup carrots, diced
    sea salt or tamari soy sauce
    1–2 Tbsp parsley, finely chopped
    1/2 lemon
    4–6 sprigs of parsley for garnish

Heat the light sesame or corn oil in a skillet and sauté the onions for 3 to 4 minutes. Place the flour in the skillet and sauté to evenly coat the onions with flour. Add the water and optional soy milk, stirring constantly to prevent lumping. When the sauce is thick and creamy, add the celery, green peas, carrots, and fish. Mix and season mildly to taste with sea salt or tamari soy sauce. Simmer for 3 to 4 minutes. Remove from the flame and mix in the chopped parsley.

Preheat the oven to 350° to 375° F and lightly oil an oblong baking dish or glass bread pan with light sesame or corn oil. Place a layer of lasagne in the bottom of the dish. Ladle a third of the creamed fish and vegetables over the lasagne. Repeat this process twice more, so that the top layer consists of creamed fish and vegetables. Bake for approximately 25 to 30 minutes until very hot and the lasagne sauce is bubbling. Remove from the oven, squeeze a little lemon juice over the top of the lasagne, and allow to cool just slightly. Slice into 4 to 6 pieces and serve with a sprig of parsley.

Broccoli Lasagne

>   5–6 oz whole grain lasagne noodles, cooked al dente
>   1 medium-sized head of broccoli, lower part of stem removed (save for soup stock)
>   and chopped into pieces
>   1 lb firm-style tofu
>   1/2 cup water
>   3–4 Tbsp umeboshi vinegar
>   water, for cooking broccoli
>   1 Tbsp light sesame oil
>   1 cup onions, diced
>   1/2 lb mushrooms, stems removed and sliced
>   1 tsp tamari soy sauce

Place the tofu, water, and umeboshi vinegar in a blender and purée until smooth and creamy. Remove and place in a bowl.

Place about 1 inch of water in a pot, cover, and bring to a boil. Add the broccoli, cover, reduce the flame to medium-low, and simmer until the broccoli is very tender. Remove the broccoli, place in a suribachi, and purée or mash until it becomes fairly smooth. You may add some of the broccoli cooking water to the suribachi to create a thick broccoli paste or cream.

Heat the light sesame oil in a skillet and sauté the onions and mushrooms for 3 to 4 minutes. Season with the tamari soy sauce and cook for another minute.

Oil an oblong baking dish or glass bread pan lightly with light sesame oil. Preheat the oven to 350° to 375° F. Place a layer of lasagne in the pan. Spread alternate layers of broccoli, sautéed vegetables, and tofu cream on top of the lasagne. Repeat twice, so that the tofu cream is the top layer. Bake for 25 to 30 minutes until hot. Remove, slice, and serve hot.

Lasagne with Carrot Sauce

>   5–6 oz whole grain lasagne noodles, cooked al dente
>   3 cups carrots, diced
>   water, for cooking carrots
>   pinch of sea salt
>   1–2 Tbsp light sesame oil

1/2 cup onions, diced
1/2 lb mushrooms, stems removed and sliced
tamari soy sauce
1 1/2 cups tofu cream (see previous recipe)
1 cup brown rice mochi, grated

Place the carrots in a saucepan and cover slightly with water. Add a small pinch of sea salt, cover, and bring to a boil. Reduce the flame to medium-low and simmer the carrots for about 20 minutes or until very soft. Place the carrots and carrot cooking water in a blender and purée to a smooth consistency.

Heat the light sesame oil in a skillet and sauté the onions and mushrooms for about 3 to 4 minutes. Pour the carrot purée into the skillet and mix with the sautéed vegetables. Season with tamari soy sauce to taste. Simmer for about 5 to 7 minutes.

Preheat the oven to 350° to 375° F and oil an oblong baking dish or glass bread pan lightly with light sesame oil. Place a layer of lasagne in the bottom of the dish. Spoon a third of the carrot sauce over the lasagne. Then spread a third of the tofu cream over the sauce. Sprinkle a third of the grated mochi on top. Repeat twice, so that the top layer consists of sauce and grated mochi. Bake for 25 to 30 minutes until hot and the sauce is bubbling. Remove, slice into 4 to 6 pieces, and serve hot.

Lasagne with Carrot-Beet Sauce

Adding a small amount of diced beets to the carrot sauce presented above gives the sauce a color like that of tomato sauce. Prepare the dish as described above, but add 2 to 3 tablespoons of diced beets to the carrots and cook together. Also, add a small amount of umeboshi vinegar to the carrot sauce while it is simmering to give it a slightly sour flavor similar to that of tomato sauce. You may also add 1/2 cup of finely diced seitan to the sauce while it is simmering for a different flavor.

Spaghetti with Carrot Sauce and Wheat Balls

1 lb whole grain spaghetti
4–5 cups carrot sauce or carrot-beet sauce (see above recipes for instructions)
Wheat Balls:
1 1/2 lb seitan, cubed
1/2 cup onions, finely diced
1/2 cup mushrooms, finely diced
1 cup whole wheat bread crumbs
light or dark sesame oil, for deep frying

Place a hand food mill over a mixing bowl or saucepan and purée the seitan through it. Add the onions, mushrooms, and bread crumbs to the bowl with the seitan. Mix thoroughly. Form the seitan mixture into about 12 balls about the size of golf ball. Pack the balls firmly so that they hold together well.

Heat the sesame oil in the deep-frying pot and deep fry several wheat balls at a time until golden brown. Remove and place on paper towels to drain. Repeat until all the wheat balls have been deep fried.

Cook the spaghetti, drain, and place the hot spaghetti in serving bowls. Place 2 to 3 wheat balls in each serving dish and ladle hot carrot or carrot-beet sauce over each serving. Wheat balls fall apart if cooked with the carrot sauce. That is why we specify spooning the sauce over them.

Seitan Stuffed Ravioli

1 lb dough, for making ravioli (see Chapter 9)
1 lb seitan, cubed
1 Tbsp olive or sesame oil
1/2 cup onions, diced
1/4 cup mushrooms, diced
1/2 cup fine whole wheat bread crumbs
2 quarts water, for boiling ravioli
1/4 tsp sea salt
3–4 cups carrot or carrot-beet sauce (pp. 144 and 145)

Place the seitan in a hand food mill and grind. Heat the olive or sesame oil in a skillet. Sauté the onions and mushrooms for 2 to 3 minutes. Mix in the seitan and sauté for another 3 to 4 minutes. Place in a mixing bowl, add the bread crumbs, and mix thoroughly.

Roll out the dough for ravioli and stuff with the seitan mixture as instructed in Chapter 9. Continue until all the seitan mixture has been used.

Place 2 quarts of water in a pot and add the sea salt. Cover and bring to a boil. Remove the cover, drop the ravioli in and simmer, without a cover, for several minutes until the ravioli are done (see Chapter 9 for time). Remove, drain, and place in serving dishes. Ladle the carrot or carrot-beet sauce over the ravioli. Serve hot.

Tofu Stuffed Ravioli

1 lb dough, for making ravioli (see Chapter 9)
1 lb firm-style tofu
3 scallions, finely sliced
3 Tbsp umeboshi vinegar
2 quarts water, for boiling ravioli
1/4 tsp sea salt
3–4 cups carrot or carrot-beet sauce (pp. 144 and 145)

Place the scallions in a suribachi and grind 1 to 2 minutes. Add the tofu and purée. Add the umeboshi vinegar and mix thoroughly.

Roll out the ravioli dough as instructed in Chapter 9. Fill each ravioli with a teaspoon of tofu mixture. Continue until all tofu is used.

Place the water and sea salt in a pot. Cover and bring to a boil. Remove the cover and drop in the ravioli. Cook, uncovered, until the ravioli are done (see Chapter 9 for time). Remove, drain, and place in serving dishes. Ladle carrot or carrot-beet sauce over the hot ravioli and serve.

Fish Stuffed Ravioli with Creamy Mushroom Sauce

    1 lb dough for making ravioli (see Chapter 9)
    1 lb cod, haddock, scrod, sole, or other white-meat fish (without bones)
    1 cup water, for boiling fish
    1–2 tsp fresh lemon juice
    1/2 cup whole wheat fine bread crumbs or 1/4 cup whole wheat pastry flour
    2 quarts water, for boiling ravioli
    1/4 tsp sea salt
   Creamy Mushroom Sauce:
    1 cup mushrooms, sliced
    1 Tbsp olive or corn oil
    1/2 cup onions, diced
    4–5 Tbsp unbleached white or whole wheat pastry flour
    1 cup water from cooking the fish
    2 cups plain soy milk or water
    1 cup plain water
    sea salt or tamari soy sauce
    2 Tbsp parsley, minced

Place 1 cup of water in a saucepan, add the fish, cover, and bring to a boil. Reduce the flame to medium-low and simmer for 3 to 4 minutes until the fish is tender. Remove the fish, drain, and place in a suribachi. Reserve the cooking water to prepare the sauce with. Purée the fish in the suribachi. Add the lemon juice and bread crumbs or just enough flour to hold the fish paste together.

    Roll out the ravioli and stuff with the fish paste mixture as described in Chapter 9. Continue until all the fish mixture is used.

    Place the water and sea salt in a pot. Cover and bring to a boil. Remove the cover and drop in the ravioli. Cook until the ravioli are done (see Chapter 9 for time). When done, remove, drain, and place in serving dishes.

    Heat the olive or corn oil in a skillet and sauté the onions and mushrooms for 4 to 5 minutes. Add the flour and sauté for another 1 to 2 minutes. Add the 4 cups of liquid, stirring constantly. Stir until the sauce becomes thick, smooth, and creamy. Add sea salt or tamari soy sauce for a mild salty flavor, cover, and reduce the flame to low. Simmer for about 5 to 7 minutes. Remove from the flame and mix in the minced parsley. Ladle over the hot ravioli and serve.

Unstuffed Ravioli with Vegetable Sauce

    1/2 lb dough, for making ravioli (see Chapter 9)
    2 quarts water, for boiling ravioli
    1/4 tsp sea salt
    3 Tbsp olive oil
    2 cloves garlic, minced
    3 Tbsp mushrooms, diced
    1/2 cup water
    few drops tamari soy sauce
    2 Tbsp parsley, minced

Roll and cut the ravioli as described in Chapter 9. Do not stuff. Cook the ravioli in 2 quarts of water with 1/4 teaspoon of sea salt until completely done. Remove, drain, and place in serving dishes.

Heat the olive oil in a small skillet and sauté the garlic for 1 to 2 minutes. Add the mushrooms and sauté for 2 to 3 minutes. Add the water and season mildly with tamari soy sauce. Simmer on a low flame for about 4 to 5 minutes. Remove from the flame, mix in the minced parsley, and spoon over the fresh ravioli. Serve hot.

Linguine with Pesto Sauce

> 1 lb whole grain linguine, cooked al dente
> 2 cloves garlic, minced
> 1/4 cup pine nuts, lightly roasted
> 1/3 cup extra-virgin olive oil, heated over a low flame until warm
> 1/2 cup water
> 2 tsp umeboshi paste
> 1/2 cup firm-style tofu

Place the garlic, pine nuts, olive oil, water, umeboshi paste, and tofu in a blender. Purée until smooth and creamy. Remove and place in a bowl. Place the drained hot linguine in serving bowls and spoon the pesto sauce over the linguine. Serve.

Spaghetti with Parsley-Walnut Pesto Sauce

> 1 lb whole grain spaghetti, cooked al dente
> 1/2 cup fresh parsley, chopped
> 1/4 cup walnuts, roasted
> 1/3 cup extra-virgin olive oil, heated over a low flame until warm
> 1/2 cup water
> 2 tsp umeboshi paste
> 1/2 cup firm-style tofu

Place parsley, walnuts, olive oil, water, umeboshi paste, and tofu in a blender. Purée until smooth and creamy. Remove and place in a bowl. Place the drained hot spaghetti in serving bowls and spoon the pesto sauce over each serving. Serve hot.

Pasta with Sesame-Parsley Pesto Sauce

> 1 lb whole grain elbows, shells, rigatoni, ziti, or spiral pasta, cooked al dente
> 1/2 cup parsley, chopped
> 1/4 cup tan sesame seeds, roasted
> 2 scallions, finely chopped
> 1/2 cup water
> 1/4–1/3 cup extra-virgin olive oil, heated over a low flame until warm
> 2 tsp umeboshi paste

Cook and drain the pasta and place in serving dishes. Place all other ingredients in a blender and purée until smooth and creamy. Place in a bowl and spoon over the hot pasta. Serve hot.

Spiral Pasta with Escarole and Navy Beans

> **1 lb whole grain spiral pasta, cooked al dente**
> **2–3 cups escarole, chopped**
> **1 1/2–2 cups navy beans, cooked and drained**
> **3–4 Tbsp extra-virgin olive oil**
> **3–4 cloves garlic, minced**
> **1/2 cup mushrooms, diced**
> **1 cup water**
> **tamari soy sauce**

Heat the olive oil in a skillet and sauté the minced garlic for 1 to 2 minutes. Add the mushrooms and sauté for another 2 to 3 minutes. Add water and navy beans, mix, and season to taste with a few drops of tamari soy sauce. Simmer for 3 minutes. Add the chopped escarole and simmer for another 2 minutes until the greens are tender but still bright green. Remove from the flame and mix with the hot spiral pasta. Place in serving dishes and serve hot.

As a variation try substituting endive, chicory, dandelion greens, or Italian broccoli for escarole. You may also use beans such as kidney, northern, or chick-peas in place of navy beans.

Spaghetti with Seitan-Mustard Sauce

> **1 lb whole grain spaghetti, cooked al dente**
> **2 lb seitan, sliced into thin strips**
> **2 Tbsp sesame oil**
> **1 large Spanish onion, sliced into thin rounds**
> **1 cup water**
> **1 Tbsp miso mustard**
> **tamari soy sauce to taste**
> **1/4 cup scallions or chives, finely chopped**

Heat the sesame oil in a skillet and sauté the onions for 3 to 4 minutes. Layer the seitan on top of the onions. Mix the water and miso mustard and pour into the skillet. Bring to a boil. Cover, reduce the flame to low, and simmer for 20 minutes or so until the onions are very tender. Season with a few drops of tamari soy sauce, mix, and sauté for another minute or so. Mix in the cooked spaghetti. Place in serving dishes and garnish with chopped scallions or chives. Serve hot.

Sautéed Sauerkraut and Cabbage with Pasta

> **8 oz whole grain fettucine, cooked al dente**
> **1 cup sauerkraut, excess liquid squeezed out**
> **1 cup cabbage, thinly shredded**

2 Tbsp dark sesame oil
1/2 cup onions, diced
1/2 lb firm-style tofu
1/4 cup water
1 1/2 Tbsp umeboshi vinegar
3 scallions, finely chopped

Heat the dark sesame oil in a skillet and sauté the onions, cabbage, and sauerkraut for about 5 minutes. Cover, reduce the flame to medium-low, and cook for another 15 minutes. Place the tofu, water, umeboshi vinegar, and scallions in a blender and purée until smooth and creamy. Place in a small bowl. Toss the hot, drained pasta, sautéed vegetables, and tofu cream together, and serve hot.

Pierogi with Sauerkraut Stuffing

This eastern European dish is similar to Italian ravioli and Chinese egg rolls. Pierogi may have several different fillings for variaiton. They are often served in soup or sautéed.

1/2 lb dough, for making pierogi wrappings (see Chapter 9)
2 cups sauerkraut, liquid squeezed out and chopped
2 Tbsp corn oil
1/2 cup onions, diced
1/2 cup mushrooms, diced
2 quarts water, for boiling pierogi
1/4 tsp sea salt
1/4 cup parsley, chopped
tamari soy sauce

Heat the corn oil in a skillet and sauté the onions, mushrooms, and sauerkraut for about 15 minutes over a medium-low flame. Remove from the flame and allow to cool.

Roll out the dough and cut into circles as instructed in Chapter 9. Fill each round with almost 1 tablespoon of the sautéed vegetables. Wet the edges of the dough circles with a little water. Fold the circles in half, covering the sautéed vegetables and creating a half-moon-shaped dumpling. Press the edges around the circular part of the half-moons with a fork to seal tightly.

Place the water and sea salt in a pot and bring to a boil. Drop in the pierogi and boil for about 10 minutes until done. Remove, place in a strainer, and drain. Sauté the cooked pierogi with a little corn oil, chopped parsley, and a few drops of tamari soy sauce. Serve hot.

Pierogi with Buckwheat and Cabbage Stuffing

1/2 lb dough, for making pierogi (see Chapter 9)
1 cup buckwheat, cooked
1 cup cabbage, diced
2 Tbsp corn oil
1 cup sauerkraut, liquid squeezed out and chopped

1 tsp tamari soy sauce
2 quarts water, for boiling pierogi
1/4 tsp sea salt
4–5 cups kombu-shiitake stock (p. 63), seasoned with 2–3 Tbsp tamari soy sauce
1/4 cup parsley, chives, or scallions, finely chopped

Heat the corn oil in a skillet and sauté the cabbage and sauerkraut for about 10 minutes. Add the cooked buckwheat and tamari soy sauce. Sauté for another 5 minutes or so. Remove from the flame and allow to cool.

Roll out, cut, and fill the pierogi as described above. Cook as above. Remove, place in a strainer, and drain. Heat the tamari seasoned kombu-shiitake broth. Place the pierogi in the broth. Ladle the pierogi and broth into soup bowls. Garnish with chopped parsley, chives, or scallions and serve hot.

Pasta and White Rice Pilaf

1/2 cup whole grain spaghetti, broken into 1/2-inch long pieces
2 cups organic white rice, washed and drained
3 Tbsp extra-virgin olive oil
1 clove garlic, minced
1/4 cup shiitake mushrooms, soaked, stems removed, and diced
1/4 cup carrots, diced
1/4 cup celery, diced
1/4 cup green peas, removed from shell
2 1/2 cups water
pinch of sea salt

Heat the olive oil in a skillet and sauté the garlic and uncooked spaghetti, stirring constantly to prevent burning. Place the white rice, sautéed spaghetti and garlic, diced vegetables, green peas, water, and sea salt in a pressure cooker. Bring up to pressure over a high flame. When the pressure comes up, reduce it immediately to medium-low, place a flame deflector under the cooker, and cook for 20 minutes. Remove from the flame and allow the pressure to come down. Remove the cover and let sit for 3 to 4 minutes. Remove the rice and pasta pilaf and place in a serving bowl.

Pasta with Peanut Sauce

8 oz whole grain pasta, cooked al dente
1/2 cup freshly ground smooth organic peanut butter
1 1/2 cups water
1 tsp umeboshi vinegar or lemon juice
1 Tbsp tamari soy sauce
1/2 cup scallions, very thinly sliced

Place the peanut butter and water in a small saucepan. Place over a low flame and stir constantly until smooth and creamy. Add the umeboshi vinegar or lemon juice, tamari soy sauce, and scallions. Simmer for 1 minute. Remove and mix with the hot drained pasta. Serve.

Canneloni with Fish Stuffing

This dish makes about 10 to 12 canneloni.

> **1/2 lb parsley pasta dough, for making canneloni (see Chapter 9)**
> **1 lb cod fillet (without bones), washed**
> **1/2 lb medium shrimp, shelled, deveined, and sliced into 1/2-inch pieces**
> **1 cup water, for cooking shrimp and cod**
> **sea salt to taste**
> **2–3 Tbsp light sesame or corn oil**
> **1/4 cup celery, diced**
> **5–6 Tbsp unbleached white flour**
> **2 cups soy milk (optional; water can be used instead)**
> **1/2 cup green peas, removed from shell**
> **2 quarts water, for cooking canneloni**
> **1/4 tsp sea salt**

Place 1 cup of water in a saucepan and bring to a boil. Place the shrimp in the saucepan, cover, and bring to a boil. Reduce the flame to low and simmer for about 7 to 8 minutes. Remove and drain the shrimp. Place the cod in the saucepan along with the sea salt. Cover and simmer for about 3 to 4 minutes. Remove the cod, drain, and place in a bowl. Measure the cooking liquid, making sure you have 1 cup. (If less than 1 cup, add a little fresh water to equal 1 cup.)

Heat light sesame or corn oil in a skillet and sauté the celery for 1 to 2 minutes. Mix in the flour and sauté for another 1 to 2 minutes. Pour in the fish cooking water and the soy milk, stirring constantly until the sauce becomes thick and creamy. Add the green peas, reduce the flame to low, cover, and simmer for about 2 to 3 minutes. Turn off the flame, remove 1 cup of the sauce, and set aside. Mix the shrimp and cooked cod with the remaining 2 cups of sauce. Let cool to room temperature.

Roll out the dough and cut into thin 5-by-4-inch pieces. Bring 2 quarts of water with 1/4 teaspoon of sea salt to a boil. Place several pieces of dough at a time into the boiling water and cook for about 1 to 1 1/2 minutes. Remove with a slotted spoon and submerge the pieces in a bowl of cold water. Remove one at a time and spread on a clean kitchen towel.

Spoon about 3 to 4 tablespoons of filling along the 5-inch long end of the canneloni wrapper. Roll the filled dough into a cylinder or log shape. Repeat until all the filling and dough are rolled.

Lightly oil a casserole or baking dish with light sesame or corn oil and place the stuffed canneloni (1 layer deep only) in the dish. Pour the cup of reserved white sauce evenly over the top of the canneloni. You may also sprinkle a little grated mochi over the sauce if you wish.

Preheat the oven to 375° to 400° F and bake the canneloni for about 15 to 20 minutes. Remove and serve.

Canneloni with Seitan Stuffing

> **1/2 lb dough, for making canneloni (see Chapter 9)**

2 lb seitan, chopped and ground in a hand food mill
2 quarts water, for cooking canneloni
1/4 tsp sea salt, for cooking canneloni
1 Tbsp corn oil
1/4 cup onions, finely diced
1/4 cup celery, finely diced
2 cups fresh whole wheat bread cubes
4 cups carrot or carrot-beet sauce (pp. 144 and 145)

Roll out, cut, and cook the canneloni wrappers as described above. Remove and place in a bowl of cold water.

Heat the corn oil in a skillet and sauté the onions and celery for 2 to 3 minutes. Place the sautéed vegetables in a bowl. Add the seitan and bread cubes and mix thoroughly.

Place about 1/4 cup of the filling on each canneloni wrapper as instructed above and roll into a cylinder or log shape. Repeat until all filling is used.

Lightly oil a baking dish, place the canneloni in (1 layer deep only), and pour the hot carrot or carrot-beet sauce over them. Preheat the oven to 350° to 400° F and bake for 15 to 20 minutes. Remove and serve.

Canneloni with Vegetable-Tofu Stuffing

1/2 lb dough, for making canneloni (see Chapter 9)
1 1/2 lb firm-style tofu
2 quarts water, for cooking canneloni
1/4 tsp sea salt, for cooking canneloni
6–7 scallions, finely chopped
4–5 Tbsp umeboshi vinegar
4 cups carrot or carrot-beet sauce (pp. 144 and 145)

Roll, cut, and cook the canneloni as described previously. Remove and place in cold water.

Place the scallions in a blender. Add the umeboshi vinegar and purée. Add the tofu, a little at a time, and purée. Remove and place in a bowl.

Fill the canneloni as in the previous recipes, but this time with the tofu filling. Roll up in cylinders. Lightly oil a baking dish. Place the filled canneloni in the dish and pour the carrot or carrot-beet sauce over them. Bake in a 375° to 400° F oven for 15 to 20 minutes. Remove and serve hot.

Deep-fried Breaded Canneloni

12 stuffed canneloni (use any of the above fillings)
1 cup whole wheat pastry flour
1 cup water
pinch of sea salt
1 tsp kuzu, diluted
1 cup fine whole wheat bread crumbs

light or dark sesame oil, for deep frying
1 lemon, sliced in wedges for garnish
4–6 sprigs parsley, for garnish

Mix flour, water, sea salt, and diluted kuzu. Dip the stuffed canneloni in the batter and then roll in the fine bread crumbs, making sure to bread the ends of the canneloni as well as the center.

Heat the sesame oil to about 375° F and deep fry 3 to 4 canneloni at a time until golden brown. Remove and place on paper towels to drain. Repeat until all the canneloni have been deep fried. Place the deep-fried canneloni on individual serving plates. Garnish each with 2 lemon wedges and a sprig of parsley. Serve hot.

Tortellini

1/2 lb dough, for making tortellini (see Chapter 9)
1 cup any of the above fish, seitan, or tofu fillings used in making canneloni
2 quarts water, for cooking tortellini
1/4 tsp sea salt
4 cups carrot, carrot-beet, or creamy mushroom sauce (pp. 144, 145, and 147)

Roll the dough into 2-inch circles. Fill with any of the above fillings as described in Chapter 9. Bring 2 quarts of water to a boil with the sea salt in it. Drop in the tortellini and cook until tender. Remove and drain. Place the hot tortellini in serving bowls and pour hot carrot, carrot-beet, or creamy mushroom sauce over them. Serve hot.

Deep-fried Tortellini

Fill the tortellini with any of the above fillings as described in Chapter 9. Heat oil in a deep-frying pot and deep fry several tortellini at a time until golden brown. Remove and drain on paper towels. Repeat until all tortellini have been deep fried. Serve with lemon juice sprinkled on top.

Cappelletti

Use the same amount of dough as in the recipes for tortellini, together with any of the stuffings or sauces indicated above. Roll the dough into 2-inch squares, fill, and boil in salted water until tender. Place in serving bowls and serve with carrot, carrot-beet, or one of the creamy sauces described in this chapter poured over them.

Deep-fried Cappelletti

Fill the cappelletti with desired stuffing and deep fry until golden brown. Remove and place on paper towels to drain. Repeat until all cappelletti have been deep fried. Sprinkle lemon juice over the cappelletti and serve.

Chapter 8: Pasta Salads

Although it is especially light and refreshing in the summer, cold pasta can be enjoyed any time of year. Whole grain noodles and pasta are delicious in salads. As we explained, Japanese noodles are usually made with salt, so sea salt does not need to be added when you cook them. American or European pastas usually do not contain salt, so you can add a pinch of sea salt to the water when you boil them.

All noodles and pasta are cooked in the same basic manner. Place the noodles, spaghetti, or pasta in a pot of boiling water. Stir occasionally to prevent the noodles from clumping together. Bring to a boil again and reduce the flame to medium. Do not cover the pot. Simmer until the noodles or pasta are done. You can tell when noodles are done by breaking a piece in half. The inside should be the same as the outside. If the inside is still light and the outside is darker, cook them a little longer. When done, place in a strainer or colander, rinse until cool with cold water, and drain for several minutes.

If you would prefer not to use any of the ingredients in the recipes, feel free to omit them and substitute others.

Pasta and Buckwheat Salad with Tamari Soy Sauce-Ginger Dressing

> 2 cups whole grain elbows or shells, cooked
> 1 cup buckwheat groats, washed
> 2 cups water, for boiling buckwheat
> pinch of sea salt
> 1/2 cup tempeh, sliced into 1/2-inch cubes
> 1 Tbsp dark sesame oil
> 1 cup water, for boiling tempeh
> 1 tsp tamari soy sauce
> 2 cups water, for blanching vegetables
> 1/4 cup sweet corn, removed from cob
> 1/2 cup kale, sliced into 1/4-inch thick slices
> 1/2 cup green peas
> 1/4 cup red radishes, quartered
> 1/4 cup red onions, sliced into thin half-moons
> 1/4 cup sauerkraut
> 1/4 cup sauerkraut juice
> *Tamari Soy Sauce-Ginger Dressing:*
> 1 Tbsp tamari soy sauce
> 1/4–1/3 tsp fresh ginger juice
> 1/2–2/3 cup water
> 2 Tbsp parsley, minced

Place 2 cups of water with a pinch of sea salt in a saucepan, cover, and bring to a boil. Add the buckwheat groats, bring to a boil again, and reduce the flame to medium-low.

Simmer for 20 minutes. Remove the buckwheat and place in a bowl. With a fork, chopsticks, or wooden spoon, make several continuous strokes through the buckwheat to fluff it up and cool it off. When thoroughly fluffed and cooled to room temperature, place the cooked buckwheat in a mixing bowl.

While the buckwheat is cooking, prepare the tempeh in the following manner. Place the dark sesame oil in a skillet and heat up. Add the tempeh cubes and pan fry until golden brown on all sides. Place 1 cup of water in the skillet, cover, and bring to a boil. Reduce the flame to medium-low and simmer for 10 minutes. Sprinkle the tempeh with several drops of tamari soy sauce, cover, and simmer for another 10 minutes. Remove the cover and cook off the remaining liquid. Remove the tempeh and place it in the mixing bowl with the buckwheat.

Place 2 cups of water in a saucepan, cover, and bring to a boil. Remove the cover and blanch the vegetables separately in the following manner: sweet corn for 1 minute and remove; kale for 1 minute and remove; green peas for 1 minute and remove; red radishes for 1 1/2 minutes and remove. Place cooked vegetables in the mixing bowl with the buckwheat and tempeh.

Place the cooked pasta, raw red onions, sauerkraut, and sauerkraut juice in the mixing bowl and mix thoroughly.

Place the water in a saucepan and bring to a boil. Reduce the flame under saucepan to low and add the tamari soy sauce. Simmer for 2 to 3 minutes. Remove from the flame and mix in ginger juice and minced parsley. Allow to cool slightly.

Pour the tamari soy sauce-ginger dressing over the salad ingredients in the mixing bowl and toss to thoroughly mix in. Place the salad in a serving bowl.

Pasta Salad with Umeboshi-Tahini Dressing

> 8 oz whole wheat or Jerusalem artichoke shells, elbows, ziti, or rigatoni, cooked
> 1 cup chick-peas, cooked
> 1/2 cup cucumber, sliced into thin quarters
> 1/2 cup red onions, sliced into thin half-moons
> 1/4 cup celery, diced or sliced on a thin diagonal
> 1/4 cup red radishes, sliced into thin rounds
> 1 cup red leaf lettuce, sliced into 1-inch pieces
> 2 Tbsp parsley, minced
> *Umeboshi-Tahini Dressing:*
> 2–3 umeboshi plums, pits removed
> 2–3 Tbsp organic tahini, roasted
> 1 tsp onion, finely grated
> 3/4–1 cup water

Place all ingredients in a bowl and thoroughly mix before adding the dressing.

Place the umeboshi in a suribachi and purée until smooth. Add the tahini and purée together with the umeboshi until smooth. Add the grated onion and purée. Next, gradually pour the water into the suribachi and purée with the other ingredients until smooth and creamy.

Pour the dressing over the salad ingredients and mix thoroughly. Place the salad in a serving bowl or line a bowl with lettuce leaves and place the salad on top.

Pasta Salad with Tofu Cream Dressing

> 8 oz whole grain elbows, shells, ziti, or rigatoni, cooked
> 1/2 cup green beans, sliced into l-inch lengths and blanched 1 minute
> 1/2 cup yellow wax beans, sliced into l-inch lengths and blanched 1 minute
> 1/4 cup red radish, sliced into thin rounds
> 1/4 cup yellow summer squash, sliced into thin quarters and blanched 45 seconds
> 1/2 cup leeks, sliced into 1/2-inch rounds and blanched 1 1/2 minutes
> 1/4 cup green peas, removed from pod and boiled 1 1/2–2 minutes
> *Tofu Cream Dressing:*
> 1 cake (1 lb) firm-style tofu
> 3–4 Tbsp umeboshi vinegar
> 2 Tbsp onion, finely grated
> 1/2 cup water

Place the pasta and vegetables in a mixing bowl.

Purée the tofu through a hand food mill into a bowl. Add the umeboshi vinegar and grated onion. Mix thoroughly with a wooden spoon or pestle. Add the water and mix again.

Place the dressing in the bowl with the cooked pasta and vegetables and mix in well. Place the salad in a serving bowl. Garnish with sprigs of parsley and serve.

Stuffed Shells with Tofu Cream and Black Olives

> 12 large whole grain stuffing shells, cooked
> 1/2 lb firm-style tofu
> 1/4 cup black olives, chopped
> 3 scallions, finely chopped
> 1–2 Tbsp water
> 1 1/2–2 Tbsp umeboshi vinegar
> 2 Tbsp red radish or red onion, minced

Place the scallions and water in the blender and purée. Add the umeboshi vinegar and tofu and purée until smooth and creamy. Remove and place in a small bowl and mix in the black olives. Stuff each cooked shell with the tofu cream and sprinkle a little red radish or red onion on top of the stuffing for garnish. Place on a serving platter or place a bed of lettuce on the platter with the stuffed pasta on top. Garnish with red radish slices and serve.

Stuffed Shells with Seitan and Vegetables

> 12 large whole grain stuffing shells, cooked
> 1/2 lb seitan
> 2 tsp dark sesame oil
> 1/4 lb fresh mushrooms, diced
> 1/4 cup onions, minced
> tamari soy sauce
> 1 Tbsp parsley, minced

Place the dark sesame oil in a skillet and heat up. Add the mushrooms and sauté for 1 minute. Add the onions and several drops of tamari soy sauce. Sauté for another 1 minute or so. Remove and place in a mixing bowl. Mix in the parsley. Place the seitan in a hand food mill and coarsely grind into the mixing bowl. Mix the ingredients.

Stuff each cooked shell with the seitan and vegetable stuffing. Place on a serving platter. Garnish the platter with sprigs of parsley and half-moon slices of lemon.

Stuffed Shells with Fish

> **12 medium or jumbo whole grain stuffing shells, cooked**
> **1 lb fresh cod, scrod, or haddock (without bones), washed**
> **water, for boiling fish**
> **tamari soy sauce**
> **1 tsp extra-virgin olive oil**
> **1/4 cup celery, minced**
> **1 Tbsp parsley, minced**
> **1/2 cup red onions, minced**
> **2 tsp fresh lemon juice**
> **4–5 lettuce leaves**

Slice the fish into chunks and place in a saucepan. Add enough water to half cover the fish. Sprinkle several drops of tamari soy sauce over the fish. Cover and bring to a boil. Reduce the flame to medium-low and simmer for about 3 to 5 minutes. Remove, place in a colander, and drain. Place the fish in a suribachi and mash.

Heat the olive oil in a skillet and add the celery and parsley. Sauté for 1 minute. Remove and place in the suribachi with the fish.

Place the red onions and lemon juice in the suribachi and mix thoroughly with the fish. Stuff each shell with the mixture. Arrange several lettuce leaves on a serving platter and place the stuffed shells on top. Garnish with several red radish slices or red onion rings and serve.

Macaroni Salad with Tofu Cheese and Black Olives

> **8 oz whole grain elbow macaroni, cooked**
> **8 oz tofu cheese (see recipe for Pickled Tofu on p. 47)**
> **1/2 cup black olives, pitted and sliced or diced**
> **1 cucumber**
> **5 red radishes, sliced into thin half-moons**
> **1/2 cup red onions, diced**
> **2 Tbsp parsley, finely chopped**
> **1/4 cup extra-virgin olive oil**
> **1 Tbsp fresh lemon juice**

Prepare the tofu cheese (pickled tofu) as described in Chapter 2. (This should be done several days in advance.)

Take the cucumber and score it with a fork, by making shallow straight lines down the skin of the cucumber. Slice the cucumber in half lengthwise and scoop the seeds with a spoon and discard them. Slice the scored cucumber into 1/4-inch thick half-moons and place in a mixing bowl. Slice the tofu cheese into cubes or dice. Place the pasta, red radishes, red onions, tofu cheese cubes, black olives, and parsley in the mixing bowl.

Place 1/2 inch of water in a saucepan and bring to a boil. Place the olive oil in a cup and place it in the saucepan. Heat up the olive oil in the cup until warm. Remove and let cool to room temperature. Mix in the lemon juice. Pour the dressing over the salad ingredients and mix well. Serve at room temperature or slightly chilled with a sprig of parsley for garnish.

Pasta Salad with Pumpkin Seed and Parsley Dressing

> 8 oz whole grain elbows, shells, or other small pasta, cooked
> 1 cup pumpkin seeds, washed and drained
> 1/4 cup parsley, minced
> 3/4 cup water
> 2 Tbsp umeboshi vinegar
> 1/4 cup carrots, coarsely grated

Heat up the skillet and add the drained pumpkin seeds. Dry roast over a high flame until most of the liquid evaporates from the surface of the seeds. Reduce the flame to medium and roast, stirring constantly, until all the seeds begin to puff up and pop. Remove and place in a suribachi. Grind with a wooden pestle until all seeds are crushed. Add the parsley and grind in with the seeds. Pour the water and umeboshi vinegar into the suribachi and mix thoroughly.

Place the pasta and carrots in a mixing bowl. Pour the pumpkin seed and parsley dressing over the pasta and carrots and mix in. Place in a serving bowl. Garnish with several carrot slices cut into flowers and serve.

Spaghetti with Sesame-Scallion Dressing

> 8 oz whole wheat or Jerusalem artichoke spaghetti, cooked
> 1 cup tan sesame seeds, roasted
> 1/4 cup scallions (or chives), finely chopped
> 2 Tbsp umeboshi vinegar
> 3/4 cup water or kombu stock (p. 62)
> 2 cups green beans, sliced into l-inch long pieces and boiled 2–3 minutes

Place the sesame seeds in a suribachi and grind with a wooden pestle until they are more than half-crushed. Add the scallions and grind in with the sesame seeds. Add the umeboshi vinegar and water or kombu stock. Mix thoroughly.

Place the cooked spaghetti and green beans in a mixing bowl and pour the sesame-scallion dressing over them. Mix and place in a serving bowl.

Pasta with Carrot Tops and Sesame eed Dressing

> 8 oz whole grain elbows, shells, or other small pasta, cooked
> 1 bunch fresh carrot tops, finely chopped
> 1/2 cup tan sesame seeds, roasted

    1 cup water
    2 tsp tamari soy sauce
    1/2 tsp fresh ginger juice
    1/2 cup carrot slices cut into flowers

Grind the sesame seeds in a suribachi until they are more than half-crushed.

Place 1/2 cup of water in a skillet, cover, and bring to a boil. Add the carrot tops and tamari soy sauce. Cover and boil for 1 minute. Remove and place liquid and carrot tops in the suribachi. Add the remaining water and ginger juice and grind to mix thoroughly.

Place the pasta and carrot flowers in a mixing bowl and pour the carrot tops and sesame seed dressing over them. Mix well and place in a serving dish.

Pasta and Seitan Salad with Mustard Dressing

    8 oz whole grain spirals, twists, or ziti pasta, cooked
    1 lb seitan, sliced into 1/4-inch thick slices and then into 1/4-inch strips
    2 tsp natural miso or dijon-style prepared mustard
    3 Tbsp extra-virgin olive or rice bran oil
    1 small clove garlic, minced (optional)
    1/2 lb mushrooms, quartered
    2 tsp tamari soy sauce
    1 tsp sweet rice vinegar
    1 Tbsp parsley, minced
    1 Tbsp scallions, minced
    3 Tbsp water
    1/2 lb green string beans, sliced into 2-inch lengths and boiled 2 minutes until tender
    1 cup carrots, cut into matchsticks and boiled 1 minute
    1/2 cup summer squash, sliced in 1/4-inch thick half-moon slices and boiled 1 minute

Place the olive or rice bran oil in a skillet and heat up. Add the garlic and mushrooms. Add the tamari soy sauce. Sauté for 1 minute and add the strips of seitan. Sauté for 2 to 3 minutes, stirring constantly. Remove from the flame and allow to cool. Mix in the miso or dijon-style mustard, sweet rice vinegar, parsley, scallions, and water.

Place the cooked pasta, green string beans, carrots, and summer squash in a mixing bowl. Pour the mustard dressing over the ingredients and mix in well. Place in a serving bowl and garnish with a sprig of parsley or watercress. Serve at room temperature or slightly chilled.

Fresh Tuna-Pasta Salad with Tofu Mayonaise

    8 oz whole grain shells, elbows, twists, or ziti, cooked
    1 lb fresh tuna, boiled 3–5 minutes until tender and flaky
    1/2 cup tofu mayonaise (available at natural food stores)
    1 cup fresh green peas, removed from pod and boiled 3 minutes until tender but still
        bright green
    5 red radishes, sliced into thin half-moons
    1 cucumber, sliced into thin half-moons

    1/2 red onion, sliced into thin half-moons
    1 cup chick-peas, cooked
    1 Tbsp parsley, minced
    4–5 lettuce leaves, for garnish

Place the cooked pasta, tuna, vegetables, and chick-peas in a mixing bowl. Mix in the tofu mayonaise and parsley. Place in a serving bowl, lined with a bed of lettuce leaves and serve.

Pasta and Bean Salad with Sesame-Vinegar Dressing

    8 oz whole grain shells, twists, or spirals, cooked
    1 cup chick-peas, cooked
    1 cup navy beans, cooked
    1 cup green string beans or fresh lima beans, boiled 2–3 minutes
    1 cup sweet corn, removed from cob and boiled 2–3 minutes
    1/2 cup tan sesame seeds, roasted
    1 tsp umeboshi vinegar
    1 tsp tamari soy sauce
    1 tsp sweet brown rice vinegar
    1 tsp parsley, minced
    1/2 cup water or kombu stock (p. 62)

Place the cooked pasta, chick-peas, navy beans, green string beans, and sweet corn in a mixing bowl.

   Place the fresh roasted sesame seeds in a suribachi and grind until they turn into a thick paste or sesame butter. Slowly add the umeboshi vinegar, tamari soy sauce, and sweet brown rice vinegar. Grind until smooth and creamy. Add the parsley and grind slightly. Gradually add the water or kombu stock, stirring constantly until smooth and creamy. Pour the dressing over the salad ingredients and mix in thoroughly. Place in a serving bowl.

Bean, Pasta, and Dandelion Salad

    8 oz whole grain shells or elbows, cooked
    1 cup kidney beans, cooked
    1 cup chick-peas, cooked
    1 cup green string beans, cooked and sliced into 2-inch lengths
    2 cups fresh dandelion greens, chopped
    1 tsp extra-virgin olive oil
    1/2 tsp tamari soy sauce
    3 umeboshi plums, pits removed
    1 Tbsp onion, grated
    1 Tbsp parsley, minced
    3/4 cup water

Place the beans and cooked pasta in a mixing bowl. Heat the olive oil in a skillet and place the dandelion greens in it. Sauté several seconds. Add the tamari soy sauce and sauté for another minute or so. Remove and place the sautéed dandelions in the mixing bowl with the other ingredients.

Place the pitted umeboshi in a suribachi and grind to a smooth paste. Add the onion and parsley and grind. Slowly add the water and grind until smooth. Pour the dressing over the salad ingredients in the mixing bowl. Mix thoroughly and place in a serving bowl.

Shrimp and Pasta Salad with White Miso Dressing

8 oz whole grain shells or elbows, cooked
1/2 lb medium shrimp, cooked and sliced into l-inch lengths
1 cup water
3 Tbsp white miso
1/2 cup tan sesame seeds, roasted
2 tsp parsley, minced
1/2 cup green peas, cooked

Place the water in a saucepan, add the white miso, and dilute. Heat up, without boiling, and simmer on a very low flame for 2 to 3 minutes. Remove from the flame and allow to cool to room temperature.

Place the hot roasted sesame seeds in a suribachi and grind to a smooth paste or butter. Add the diluted miso and minced parsley. Grind to a smooth consistency. Place all ingredients in a mixing bowl and pour the dressing over them. Mix well and place in a serving bowl.

Pasta and Hijiki Salad with Tofu Dressing

4 oz whole grain elbows, small shells, or other small pasta, cooked
1 cup hijiki, washed, soaked 3–5 minutes, and chopped
1 lb firm-style tofu
1 cup water, for boiling hijiki
1/2 cup sweet corn, removed from cob and boiled 2–3 minutes
1/2 cup carrots, cut into matchsticks and boiled 1 minute
1/2 cup green string beans, sliced into 2-inch lengths and boiled 2 minutes
1/2 cup red onions, sliced into half-moons
1/4 cup red radishes, sliced into thin rounds
1 cup broccoli, sliced into small flowerettes and boiled 1 1/2 minutes
3 Tbsp umeboshi vinegar
2 Tbsp onion, finely grated
1/2 cup water

Place the hijiki in a saucepan, add 1 cup of water, cover, and bring to a boil. Reduce the flame to medium-low and simmer for about 15 to 20 minutes. Remove, place in a strainer, and rinse under cold water. Place the hijiki in a mixing bowl. Add the cooked pasta, sweet corn, carrots, green string beans, red onions, red radishes, and broccoli. Place the tofu in a hand food mill and purée into a bowl. Add the umeboshi vinegar and grated onion. Mix well with a wooden pestle. Add the water and mix again. Place the tofu dressing in the mixing bowl with the other salad ingredients and mix well. Place in a serving dish.

Pasta with Parsley and Sunflower Seed Pesto

8 oz whole grain shells, twists, spirals, or other small pasta
1/3 cup fresh parsley, minced
1/3 cup sunflower seeds, roasted
1 Tbsp shiso condiment (roasted and chopped shiso leaves)
1 clove garlic, minced (optional; you may substitute 2 Tbsp diced onion or 3 Tbsp chopped scallion)
2 Tbsp fresh lemon juice
1/4 cup rice bran oil, heated
1/4 cup water

Cook the pasta al dente, rinse, and drain. Place in a bowl and set aside. Place the parsley, sunflower seeds, shiso condiment, garlic, lemon juice, heated rice bran oil, and water in a blender, and chop.

Place the cooked pasta in a individual serving dishes and spoon 2 to 3 tablespoons of the pesto sauce over each. Mix before eating.

Pasta with Green Goddess Dressing

8 oz whole grain spaghetti, fettucine, or ribbon pasta, cooked
2 cups broccoli, sliced into small flowerettes and boiled 2 minutes
1/2 cup red radishes, sliced into thin rounds
1/4 cup black olives, diced
2–3 umeboshi plums, pits removed
1 cup water
2 Tbsp onion, minced
3/4 cup brown rice, cooked
1/2 cup parsley, chopped
2 Tbsp organic tahini, roasted
1 Tbsp tamari soy sauce

Place the pasta, broccoli, red radish slices, and black olives in a mixing bowl.

Place the umeboshi plums, water, onion, brown rice, parsley, tahini, and tamari soy sauce in a blender. Purée until smooth and creamy. Pour the dressing over the salad ingredients and toss or spoon over individual servings of pasta and vegetables.

Pasta and Marinated Tofu Salad

8 oz whole grain spaghetti or linguine, cooked
1 lb firm-style tofu, sliced into 1/2-inch cubes
1 Tbsp tamari soy sauce
1/2 lb snow peas, stems removed and boiled 1 minute
1/4 cup summer squash, sliced into thin quarters and boiled 1 minute
1/2 cup broccoli, sliced into small flowerettes and boiled 1 1/2–2 minutes

1/2–2/3 cup water or kombu stock (p. 62)
1 Tbsp tamari soy sauce, for dressing
1/4–1/3 tsp fresh ginger juice

Place the cubed tofu in a bowl and sprinkle 1 tablespoonful of tamari soy sauce over it. Mix gently and marinate for 1 hour (mix occasionally to evenly marinate). Remove and place the tofu, cooked pasta, snow peas, summer squash, and broccoli in a mixing bowl.

Place the water or kombu stock and the tamari soy sauce in a saucepan and heat over a medium flame. Do not boil. Remove from the heat and add the ginger juice. Allow to cool to room temperature and pour over the pasta salad ingredients. Mix and place in a serving dish.

Spiral Pasta with Scallion-Sunflower Seed Pesto

8 oz whole grain spiral pasta (any type)
1/2 cup scallions, chopped
1/4–1/3 cup sunflower seeds, roasted
1/4 cup rice bran oil, heated
1 Tbsp tamari soy sauce
2 Tbsp fresh lemon juice
1/4 cup water

Cook the spiral pasta al dente, rinse, and drain. Place in a bowl and set aside. Place the scallions, sunflower seeds, heated rice bran oil, tamari soy sauce, lemon juice, and water in a blender, and chop. Place the cooked pasta in individual serving dishes and spoon 2 to 3 tablespoons of the pesto sauce over each. Mix before eating.

Spaghetti with Watercress-Pumpkin Seed Pesto

8 oz whole grain spaghetti (any type)
1/2 cup watercress, chopped
1/4–1/3 cup pumpkin seeds, roasted
2 Tbsp scallions or chives, chopped
1 clove garlic, minced (optional; you may substitute 2 Tbsp chopped onion or use
**   more scallions or chives)**
1/4 cup rice bran oil, heated
1/4 cup water
2 Tbsp fresh lemon juice
1 Tbsp tamari soy sauce

Cook the spaghetti al dente, rinse, drain, and place in a bowl. Set aside. Place the watercress, pumpkin seeds, scallions or chives, garlic, heated rice bran oil, water, lemon juice, and tamari soy sauce in a blender, and chop.

Place the spaghetti in individual serving dishes and spoon 2 to 3 tablespoons of the pesto sauce over each. Mix before eating.

Pasta with Watercress-Almond Pesto

> **8 oz whole grain pasta (any type)**
> **1/2 cup watercress, chopped**
> **1/4–1/3 cup almonds, roasted and chopped**
> **2 Tbsp parsley, chopped**
> **1/4 cup rice bran oil, heated**
> **1/4 cup water**
> **2 tsp shiso condiment (p. 163)**
> **1 1/2 Tbsp fresh lemon juice**
> **2 tsp tamari soy sauce**

Cook the pasta al dente, rinse, and drain. Place in a bowl and set aside. Place the watercress, parsley, almonds, heated rice bran oil, water, shiso condiment, lemon juice, and tamari soy sauce in a blender, and chop.

Place the cooked pasta in individual serving dishes and spoon 2 to 3 tablespoons of the pesto sauce over each. Mix before eating.

Pasta with Chick-pea-Parsley Dressing

> **8 oz whole grain pasta (any type)**
> **1 cup chick-peas, cooked**
> **1/2 cup parsley, chopped**
> **1/4 cup carrots, diced**
> **2 Tbsp sesame butter**
> **1/4 cup onions, diced**
> **2 Tbsp umeboshi vinegar**
> **1/2 cup water**

Cook the pasta al dente, rinse, and drain. Place in a bowl and set aside. Place the cooked chick-peas, carrots, sesame butter, onions, parsley, umeboshi vinegar, and water in a blender, and chop.

Place the cooked pasta in individual serving dishes and spoon 2 to 3 tablespoons of dressing over each. Mix before eating.

Fettucine with Pumpkin Seed-Celery Leaf Pesto

> **8 oz whole grain fettucine**
> **1/4 cup pumpkin seeds, roasted**
> **1/4 cup celery leaves, chopped**
> **2 Tbsp onion, diced**
> **3 Tbsp parsley, chopped**
> **1 Tbsp umeboshi vinegar**
> **1 Tbsp tamari soy sauce**
> **2 Tbsp organic tahini, roasted**
> **1/4 cup water**

Cook the fettucine al dente, rinse, and drain. Place in a bowl and set aside. Place the pumpkin seeds, celery leaves, onion, parsley, umeboshi vinegar, tamari soy sauce, tahini, and water in a blender, and chop.

Place the fettucine in individual serving dishes and spoon 2 to 3 tablespoons of the pesto sauce over each. Mix before eating.

Macaroni and Hijiki Salad with Ume-Sesame Seed Dressing

> 8 oz whole grain elbow macaroni, cooked
> 1 cup hijiki, washed, soaked 3–5 minutes, boiled 15 minutes, and rinsed
> 2–3 Tbsp umeboshi vinegar
> 1/2 cup tan sesame seeds, roasted
> 1/2 cup sweet corn, removed from cob, boiled 2–3 minutes
> 1/4 cup broccoli flowerettes, boiled 1–1 1/2 minutes
> 1/4 cup carrots, cut into matchsticks and boiled 1 minute
> 1/4 cup cauliflower flowerettes, boiled 2–3 minutes
> 1/4 cup green peas or green beans, boiled 2 minutes
> 1/4 cup parsley, chopped
> 1/2 cup water
> 1 Tbsp fresh lemon juice

Place the cooked macaroni, hijiki, sweet corn, broccoli, carrots, cauliflower, and green peas or green beans in a bowl and toss to mix. Place the sesame seeds, parsley, umeboshi vinegar, water, and lemon juice in a blender or grind in a suribachi until smooth.

Pour the dressing over the salad and mix thoroughly, or spoon over individual servings of the salad, and serve.

Spaghetti with Peanut-Mustard Pesto

> 8 oz whole grain spaghetti, cooked
> 1/2 cup peanuts, roasted
> 1 Tbsp miso or dijon-style mustard
> 1/2 cup kale, chopped and boiled 1 minute
> 1/4 cup carrots, cut into matchsticks and boiled 1 minute
> 1/3 cup scallions or chives, chopped
> 1 Tbsp tamari soy sauce
> 1/2 cup water
> 1 Tbsp fresh lemon juice

Combine the cooked spaghetti, kale, and carrot matchsticks in a bowl and toss. Place the peanuts, miso or dijon-style mustard, scallions or chives, tamari soy sauce, water, and lemon juice in a blender, and chop.

Mix the pesto sauce in with the salad or spoon over individual servings of the spaghetti and vegetables.

Spiral Pasta with Walnut Pesto

> **8 oz whole grain spiral pasta**
> **1/2 cup walnuts, roasted**
> **1/2 cup parsley, chopped**
> **1/2 cup water**
> **2 Tbsp fresh lemon juice**
> **2 Tbsp tamari soy sauce**
> **1 1/4 Tbsp umeboshi vinegar**
> **2 tsp scallions, chopped**
> **1/4 tsp ginger, finely grated**

Cook the pasta al dente, rinse, drain, and place in a bowl. Set aside. Place the walnuts, parsley, water, lemon juice, tamari soy sauce, umeboshi vinegar, scallions, and ginger in a blender, and chop.

Place the pasta in individual serving dishes and spoon 2 to 3 tablespoons of the pesto sauce over each. Mix before eating.

Spaghetti with Hazelnut Pesto

> **8 oz spaghetti or any other type of whole grain pasta**
> **1/2 cup hazelnuts, roasted**
> **1/2 cup watercress, chopped**
> **2 Tbsp parsley, chopped**
> **2 Tbsp rice bran oil, heated**
> **1/4 cup water**
> **2 tsp shiso condiment (p. 163)**
> **1 Tbsp fresh lemon juice**
> **2 tsp tamari soy sauce**

Cook the spaghetti al dente, rinse, drain, and place in a bowl. Set aside. Place the watercress, parsley, hazelnuts, heated rice bran oil, water, shiso condiment, lemon juice, and tamari soy sauce in a blender, and chop.

Spoon the hazelnut pesto sauce over individual servings of spaghetti or mix in with the entire bowl of spaghetti and serve.

Pasta with Mustard-Parsley Pesto

> **8 oz whole grain pasta (any type)**
> **1 Tbsp miso or dijon-style mustard**
> **1 Tbsp parsley, minced**
> **1/2 cup scallions, chopped**
> **1 Tbsp tamari soy sauce**
> **1/2 cup water**
> **1/4 cup rice bran oil, heated**
> **1 Tbsp fresh lemon juice**

Cook the pasta al dente, rinse, drain, and place in a bowl. Set aside. Place the scallions, miso or dijon-style mustard, tamari soy sauce, water, heated rice bran oil, lemon juice, and minced parsley in a blender, and purée.

Spoon 2 to 3 tablespoons of mustard-parsley pesto sauce over each serving of pasta. Mix before eating

Ziti with Tofu Cheese-Sunflower Seed Pesto

8 oz whole grain ziti
1/2 cup tofu cheese (see recipe for Pickled Tofu on p. 47), minced
1/3 cup sunflower seeds, roasted
1/4 cup rice bran oil, heated
1/2 cup scallions, chopped
1 Tbsp tamari soy sauce
2 Tbsp lemon juice
1/4 cup water

Cook the ziti al dente, rinse, drain, and place in a bowl. Set aside. Place the sunflower seeds, heated rice bran oil, scallions, tamari soy sauce, lemon juice, and water in a blender, and chop. Mix in the minced tofu cheese, but do not blend.

Spoon the pesto sauce over individual servings of ziti or mix in with the ziti, and serve.

Greek Pasta Salad with Tofu Cheese

4–6 oz whole grain spiral pasta, cooked, rinsed, and drained
4 oz tofu cheese (made with mellow barley miso; see recipe for Pickled Tofu on p. 47)
1 cup red leaf lettuce, chopped
1/4 cup black olives, diced
1/4 cup natural mushrooms, thinly sliced
1/4 cup red onions, sliced into thin half-moons
1 1/2 Tbsp rice bran oil, heated
1 Tbsp fresh lemon juice
1/2 tsp garlic, finely minced
1/4 cup water
1 tsp umeboshi vinegar

Place the spiral pasta, red leaf lettuce, black olives, mushrooms, and red onions in a bowl, and toss to mix. Place the heated rice bran oil, lemon juice, garlic, water, and umeboshi vinegar in a blender, and purée.

Pour the dressing over the salad ingredients and toss. Crumble the tofu cheese over the salad and let sit for 10 to 15 minutes. Serve.

Saifun (Baifun) with Bonito Flakes

6–8 saifun (mung bean thread noodles)
3–4 Tbsp bonito flakes (small, ground flakes for garnish)
4 cups water

ginger, finely grated
1/4 cup scallions or chives, chopped
tamari soy saurce

Place the water in a pot, cover, and bring to a boil. Place the saifun noodles in the boiling water, cover, and turn off the flame. Let sit for 10 to 15 minutes. Remove, place in a strainer, and rinse with cold water.

Place the saifun in individual serving dishes. Garnish with a teaspoon or so of bonito flakes, a dash of finely grated ginger, a tablespoonful of chopped scallions or chives, and several drops of tamari soy sauce. Serve at room temperature or slightly chilled.

Kuzu-kiri (Kuzu Starch Noodles) Salad

4 oz kuzu-kiri
4 cups water, for cooking kuzu-kiri
water, for cooking vegetables
2 cups Chinese cabbage, sliced into l-inch thick slices
1/4 cup daikon, sliced into very thin rounds and then into very thin matchsticks
1/4 cup fresh shiitake mushrooms, quartered
1/4 cup carrots, cut into matchsticks
1/4 cup snow peas
2 Tbsp green nori flakes (aonori)
2 tsp ginger, finely grated
3 Tbsp finely ground bonito flakes
tamari soy sauce

Place 4 cups of water in a saucepan and bring to a boil. Slowly and carefully place the kuzu noodles in the water, so that they do not stick together. Simmer over a medium flame for about 4 to 5 minutes. Turn off the flame and let the noodles sit for 5 to 7 minutes. Place in a strainer and rinse under cold water. Place the cooked kuzu-kiri in a bowl.

Place about 3 inches of water in a pot, cover, and bring to a boil. Add the Chinese cabbage and cook for 1 minute. Remove, rinse, and drain. Place the Chinese cabbage in the bowl with the kuzu-kiri. Next, cook the remaining vegetables as follows: daikon for 1 minute; shiitake mushrooms for 2 minutes; carrots for 1 minute; snow peas for 1 minute. As each finishes cooking, rinse, drain, and mix in with the kuzu-kiri.

Place the salad ingredients in individual serving dishes. Garnish each with green nori flakes, ginger, bonito flakes, and several drops of tamari soy sauce. Serve at room temperature or slightly chilled.

Chilled Somen with Natto

8 oz somen
6 oz natto
1–1 1/2 Tbsp tamari soy sauce
1/4 cup daikon, finely grated

1/4 cup scallions or chives, finely chopped
2 Tbsp finely ground bonito flakes (optional)

Cook the somen al dente and rinse under cold water until completely chilled. Place the natto, tamari soy sauce, grated daikon, scallions or chives, and bonito flakes in a bowl, and mix well.

Combine the natto mixture and somen and mix well. Place in individual serving dishes.

Udon or Soba with Tamari-Ginger Sauce

8 oz udon or soba, cooked, rinsed, and drained
1/2 cup cucumber, quartered and thinly sliced
1/4 cup red radishes, sliced into thin rounds
1/4 cup celery, sliced into thin diagonals
1 cup tofu, cubed and marinated for 30 minutes in 1/4 cup tamari soy sauce, 1/4 cup water, and a dab of grated ginger
1/4 cup red onions, halved and sliced into thin half-moons
2 Tbsp black sesame seeds, toasted
Tamari-Ginger Sauce:
1 Tbsp tamari soy sauce
1/4–1/2 tsp ginger, finely grated
1/2–2/3 cup water
1 Tbsp parsley, minced
1 tsp scallions, finely minced

Place all salad ingredients in a mixing bowl and set aside.

Place the water and tamari soy sauce in a saucepan and bring almost to a boil. Reduce the flame to very low and simmer for 1 to 2 minutes. Remove and cool to room temperature. Mix in the parsley, scallions, and ginger.

Place the udon or soba salad in individual serving dishes and spoon the sauce over each. Mix before eating.

Soba Salad with Daikon-Carrot Dressing

8 oz jinenjo soba, cooked, rinsed, and drained
1/3 cup daikon, finely grated
1/3 cup carrots, finely grated
tamari soy sauce
1/4 cup nori, toasted and cut into strips
1/4 cup scallions or chives, finely chopped

Mix the daikon and carrots in a bowl. Add several drops of tamari soy sauce for a slightly salty flavor. Add the carrot-daikon mixture to the cooked soba. Place in individual serving dishes. Garnish each with 2 to 3 teaspoons toasted nori strips and 2 to 3 teaspoons of chopped scallions or chives. Serve at room temperature or slightly chilled.

Chapter 9: Making Your Own Noodles and Pasta

There is a tremendous difference between fresh homemade pasta and the pasta that comes in a package. Fresh noodles and pasta are very light and easy to digest and make deliciously sweet dishes. Professional pasta makers and experienced homemade pasta makers all agree that fresh pasta tastes the best. Homemade pasta can be hand rolled and cut or made in a small machine that rolls and cuts the dough. It takes about an hour to an-hour-and-a-half to make a batch of noodles or pasta. It takes about thirty minutes to knead the dough and another thirty minutes to let the dough sit before you cut it. These steps are the most time-consuming.

Homemade pasta is inexpensive as well as easy to make. One cup of flour will produce about eight to ten ounces of pasta, which is usually enough for two or three people. Pasta-making is also a lot of fun. Your whole family can join in the noodle-making process.

Types of Flour

A wide variety of noodles and pastas can be made at home by combining various flours. Each combination of flours will give its own very unique and delicious flavor as well as unique texture. Please experiment with any of the flours listed below to create new and exciting varieties of pasta.

Whole Wheat Bread Flour—This tan-colored flour is made from hard wheat—*Triticum aestivum* or *Triticum vulgare*—that is high in gluten. Whole wheat bread flour is made from whole wheat berries and still has its endosperm intact. It is also high in wheat bran and this gives the noodles or pasta a coarser texture. This is the flour that is used most often in macrobiotic kitchens. It can be combined with other flours to make noodles with a variety of textures and flavors.

Unbleached White Flour—This off-white, high-gluten bread flour is milled in such way as to remove the bran and endosperm, producing a white rather than yellow-tan color. Unlike all-purpose white flour, it is not processed and bleached. It is not "enriched" with artificial additives. It can be used in combination with whole wheat bread flour or any of the flours listed below to produce noodles or pasta with a lighter texture and color.

Buckwheat Flour—This flour is made from whole buckwheat groats and is used to make Japanese noodles called *soba*. You can use 100 percent buckwheat flour for heavier, chewier soba, or you may combine buckwheat flour with whole wheat or unbleached white flour to produce lighter, more delicately textured soba.

Brown Rice Flour—Brown rice can be milled into flour and combined with either whole wheat or unbleached white flour to produce light and delicious udon or somen. Brown rice flour can be used by itself to make pasta, but the process is quite complicated and requires special equipment.

Barley Flour—This flour can be made from either the more white "pearled" barley (barley with the outer skin removed) or hulled barley. When combined with either whole wheat or unbleached white flour, barley flours produce deliciously sweet noodles or pasta.

Corn Flour—Hard dent or flint corn may be finely milled into flour and combined with unbleached white or sifted whole wheat flour to produce very light, delicious pasta.

Oat Flour—In China they sometimes mill whole oats into flour and combine it with whole wheat or unbleached white flour to create a delicious variety of noodles.

Spelt Flour—For those with wheat allergies, the whole grain spelt—*Triticum spelta*—an ancient relative of wheat, can be milled into flour. It can be substituted for whole wheat flour in any of the recipes below.

Semolina Flour—This flour is made from a different type of wheat than whole wheat bread flour. It is made from sifted durum wheat. It has an amber or yellowish color and a fine texture. It is high in gluten, holds together well, and is more resistant to heat than unbleached white flour. Most commercial Italian pastas are made from this flour.

Basic Dough

There are two basic doughs that can be used to make noodles or pasta with any size or shape. The volume of ingredients in the recipes yield a quantity of dough that is easy to knead, although larger batches can be made by increasing the amount of ingredients. If you are making a larger batch, you may want to make them separately so that kneading will be easier. These recipes yield enough noodles for four or five people.

Basic Whole Wheat and Unbleached White Flour Dough

> 1 1/2 cups whole wheat bread flour, sifted
> 1 1/2 cups unbleached white flour
> 1 tsp sea salt
> 1 cup cold water

Place the flours and sea salt in a bowl and mix thoroughly. Slowly pour in the water and form into a spongy dough. Lightly flour a table or shallow wood bowl and knead (as if you were making bread) for about 20 to 25 minutes, flouring the table or bowl

Fig. 12

Fig. 13

Fig. 14

Fig. 15

very lightly if the dough becomes too sticky to handle. The dough is finished when it becomes very smooth and silky. Experienced pasta makers say that it has a texture similar to that of your earlobe when it is ready.

Take a clean, damp kitchen towel and wrap the dough in it. Let it sit for about 30 minutes, then divide the dough into 4 equal-sized pieces for easier rolling and cutting.

Basic Soba Dough

> 1 cup unroasted or roasted buckwheat flour
> 1 cup unbleached white flour
> 1 tsp sea salt
> 3/4 cup cold water

Place the flours and sea salt in a bowl and mix thoroughly. Slowly add the water, forming a spongy dough as above.

Lightly flour a tabletop or shallow wood bowl and knead the dough for 20 to 25 minutes, until smooth and silky to the touch.

Wrap the dough in a clean, damp kitchen towel. Let it sit for 30 minutes. Divide the dough into 4 equal-sized pieces for easier handling, rolling, and cutting.

Natural Flavorings and Colorings

A wide variety of colored or flavored pasta can be made by adding vegetables, seeds, fish or seafood, or fresh and wild grasses such as chives or dandelion to your basic dough. When adding vegetables, quickly blanch or boil them until they are soft enough to be chopped or puréed. When adding puréed vegetables to your pasta dough, you may need to use more flour because of the additional moisture in the vegetables, or you may decrease the volume of water called for in the recipe. When cooking greens such as parsley or watercress, squeeze out excess liquid before mincing and adding them to the dough. Some possible combinations include:

Watercress—Take 1/2 bunch of watercress and blanch it for 1 minute. Rinse and squeeze out liquid. Chop fine and grind in a suribachi. Pour the water called for in the recipe for dough into the suribachi to remove watercress from the grooves of the bowl. Combine with flour or flours and sea salt. Form into dough and knead as above.

Parsley—Cook 1/2 bunch of fresh parsley, rinse, and squeeze as above. Chop and grind as for watercress above. Pour the amount of water called for in the recipe into the suribachi to remove parsley. Combine with flour or flours and sea salt. Form into dough and knead as above. Instead of cooking the parsley, leave it raw and mince it very finely and combine it with the other ingredients in the dough.

Chives—Finely mince 3 to 4 tablespoons of fresh chives. Mix with flour, water, and sea salt. Form into dough and knead as above.

Green Shiso—This type of shiso leaf is usually used as a garnish in sushi. It is very delicious when used in pasta. Finely chop or mince several shiso leaves and mix with the pasta dough. (Use the same proportions as you would parsley.) Fresh green shiso can be obtained at natural food stores and Japanese specialty stores. You may also purchase seeds and grow your own shiso.

Red Shiso—This herb is known in the West as "beefsteak plant" or "perilla" and can be found mixed in with umeboshi plums. The red color of the shiso leaves gives the umeboshi plums their pink or red color. These pieces of shiso can be chopped and added to noodle dough, or you may use pickled whole shiso leaves. Shiso leaves are especially nice when combined with dough for making soba or buckwheat noodles. For 2 cups of flour, very finely mince about 3 tablespoonfuls of shiso. If fresh red shiso leaves are not available, you may substitute 2 level tablespoons of powdered shiso condiment. When using powdered shiso condiment, which is salty, you may reduce the amount of sea salt called for in the basic dough.

Carrots—Very finely dice 1 cup of carrots. Place in a saucepan with enough water to about half cover. Add a pinch of sea salt. Cover, bring to a boil, and simmer over a low flame for about 10 to 15 minutes until the carrots are tender. Remove and place in a blender, or purée in a suribachi until very smooth. Place the puréed carrots in a saucepan again and simmer for another 3 to 5 minutes over a low flame to cook off excess liquid (do not burn). For 3 cups of flour, add approximately 1 cup of puréed carrots. Mix, form into a dough, and knead.

Squash—Any hard winter squash can be cooked (after peeling) the same as carrots and kneaded into dough to give the pasta an orange color. (You may leave the skin on the squash for a pale green effect.) Use the same proportions as for carrot dough above. Very old recipes from Italy refer to "gnocchi" as being originally made with puréed squash or chestnuts instead of potatoes.

Dried Chestnut Purée—Dry roast 1/2 cup of whole dried chestnuts. Then pressure cook them for about 35 minutes or so with enough water to almost cover. Then purée the chestnuts (with their cooking water) to a thick, smooth paste. Knead into your basic whole wheat or unbleached white flour dough.

Sesame Seeds—Adding sesame seeds to dough creates a deliciously nutty flavored pasta. Dry roast either tan or black sesame seeds. Chop them finely or grind them in a suribachi and then knead into the basic wheat or buckwheat dough. Black sesame seeds give the dough a black and tan-speckled look. Use 1/4 cup of either type of sesame seeds for 2 to 3 cups of flour.

Bonito Flakes—Knead 1 package of the very finely ground bonito flakes into basic whole wheat or unbleached white flour dough for a delicious smoked flavor.

Fresh or Smoked Fish—You can also knead about 6 ounces of very finely minced or puréed smoked or fresh fish or seafood into 2 to 3 cups of basic wheat dough for a delicious, hearty flavored pasta.

Garlic—To make garlic pasta, remove the skin from 3 cloves of garlic and finely mince or purée. Knead into basic wheat dough for a spicy effect.

Fresh Ginger—To make ginger pasta, grate fresh ginger and squeeze 2 to 3 teaspoons of the juice into the basic dough. Reduce the amount of water that you add to the dough slightly in order to compensate for the ginger. Ginger pasta has a very spicy, refreshing flavor.

Green Tea—Noodles are very delicious when you add green tea to them. Place 1/4 cup of green tea in a blender and finely chop. Add to basic wheat or buckwheat dough.

Azuki Beans—You may cook and purée azuki beans or grind whole dried azuki beans into flour and add to the basic wheat dough. If using flour, you may need to reduce the amount of wheat flour or increase the amount of water in the recipe to compensate.

Green Nori (Aonori) Flakes—Green nori flakes give pasta a delicious flavor and a speckled green color. Add 1/4 cup of green nori flakes to basic wheat or buckwheat dough. Add slightly more water to buckwheat dough, as the green nori flakes are also dry.

Lemon Juice and Skin—You can also add approximately 3 tablespoons of fresh lemon juice or 3 tablespoons of freshly grated lemon skin to your basic dough.

Tangerine Juice and Skin—When adding tangerine juice or skin, use the same proportions as you would for lemon.

Black Olives—Chop 2 to 3 tablespoons of organic black olives and purée. Add to basic wheat dough for a black effect. For a speckled effect, do not purée, but instead mince very finely and knead into the dough.

Hand Rolling and Cutting

To roll out fresh pasta or noodle dough by hand you will need a 24- to 36-inch long rolling pin as described in the section on cooking utensils in Chapter 2. You will also need a large, clean working surface such as a table or cutting board.

Step 1: Lightly sprinkle a little flour on your working surface or cutting board and spread it evenly around.

Step 2: Take one of the balls of dough out of the damp towel, wrapping the others up again to prevent drying until you are ready to roll the next one. Form the dough into a smooth round ball and place it on the floured working surface. Sprinkle a little flour over the ball of dough.

Step 3: Press the dough down with the palm of your hand to flatten it, rotating the flat dough, 45 degrees at a time, until it is evenly flattened all around.

Step 4: Next, if necessary, sprinkle a little more flour over the flattened dough to prevent sticking and take the long rolling pin in hand. Roll the pin over the dough, rolling away from you, stretching the dough as you roll. Rotate the dough 45 degrees at a time, roll again, rotate, and roll again. Repeat until the dough forms an oval or round shape that is about 1/8 of an inch thick. You may also lift or roll the dough up

Fig. 16 **Fig. 17**

Fig. 18   Fig. 19

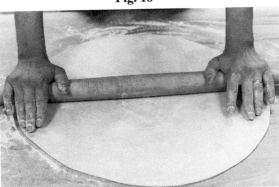

onto the rolling pin and gently roll or stretch the dough away from you. As the sheet of dough becomes larger and larger you can let it hang over the edge of a table to stretch even more.

Step 5: Take a piece of wax paper and sprinkle a little flour over it, spreading it out evenly. Place the rolled-out sheet of dough on top of the floured wax paper and cover with wax paper to prevent drying.

Step 6: Repeat with the remaining balls of dough. As you roll out each ball of dough to the proper thickness, place each layer of dough on the previous layer that is wrapped in wax paper, making sure to sprinkle a little flour between each layer to prevent them from sticking together.

Step 7: Now the flattened pasta or noodle dough is ready to be cut into any shape you desire. Please refer to the section below for directions for cutting pasta or noodles into various shapes and sizes. If you are making long strands of pasta or noodles, allow the dough to dry out for about 15 to 20 minutes before cutting. If you are making various stuffed pastas from the dough, such as ravioli or canneloni, you may cut the dough immediately without drying.

Step 8: There are several ways to go about cutting long strands of somen, udon, fettucine, and so on. You can take the entire stack of pasta dough, fold it in half, and slice into the desired thickness, or you can fold each individual sheet of rolled dough into quarters, and slice into the desired width. A long-bladed, sharp knife is very useful for cutting long thin strands. Repeat the process until all dough has been cut.

Machine Rolling and Cutting

A hand cranked pasta machine can be used to roll out the pasta dough to the correct thickness. Pasta machines have roller attachments that automatically roll out the dough into various sizes or widths. The basic rollers that come with the machine are suitable for making fettucine, spaghetti, somen, and soba. Other attachments may be purchased from the manufacturer.

Step 1: Take one piece of the divided dough and form it into a ball. Lightly flour the working surface and knead for 3 to 5 minutes until smooth.

Fig. 20   **Fig. 21**

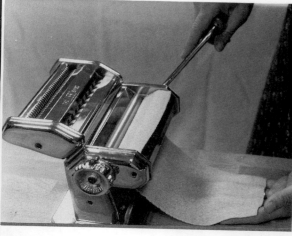

Step 2:   With the palm of your hand, flatten the dough into an oblong or 3- to 4-inch square. Take one end of the dough and fold it into the center. Now, fold the other end into the center so that the two ends meet. Dust the area where the two ends touch with a little flour. Flatten again with your palm.

Step 3:   Set the rollers of the pasta rolling machine to the widest setting. Hold the dough up against the rollers and turn the hand crank slowly, running the dough through the rollers. Do not pull on the dough as it comes out the other end, as this may cause it to break. Catch the dough with your free hand as it comes out the other end. When the dough has been completely run through the rollers, set the roller setting to the next notch.

Step 4:   Take the dough and fold the ends into the center again, as you did previously. Flour the dough and press down again with your palm. Roll the dough through the rollers again, catching it as it comes out the other end. Repeat the above process several times, setting the width of the rollers one notch lower each time, and roll the dough through until it is smooth and silky to the touch. After you roll the dough through the narrowest roller setting, it is ready to be cut. The dough should now be between 1/8 to 1/16 of an inch thick, depending on the type of pasta or noodle you are making.

Step 5:   Hang the sheet of dough over a pasta drying rack, towel rack, clothesline, or back of a chair to dry slightly. (If making various stuffed pastas such as ravioli, canneloni, and so on, this step may be omitted and the dough may be cut to the proper shape.) Repeat the above rolling process with the remaining balls of dough until all pieces have been rolled to the proper thickness.

Step 6:   If the sheets of dough are very long, you may cut them in half, across the width, before running the dough through the cutting rollers.

Step 7: Take one sheet of rolled dough at a time and run it through the desired cutting rollers, catching the strands as they come out the opposite end. Roll slowly to prevent the dough from bunching up in the rollers. Hang the cut pasta over a drying rack, towel rack, clothesline, or back of a chair.

Step 8: Repeat the above process with the remaining sheets of dough until it has all been cut. Your pasta or noodles are now ready to cook.

Fig. 22

Fig. 23

Cooking Fresh Pasta

Freshly made pasta or noodles cook slightly faster than dried pasta, so check frequently for doneness. The type of flour used in the dough will also influence the cooking time. Please refer to the previous chapter at the beginning of this book for basic instructions on cooking the pasta or noodles.

Pasta Shapes

Instead of cutting the dough into long strands, you may cut the rolled-out sheets of dough into a wide variety of shapes and sizes. The following instructions are for making some of the more well-known or frequently used shapes. A fluted pasta or pastry wheel is essential for some of the shapes below. Special square or round ravioli cutting tools can be purchased but are not essential. The fluted pasta wheel is sufficient. A sharpe knife is also essential in cutting the various shapes.

Square Ravioli

After rolling out the dough into thin sheets, take one sheet at a time and cut it into strips about 10 to 12 inches long by 2 inches wide. Lay the cut strips on a floured surface, keeping the remaining dough covered with a damp towel until you are ready to cut it.

Take one strip and lay it on a lightly floured surface. Take about 1/2 to 1 teaspoon of seitan, tofu, vegetable, or fish stuffing (see previous chapter for recipes) and place the filling on the sheet of dough, leaving about 1 1/2 inches between each spoon of filling.

Take another sheet of cut pasta dough and place it on top of the filling. With your fingers, press down firmly between the mounds of filling and along the sides of the dough strips to seal the two layers of dough together.

Fig. 24

Take a fluted pasta wheel and cut down the entire length of the filled dough strips, creating fluted edges. Next, take the pasta wheel and cut between the mounds of filling.

Take the cut ravioli and spread them out on a floured surface to dry for about 15 to 20 minutes. Turn the filled ravioli over and allow to dry for another 15 minutes. Make sure that the ravioli do not touch each other or they will stick together.

Repeat the above process until all the dough strips have been filled, cut, and allowed to dry.

The ravioli are now ready to cook (approximately 10 minutes), before serving with your favorite sauce.

Fig. 25

Round Ravioli

Take the cut strips of rolled pasta dough, one at a time, and fill same as above. Place another sheet of pasta dough over the filling and press all along the edges and in-between the filling as above. These are a little more difficult to cut than straight, square ravioli. Take the fluted pasta wheel and cut circles around the filling. Special round ravioli cutters can be purchased at kitchen specialty shops that make this process much easier.

The round ravioli are now ready to be cooked and served with your favorite sauce.

Lasagne

Take one sheet of rolled dough at a time and cut it into strips that are approximately 10 inches long by 2 inches wide. This may be done with a fluted pasta wheel or a serrated knife. Set the cut strips aside on a floured surface.

Repeat the above process with the remaining sheets of rolled dough until all dough has been cut.

Allow the lasagne to dry for 15 to 20 minutes, turn over, and allow to dry for another 15 minutes before cooking. Approximate cooking time for al dente style is about 5 minutes. The noodles can now be rinsed and drained. They are now ready to layer and bake with your favorite filling. Please see the previous chapter for various seitan, tofu, carrot sauce, vegetable, or fish fillings and sauces.

Canneloni (Can also use as pierogi wrappers)

Take one sheet of rolled pasta dough at a time and cut it into rectangular shapes about 4 inches wide by 5 inches long. This can be done with a sharp knife or even with a pizza cutting wheel. Set the sheets aside on a floured surface. Repeat until all dough has been cut to the desired size. Allow the dough to dry for 15 minutes, turn over, and dry for another 15 minutes.

Fig. 26

Fig. 27

Place the cut strips of dough into boiling, salted water and cook for approximately 5 minutes until al dente. Remove, rinse, and drain. Place the cooked strips of pasta in a bowl of cold water to prevent sticking. Remove one at a time and fill with your favorite filling. Instructions for filling and recipes for various fillings from vegetables to seafood, as well as sauces are given in previous chapters.

Tagliatelle (Thin Strips)

Fig. 28

The shape of the tagliatelle is very similar to fettucine and is very easy to cut, requiring no special tools other than a sharp knife.

Roll up the sheets of pasta dough into a loose cylinder or log shape.

Take a sharp knife and cut the cylinder crosswise into 1/4-inch widths. Separate or unroll the coils of cut pasta and set aside in small piles.

Repeat with the remaining sheets of rolled pasta dough until all dough has been cut. This type of pasta may be cooked immediately and served with your favorite sauce, or placed in soup or broth.

Bow Ties or Butterflies (Farfalla)

Take one sheet of rolled pasta dough at a time and cut with a fluted pasta wheel into thin strips about 10 to 12 inches long by 1 to 2 inches wide (1 inch wide will give you small bows; 2 inches wide larger bows).

Fig. 29

Take a knife and cut straight across the width of the strips at 1/2- to 1-inch intervals so that you have several pieces of dough 1 to 2 inches wide by 1/2 to 1 inch long.

With your thumb and index finger, pinch each small piece of dough in the center to create a bow tie or butterfly effect.

Set the pasta aside on a floured surface. Repeat the above process until all dough has been shaped into bows or butterflies. Allow to dry for 15 minutes or so. The pasta is now ready to cook and serve with your favorite sauce or placed in soups or salads.

Fluted Edged Ribbons (Pappardelle or Lasagnette)

Fluted edged ribbons are simply smaller version of lasagne noodles. Take one sheet of rolled pasta dough at a time and place on a floured surface. With a fluted pasta wheel, cut the dough into strips approximately 1inch wide by 10 to 12 inches long.

Set aside on a floured surface and allow to dry for 15 minutes. Turn over and dry for another 15 minutes.

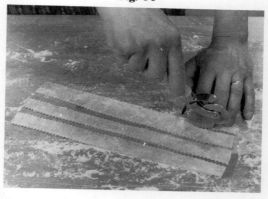

Fig. 30

Repeat the above process until all dough has been cut and dried. The pasta is now ready to cook and serve with your favorite sauce.

Gnocchi

Gnocchi are small dumpling-like pastas, that are commercially, although not traditionally, made with potato and flour. Use either squash, carrot, or chestnut purée combined with whole wheat or unbleached white flour for the dough. Traditionally these vegetables and nuts were used to make "gnocchi."

Prepare the dough, knead, and divide into 4 balls. Place one ball at a time on a floured surface. Do not roll it out.

Pinch off pieces of dough and form into round balls about the size of a marble or slightly larger. Take the ball with your thumb and index finger and press it against the back of a fork or special gnocchi tool called *comb*. The back side of the gnocchi will have the ridges of the fork or comb imprinted on it and the front of the gnocchi will be deep and hollow from your thumbprint.

Repeat until all dough has been used. Set aside on a floured surface and allow to dry for about 30 minutes. The gnocchi are now ready to cook.

Fig. 31

Half-moon-shaped Ravioli

Half-moon-shaped ravioli can be made either by cutting circular pieces of dough or with a fluted pasta wheel or a knife. They are approximately 2 inches in diameter.

Form 1/2 teaspoon of your favorite vegetable, seitan, tofu, or seafood filling into a round ball. Place the ball of filling in the center of one-half of the circular piece of dough. Fold the dough in half over the filling. Press the edges of the dough circles down firmly to seal.

Place the filled half-moon ravioli on a floured surface and allow to dry for about 15 minutes. Turn the ravioli over and allow to dry for another 15 minutes.

Repeat the above process until all dough has been cut, filled, and dried.

The ravioli are now ready to cook.

Tortellini (Rounded Caps or Hats)

Cut out 2-inch diameter circles of pasta dough the same way as for making half-moon-shaped ravioli. Take 1/4 teaspoon of your favorite filling and form it into a ball

Fig. 32

Fig. 33

Fig. 34

about the size of a chick-pea. Place the ball of filling in the center of one-half of the circle and fold the dough over the filling the same as for half-moon-shaped ravioli.

Next, fold each side of the half-moon into the center and pinch each end together with your thumb and index finger so that they are firmly sealed together. Set aside on a floured surface and allow to dry for 30 minutes.

Repeat until all dough has been cut, filled, and formed into caps.

The filled caps are now ready to boil or deep fry.

Cappelletti (Square Caps or Hats)

The shape of the cappelletti is cut into 2-inch squares instead of a 2-inch diameter circle.

Take 1/4 to 1/2 teaspoon of your favorite filling and form it into a round ball. Place the filling in the center of the square. Fold the square so that it forms a triangle. Press the edges of the triangle to firmly seal. Place your index finger on the center

Fig. 35

of the triangle and bring each of the two corners into the center so that both ends of the triangle overlap. Press the ends together with your index finger and thumb to seal. Place on a floured surface and allow to dry for about 30 minutes.

Repeat the above process until all dough has been cut, filled, and formed into caps or hats.

The cappelletti are now ready to boil or deep fry. Serve with your favorite sauce.

Fig. 36

Hollow Pasta (Tubes, Spirals, and Others)

For this type of hollow pasta, you will need a 1/4-inch or 1/8-inch thick twig or you may purchase a dowel rod from any lumberyard.

Cut the rolled-out sheets of pasta dough, one at a time, into 2-inch-by-1-inch strips, or even 2-inch-by-1/2-inch strips. Wrap the dough around the twig or rod and press to tightly seal. Let sit for several minutes. Several pieces of dough can be molded around the twig or rod at the same time. Slip the dough off the end of the twig or rod and allow to dry for several minutes before boiling.

Repeat the above process until all dough has been cut and formed into hollow tubes.

To form spirals, simply take thickly rolled strands of pasta dough and wrap around the twig or rod in a coiled spiral.

Drying Fresh Pasta

To dry fresh homemade pasta and noodles, simply roll out and cut the dough. Then hang the cut pasta over a pasta drying rack, towel rack, wooden clothes rack, or clothesline. Leave the window open so that a breeze comes through and allow the pasta to dry for approximately 3 days, until brittle. The volume of pasta will reduce by about half when dried. Store in tightly sealed glass containers.

To dry various smaller shaped pasta, simply place on a floured baking sheet or even a bamboo mat and allow to dry for about 3 days before storing in a tightly sealed glass jar.

If you choose not to dry the pasta, but do not want to cook it all at once, it may be wrapped in wax paper and kept in the refrigerator for about 3 to 4 days before cooking.

Eggless Egg Roll Wrappers

Eggless wrappers can be made very simply by adding either arrowroot flour or ground kuzu starch flour to your basic unbleached white flour dough, to form a more stiff dough. Roll out the dough into thin sheets and dust with arrowroot flour or kuzu starch flour. Cut into 4-inch-by-4-inch squares before stuffing and cooking.

For the basic dough, use all unbleached white flour instead of combining whole wheat bread flour and unbleached white flour. You may also knead a little corn or light sesame oil into the dough for elasticity.

List of Recipes